The Power of American Governors
Winning on Budgets and Losing on Policy

With limited authority over state lawmaking, but ultimate responsibility for the performance of government, how effective are governors in moving their programs through the legislature? This book advances a new theory about what makes chief executives most successful and explores this theory through original data. Thad Kousser and Justin H. Phillips argue that negotiations over the budget, on one hand, and policy bills, on the other, are driven by fundamentally different dynamics. They capture these dynamics in models informed by interviews with gubernatorial advisors, cabinet members, press secretaries, and governors themselves. Through a series of novel empirical analyses and rich case studies, the authors demonstrate that governors can be powerful actors in the lawmaking process but that whether they are bargaining over the budget or policy shapes both how they play the game and how often they can win it. In addition to assessing the power of American governors, this book contributes broadly to our understanding of the determinants of executive power.

Thad Kousser is associate professor in the Department of Political Science at the University of California, San Diego. He has written or edited several books, including *Politics in the American States* (10th ed., 2012), *The Logic of American Politics* (5th ed., 2011), and *Term Limits and the Dismantling of State Legislative Professionalism* (2005). He is a recipient of the UCSD Academic Senate's Distinguished Teaching Award as well as the Faculty Mentor of the Year Award.

Justin H. Phillips is associate professor in the Department of Political Science at Columbia University. His research has been published in the *American Political Science Review* and the *American Journal of Political Science*. He is a Fellow at the Columbia University Applied Statistics Center and at the Institute for Social and Economic Research.

Purchased Tues 8/2/22

The Power of American Governors

Winning on Budgets and Losing on Policy

THAD KOUSSER

Department of Political Science
University of California, San Diego

JUSTIN H. PHILLIPS

Department of Political Science
Columbia University

Hofstra Univ. Bookstore
200 Hofstra Univ.
Hempstead, N.Y.

CAMBRIDGE
UNIVERSITY PRESS

CAMBRIDGE
UNIVERSITY PRESS

University Printing House, Cambridge CB2 8BS, United Kingdom

One Liberty Plaza, 20th Floor, New York, NY 10006, USA

477 Williamstown Road, Port Melbourne, VIC 3207, Australia

314-321, 3rd Floor, Plot 3, Splendor Forum, Jasola District Centre, New Delhi - 110025, India

103 Penang Road, #05-06/07, Visioncrest Commercial, Singapore 238467

Cambridge University Press is part of the University of Cambridge.

It furthers the University's mission by disseminating knowledge in the pursuit of education, learning and research at the highest international levels of excellence.

www.cambridge.org
Information on this title: www.cambridge.org/9781107611177

First published 2012

A catalogue record for this publication is available from the British Library

Library of Congress Cataloging in Publication data
Kousser, Thad, 1974–
The Power of American governors : winning on budgets and losing on policy / Thad Kousser, Justin H. Phillips.
p.   cm.
Includes bibliographical references and index.
ISBN 978-1-107-02224-9 (hardback) – ISBN 978-1-107-61117-7 (paperback)
1. Governors – United States – Powers and duties.   2. Executive power – United States – States.   3. Legislative power – United States – States.   4. Veto – United States – States.   5. Political leadership – United States – States. I. Phillips, Justin H. (Justin Huhtelin)
II. Title.
JK2447.K68   2012
352.23´52130973–dc23   2012012193

ISBN 978-1-107-02224-9 Hardback
ISBN 978-1-107-61117-7 Paperback

To William and Kat, my governors of unchecked power

– TK

To my parents, Michael and Patricia

– JHP

Contents

List of Figures

ix

List of Tables

Sat 8/6/22

Acknowledgments

Many people and institutions provided the sage guidance, encouraging enthusiasm, and essential resources (in addition to helping with tedious data collection) that made this book possible. We cannot thank them all, but here is a start.

The talented team of research assistants who spent many hours on painstaking searches through newspaper search engines, archives, and microfilm were an invaluable part of this project. At Columbia University, Leslie Huang did an immense amount of work identifying gubernatorial proposals in State of the State addresses and then tracking down their outcomes; without her diligence, organization, and persistence, our dataset would not have had nearly as broad a scope. At the University of California, San Diego, a team of researchers shared in this task, which includes Kristi Dunne, Sarah Debel, Erika Kociolek, Kailyn Fitzgerald, Jonathan Chu, Kathryn Alpago, Jessica Lasky-Fink, Ashwan Reddy, Sandy Luong, Sam Deddeh, Demian Hernandez, Allison Henderson, Krishan Banwait, Sebastian Brady, and Nicole Ozeran. At Stanford, research assistants Alana Kirkland and Kelsey Davidson combed through archival sources to help us prepare the case studies of California governors. Finally, we thank the UC, San Diego, graduate students who helped to supervise our research team and to edit, proof, and index this manuscript: Mike Rivera, Vlad Kogan, and Mike Binder.

For the important task of gauging the ideological direction and scale of gubernatorial proposals, we began by using computerized news searches and text scaling procedures but soon decided that we were better off relying on the judgments of political experts than on robotic algorithms. For their attentive and thoughtful measurements, we are indebted to a

xiii

group of elected officials, capitol observers, and state politics scholars from across the nation: Montana state senator Cliff Larsen; Karl Kurtz and Jennie Bowser of the National Conference of State Legislatures; Ann Lousin of John Marshall School of Law and former Parliamentarian of the Illinois House of Representatives; Tim Gage, former Director of Finance, California; Dr. Rick Farmer, Director of Committee Staff, Oklahoma House of Representatives; Gary Hart, former California state senator and secretary of education; Ethan Rarick, former statehouse reporter in Oregon and California; Paul Schuler, former statehouse reporter in North Carolina; Richard Winters of Dartmouth College; Ron Weber, professor emeritus at the University of Wisconsin, Milwaukee; Chris Mooney of the University of Illinois, Springfield; Gary Moncrief of Boise State University; John Straayer of Colorado State University; Seth Masket of Denver University; Burdett Loomis of the University of Kansas; Lynda Powell of the University of Rochester; Ray La Raja at the University of Massachusetts, Amherst; and Alan Rosenthal of Rutgers University.

The most important gifts that a scholar can receive are the thoughtful, constructive, and challenging questions of seminar audiences, reviewers, and colleagues. We received a Christmas morning's worth of these gifts. For inviting us to present this work at various stages, we thank Gerald Gamm at the University of Rochester, Alan Rosenthal at Rutgers' Eagleton Institute of Politics, Simon Jackman at Stanford University, Will Howell at the University of Chicago, and Bob Huckfeldt at the UC in Sacramento Center, along with all of the seminar participants at each institution. Our colleagues, including Sam Popkin, Sam Kernell, Sebastian Saiegh, Gary Jacobson, Mat McCubbins, Amy Bridges, Scott Desposato, James Fowler, Keith Poole, and Gary Cox at UC, San Diego, and Jeffrey Lax, Robert Erikson, and Robert Shapiro at Columbia University gave us very helpful feedback from beginning to end. We also thank those who commented on papers from this project at many conferences. Some parts of Chapter 5 come from a paper published in the journal *Legislative Studies Quarterly*, and we are grateful to that journal's reviewers and editor Peverill Squire for their guidance and publication permission. Finally, we are indebted to the two anonymous reviewers for Cambridge University Press who were supportive and constructive through the editorial process.

Another valuable resource for an academic is time, and each of us is grateful to the institutions that gave us the opportunity to focus on this project. In the 2009–2010 academic year, Thad Kousser was very grateful to be a Visiting Associate Professor at Stanford's Bill Lane Center for the American West and a W. Glenn Campbell and Rita Ricardo-Campbell

National Fellow and Robert Eckles Swain National Fellow at the Hoover Institution. He thanks David Kennedy, David Brady, Morris Fiorina, and Jon Christensen for their support at Stanford.

No matter how many datasets we assembled and formal models we outlined, the research technique that taught us the most about chief executives was interviewing the governors and gubernatorial advisors who lived the story we try to tell. Our theories were guided by their testimony and our book enlivened by their recollections. We thank Gov. Parris Glendening of Maryland, Gov. Bob Taft of Ohio, Gov. Gray Davis of California, along with Lynn Schenk, Burdett Loomis, Bill Hauck, Larry Thomas, Dan Schnur, Phil Trounstine, Tim Gage, Joe Rodota, Gary Hart, Bill Hauck, Tom Hayes, Sal Russo, Kevin Eckery, Bill Whalen, and Pat Johnston.

Finally, we are deeply grateful to the editors and staff at Cambridge University Press, who have been supportive of the project throughout its journey from idea to manuscript to book, patient with us as we took years to complete the process, always constructive with their feedback, and ever-helpful in bringing it to fruition. We owe much to our editor, Eric Crahan, as well as to Lew Bateman, Abigail Zorbaugh, and Adrian Pereira.

One Problem Shared by 50 Governors

Governors, just like American presidents, face a singular disadvantage when it comes to lawmaking. Though the public may look to governors to lead their states, credit them with any successes, and hold them accountable for most failures, state constitutions strip governors of any direct ✳ power to craft legislation. Legislators in this country hold a monopoly over the power to introduce, amend, and pass bills, giving them the ability to write laws and then present them as take-it-or-leave-it offers to America's chief executives. A governor's only formal legislative power is a reactive one – the ability to veto or sign bills that are passed by the other branch – and comes at the end of the lawmaking process.   ⎤ ₵ α13

The dynamics of this relationship can be seen in the logistics of the annual rituals that bring the branches together. When presidents lay out legislative agendas in their State of the Union addresses, they head down Pennsylvania Avenue to do so from the speaker's rostrum before a joint session of Congress. Likewise, governors typically deliver their State of the State speeches to lawmakers in their respective legislatures' lower houses. Governors recognize who the home team is when it comes to playing the legislative game and know that their ability to shape policy depends crucially on the actions of the men and women who serve in the legislative branch. With respect to many of the formal prerogatives of lawmaking, each state's chief executive stands behind even the most junior rank-and-file legislator.

In their direct and even indirect power to create laws, governors also trail far behind chief executives throughout the world. Unlike the leaders of most parliamentary governments, they cannot reasonably expect the support of the majority coalition in the legislature, and their cabinet officers do not serve as legislative leaders with the power to introduce key bills and shepherd them through the lawmaking process. They are thus prevented from moving their agendas as quickly and successfully as prime ministers in Europe and Japan. Presidents in Latin America have the ability to introduce laws, and many possess that right exclusively for their nations' budgets, elevating them above legislators, who often serve simply to cast up or down votes on presidential agendas (Payne et al. 2002; Aleman and Tsebelis 2005; Saiegh 2011). In some countries, presidents possess decree authority, allowing them to establish the law in lieu of legislative action (Carey and Shugart 1998). The separation of powers in the United States, by contrast, dictates that our chief executives cannot author legislation.[1] Whether they wish to pass a new budget or make any statutory policy change, they are dependent on the legislature to do so.

Yet, governors are granted many opportunities to overcome this constitutional obstacle. They are the central figures of state politics, allowing governors who shine in the spotlight to shape a state's agenda (though executives who suffer under its glare gain no automatic advantage from their prominence). Chief executives possess many informal weapons to counteract their formal weakness, sticks and carrots that may compel legislative cooperation if used wisely. Although there are no guarantees that governors will move their agendas through legislatures, many are able to harness their assorted powers to pile up wins. Some governors are unqualified successes, whereas others are undeniable failures. What they share are unlimited expectations but limited powers. All governors are expected to be their states' "legislator in chief" (Lipson 1939; Beyle 1983; Rosenthal 1990; Gross 1991; Bernick and Wiggins 1991; Morehouse 1998; Ferguson 2003). Voters demand policy leadership and results from the governors whom they send to office, overlooking the mismatch between these expectations and the constitutional authority of the executive.

In this book, we consider whether American governors can use their varied powers to overcome their common challenge – the institutional advantage that legislators hold in the realm of lawmaking. Just how successful are governors in moving their programs through the legislature?

[1] While the bills proposed by governors and introduced into legislatures are in some states explicitly referred to as *governor's bills* (Rosenthal, 1990, p. 103), this is an informal arrangement that does not confer constitutional powers on governors. The legislative authors of governor's bills still control their content and shepherd them through the process, and the legislative branch as a whole maintains complete authority over their fates.

Under which institutional and strategic settings should state chief executives be most successful? When might they be most likely to fail? In short, can governors govern, and which ones are likely to govern most effectively?[2]

In formulating answers to these questions, we are guided by prior research on chief executives as well as interviews we conducted with dozens of key statehouse players. Talking with governors, their top advisors, and legislative leaders has given us insight into the goals of governors and the strategies they employ to pursue them. Combining this eyewitness testimony with lessons learned from past scholarship, we argue that critically different dynamics drive bargaining over the budget and over policy bills. As a result, we develop a model (or game) for each type of negotiation, building on existing game theoretic approaches to interbranch bargaining. Our models demonstrate the various ways in which governors can use their formal and informal powers to influence the lawmaking process, allowing us to make predictions about the factors that will shape gubernatorial success. Additionally, the models point to the subtle and complex ways in which features of a governor's public agenda, including its size, scope, and ideological content, are functions of bargaining circumstances and the value that governors place on taking uncompromising policy positions.

In general, our models predict that governors will be most successful when playing the budget game. In this game, fiscal, legal, and political realities dictate that legislators must come to the negotiating table. Lawmakers are required by law to pass a new state budget every year or biennium, and a failure to do so brings dire political consequences for both branches, including (in many states) an automatic government shutdown. These consequences transform negotiations into a staring match, eroding many of the legislature's traditional bargaining advantages. The staring-match dynamic empowers governors everywhere but should be particularly helpful to those executives who are bargaining with impatient legislatures. All governorships are well-paid, full-time jobs that allow their occupants to reside in the state capital year round and engage in protracted negotiations. Many legislatures, however, only meet in short

---

[2] Because we want to examine closely the ability of governors to move their favored policies and spending plans through legislatures, we do not address other important gubernatorial functions such as unilateral policy making through executive orders (Ferguson and Foy 2009), influencing the bureaucracy (Wright et al. 1983; Sigelman and Dometrius 1988), or overseeing the implementation of laws. These are important areas of executive strength but lie beyond the scope of this volume.

sessions, and their members maintain outside careers. In these states, governors should be able to leverage their bargaining patience into additional budgetary concessions.

When the governor is playing the policy game, conversely, the legislature enjoys a particularly advantaged position. Lawmakers are free to ignore the governor's requests, and nothing very bad happens – policy simply remains at the status quo. In this game, governors will have a hard time convincing lawmakers to come to the bargaining table, let alone getting them to pass executive agenda items without significant amendment. The governors who are most likely to succeed will be those who want to move the status quo in the same direction as the legislature or those who can promise lawmakers large rewards for cooperation or stiff penalties for opposition.

What types of rewards and punishments can state chief executives dole out? Lawmakers who work toward the passage of the executive agenda can expect to receive favors such as support for their reelection campaigns and fund-raising efforts, plumb appointments for their political allies, and joint appearances with the governor in their districts. Correspondingly, chief executives can threaten to use their high-profile positions to attack uncooperative officeholders or campaign for their challengers. The governor can also transform her veto authority from a negative to a positive power by promising to sign bills that are important to individual lawmakers in exchange for their support of her proposals. Ultimately, however, the size of the carrots and sticks that a governor wields and her ability to use them should be a function of the governor's political capital, which is shaped by her popularity with voters, the extent to which she can credibly make veto threats, and the amount of time she has remaining in office.

We evaluate the predictions of our models using several new sources of evidence. First, we use journalistic and legislative archives to track the success of the policy and budgetary agenda items that governors propose in their State of the State addresses, creating a data set that records the characteristics and ultimate fates of over 1,000 proposals made by a sample of governors in 28 states. The literature on the American presidency (Wildavsky 1966; Rivers and Rose 1985; Bond and Fleisher 1990) and studies of Latin America (Haggard and McCubbins 2001; Morgenstern and Nacif 2002; Saiegh 2010) have relied on similar types of data for measuring and estimating the determinants of executive success. Second, we study negotiations over the size of state government by assembling a data set comparing what governors ask for at the beginning of budget battles with what they get in the final deal. This data set includes all states over 20 fiscal years. Finally, we supplement these large quantitative analyses with a series of case studies carefully chosen to isolate the causal impact of variations in governors' powers, formal and informal. The case studies use a natural disaster and political scandal to evaluate the effects of gubernatorial popularity, an Iowa Supreme Court ruling to consider the importance of the line-item veto, and a Californian ballot measure to test for the effects of legislative professionalization.

Together, these comprehensive new data sets outline some of the basic but important facts about what state chief executives ask for in their public agendas and what they get. Our data show that governors' agendas vary significantly in terms of their content, size, and scope. Although governors enjoy and exercise a great deal of ideological flexibility when setting their fiscal and policy priorities, we observe (perhaps unsurprisingly) that their partisanship remains the single best predictor of the ideological tilt of their proposals. In formulating their agendas, particularly their policy proposals, chief executives respond to their bargaining circumstances.

We find that state chief executives can be, and often are, powerful players in the lawmaking process. Our analysis of 1,088 policy and budgetary proposals in State of the State addresses shows that governors frequently get a good portion of what they ask for – legislators pass 41 percent of executive agenda items and deliver a compromise measure on an additional 18 percent. In budget negotiations over the size of state government, each dollar of overall spending or revenue changes proposed by the governor in January translates into roughly 70 cents in the final budget deal reached with the legislature. Importantly, we also find that success varies across governors and bargaining games and does so in the ways anticipated by our models. Governors are more successful when it comes to negotiating over the budget than they are over policy bills. In the budget realm, the governors who do best are those who bargain with an impatient legislature – a legislature in which lawmakers will face personal costs if they engage in protracted budget negotiations. By contrast, the governors who succeed with their policy proposals are those who are lucky enough to negotiate with an ideologically similar legislature or who have a large amount of political capital that can be expended in pursuit of legislative achievement.

In addition, our investigations reveal the often hidden powers of American governors. Even though past studies have reached the puzzling conclusion that budgets passed by Democratic governors spend no more money than those signed by Republicans, we use new data sources and analytical approaches to show that chief executives nonetheless exert impressive power over the size of state government. To understand the sources of state executive power, we show that it is critical to view the budget and policy-making processes separately. When they are combined, the factors that make for strong governorships are obscured. When budgeting and policymaking are kept analytically and empirically distinct, the most important powers of governors in each realm become clear. While at first glance, popular governors seem to pass fewer of the bills that they propose than unpopular ones do, a closer look shows that political capital can indeed pay dividends. Over and over again, we show that one of the strongest determinants of gubernatorial power lies outside of the executive branch altogether – the professionalization of the legislature.

In this introductory chapter, we begin by making the case that a study of governors in the American states can learn from and contribute to the wider literature on executive power. Next, we sketch our view of governors and introduce our arguments about the ways in which they attempt to wield power over legislatures. We lay out the types of evidence that we assemble to explore our hypotheses and then preview in greater detail how some of the hidden powers of governors are revealed. Finally, we map out the way in which we will interweave theory, close examination of cases, and large-scale data analysis.

1.1. States as Laboratories for the Study of Executive Power

Although our empirical focus is squarely on American governors, broad questions about the nature and dynamics of executive power motivate our inquiry. The states provide a unique laboratory in which to investigate executive power over lawmaking. A close study of governors, especially one looking at how their influence varies across the wide range of institutional structures and political dynamics present in American states, can yield larger lessons. In particular, studying governors can teach us something about American presidents. Because state constitutions are based, by and large, on the federal structure, the office of the governor operates much like the presidency. Except in the realm of foreign policy, governors and presidents deal with a similar set of policy issues. In the modern era, with the exception of a few independent governors, both types of chief executives have worked within the same two-party system. Many people have held both offices, with Jimmy Carter, Ronald Reagan, Bill Clinton, and George W. Bush ascending from the governorship to the White House, and today, statehouses are full of presidential aspirants.

Most important, presidents face the same constitutional quandary as governors, needing to summon all their informal strength to combat the legislature's advantage in formal powers. Writing about presidents, Kernell and Jacobson (2006, p. 283) speak of how "modern executives do all they can to break out of the Constitution's 'take it or leave it' bind." They could just as easily have been talking about governors. Presidents and governors have many of the same tools to draw on, with governors using their political preeminence and personal popularity to "go public" in the same way that presidents do (Kernell 1986). States can give us additional empirical traction to expand the presidential literature, providing out-of-sample cases to test new theories and explore well-trodden fields that have yielded mixed results, including the literature linking presidential popularity to legislative success.[3]

But states provide more than just a larger number of observations to study politics – the powers that governors possess and the political dynamics that they face vary in ways that do not fluctuate across presidents. This variation is richly cataloged in Rosenthal (1990) and Ferguson (2006) and quantified by Schlesinger (1965) and Beyle (1983, 2004). The critical details of veto powers, for instance, vary widely at the state level. Governors in a few states may be overridden by a simple majority of legislators (as in Kentucky), while others require very large supermajorities to do so. In 44 states, governors not only possess the blanket veto but also have line-item veto power, giving them the ability to nullify or reduce individual expenditures in appropriations bills. Some governors even have the ability to veto individual lines of policy bills, and at least one – the governor of Wisconsin – can, through the creative use of that state's "Vanna White" item veto, strike out individual letters and digits to alter the intent of legislative language.[4] Governors also vary widely in their levels of popularity. The comprehensive archive of gubernatorial approval ratings recently collected[5] shows just how much their popularity fluctuates, providing the opportunity for a comprehensive evaluation of the impact of the ever-elusive concept of political capital. As Squire

[3] National studies by Collier and Sullivan (1995), Covington and Kinney (1999), and Cohen et al. (2000) find little support for the idea that presidential popularity helps to sway congressional votes, while Edwards (1980), Bond and Fleisher (1990), and Canes-Wrone and de Marchi (2002) show that popularity helps presidents move their agendas under specific conditions.

[4] Daniel C. Vock, "Govs Enjoy Quirky Veto Power," accessed at Stateline.org on April 24, 2007.

[5] Richard Niemi, Thad Beyle, and Lee Sigelman, "Job Approval Ratings," accessed at http://www.wnc.edu/beyle/jars.html in January 2007.

and Hamm's (2005) sweeping overview of legislative institutions shows, the houses with which governors negotiate vary enormously in their levels of professionalization, that is, the length of their regularly scheduled sessions, the salary they pay lawmakers, and the number of staff they employ. Unlike the American president, many governors find themselves bargaining with citizen legislators. The states allow scholars to ask questions that we cannot answer by studying presidents alone and to anticipate the effects of proposed reforms – such as the line-item veto – on the presidency.

The study of legislatures has made tremendous use of the variation in state legislative institutions to test and further develop theories about committee organization (Overby and Kazee 2000; Overby et al. 2004), party power (Aldrich and Battista 2002; Wright and Schafner 2002; Kim and Phillips 2009; Cox et al. 2010), and ideological mobility (Kousser et al. 2007). In the same way, scholars should examine governors as part of a wider research agenda on executive power. Governors are not exactly like American presidents, just as state legislatures are not perfect copies of Congress.[6] But in the differences lies the great research design opportunity offered by the states, and the similarities are strong enough to make the states fertile ground for exploring more general theories about chief executives.

1.2. How We View Governors

The starting point of our argument is the formal institutional weakness of American chief executives. This weakness – the fact that the highest elected lawmakers of our land cannot themselves introduce or pass laws – poses a fundamental challenge to American chief executives. The dilemma of American executives has long been recognized at the national level and continues to shape how we view the actions of presidents today. Richard Neustadt (1960) famously deemed presidential power "the power to persuade," whereas a recent description of President Obama's efforts to convince wavering Democrats to support his health care reform characterized the president as the "cajoler in chief."[7]

---

[6] In fact, a key point we make in the next chapter is that formal models of bargaining between the branches of the federal government should not be automatically applied to every state.

[7] David M. Herszenhorn, "A National Measure, Inextricably Enmeshed with Local Interests," *New York Times*, March 15, 2010, p. A13.

Yet, of course, this institutional weakness does not make governors impotent, any more than it renders presidents powerless. Governors monopolize the power to sign legislation and control a host of other informal sticks and carrots that may help them compel the cooperation of legislators. The question is, when will legislators agree to enact the gubernatorial proposals? Legislators move first, governors act last. How does this bare set of rules shape their complex bargaining game?

A major theme that guides both the approach of our study and the organization of this book is that what governors are able to achieve in the legislative process depends crucially on what they are bargaining over: the budget or policy bills. Although both the state spending plan and policy bills move through the same basic legislative process, the consequences of an impasse are radically different for each type of legislation. If legislators fail to pass a policy bill that the governor proposes, state policy in that area remains where it was before. Legislators face the governor's wrath, but they may be quite happy with the status quo policy. By contrast, if legislators fail to pass a budget that the governor will sign, the consequences can be dire. Both sides will face political heat from a late budget, and the operations of state government can be stalled or thrown into uncertainty. Neither branch will look forward to this outcome, motivating all sides to work hard to avoid it.

Legislators and the governor can see the endgame, and this changes how they play from the start. In the policy realm, knowing that no catastrophe will ensue if they fail to pass one of the governor's proposals, legislators can often stick to their positions. If they like an existing policy better than the governor's plan, and the governor has insufficient charm or threats to move them, they will not budge at all. That is why executive proposals contained in State of the State addresses can soon become dead letters. When bargaining over policy bills, legislators can take full advantage of their monopoly power to write and pass legislation on even the biggest issues of the day. In his 2003 State of the State address, the first item that Republican governor Jeb Bush of Florida requested was a legislative referendum asking voters to overturn (or pay for) the class size reduction plan they had approved in a recent ballot measure. Democrats in the legislature opposed such an effort, not wanting to see the state's effort at class size reduction killed just as it was getting started. Despite the governor's best efforts, lawmakers were able to hold out. "Bush constantly warned citizens that the class-size amendment will be costly to implement and asked lawmakers to put a repeal of the amendment on the ballot," according to one statehouse reporter. "The lawmakers ignored his plea."[8]

Even when they want to curry favor with a governor by cooperating on a policy bill, legislators, as long as they can live with the status quo should the governor veto their bill, can use their ability to make a take-it-or-leave-it offer to dictate the terms of the deal. In 2006, New Hampshire governor John Lynch asked the legislature for a bipartisan ethics reform bill. Republicans in the legislature responded with SB 206, which Lynch threatened to veto because it contained provisions that would have barred lobbyists from volunteering in the executive branch, while still allowing them to spend an unlimited amount of money on free meals for legislators. According to the *Nashua Telegraph*, "House Republican leaders dealt a startling defeat to Gov. John Lynch...ramming through their own version of ethics reform for the executive branch."[9] Governor Lynch, who had made ethics a key plank of his 2004 campaign, eventually signed into law a compromise version of the Republicans' bill. This compromise tightened reporting requirements for lobbyists but still imposed restrictions on the use of volunteers in the executive branch and placed only minor limits on legislators' free meals. Though the bill was far from what he originally called for, Gov. Lynch hailed it in the press as "comprehensive ethics reform legislation that ensures the highest codes of conduct for public officials."[10] It is doubtful, however, that the governor was as jubilant in private about the deal he cut. Simply put, legislators hold enormous sway over bills when they are content with the status quo but know that a governor is desperate to reach a deal.

The bargaining benefits of legislatures' formal monopoly over the lawmaking process wash away, by contrast, in the budget because neither side can live with inaction. This puts the governor on equal footing with the legislature, even while it does not guarantee executive success. After a governor issues a set of budget proposals, legislators cannot believably boast that they will do nothing on fiscal policy, or make a take-it-or-leave-it offer tilted dramatically in their favor, because the status quo of a budget meltdown is untenable. For the same reason, the governor cannot credibly threaten to veto any and all state spending plans. Both sides must

---

[8] Diane Hirth, "Teachers' Raises Cut for Smaller Classes," *Tallahassee Democrat*, May 28, 2003.

[9] Kevin Landrigan, "House Passes Ethics Commission Bill," *The Telegraph* (Nashua, NH), January 2, 2006.

[10] Tom Fahey, "Governor Hails Ethics Law Changes," *New Hampshire Union Leader*, March 31, 2006, p. A2.

come to the table and compromise. Backroom dealings replace the formal legislative process, and negotiations become staring matches that patient governors can often win.

Governor Bill Graves's record after he gave Kansas's 2001 State of the State address illustrates how successful governors can be on the budget, even when they struggle to move items on their legislative agendas. Though the Republican governor's party held firm control over both houses of the state legislature, Gov. Graves's policy agenda was consistently defeated in Topeka. He included seven policy ideas in his State of the State address in 2001 but could pass only two of them in anything near their original form. The legislature dealt him defeats even on fairly innocuous items like a seat belt law. Lawmakers, many of whom viewed the governor's proposal as an "affront to individual liberty,"[11] preferred the status quo and never even brought governor-backed HB 2012 up for a vote. Contrast this with the budget, where Graves won victory after victory. He was able to secure passage for 13 of the 22 items that he included in his lengthy budget agenda, including a $21 million expansion in higher education funding and $19 million in additional money for special education. At the end of the budget process, Gov. Graves proudly concluded that "overall, this bill [the budget] effectively deals with the financial needs of Kansas during the next fiscal year."[12] He could not claim this sort of victory in the legislative realm.

The implication behind our view of governors is that their disadvantages in the legislative process are in some situations quite real and in others ephemeral. State chief executives will find it harder to shift state policy than to influence the budget. Experiences similar to those of Gov. Graves should be observed in many states. Indeed, our analysis of the policy and fiscal proposals made at the same time in State of the State speeches shows that legislators take action on 54 percent of bill proposals but pass in some form 66 percent of the budget ideas set forth in these speeches. This difference is significant, if not radical. More important is that different dynamics drive bargaining over the budget and over policy bills. We make concrete predictions about how each process will be played out by applying game theoretic models of bargaining. To our eye, bargaining over legislation looks much like Romer and Rosenthal's (1978) classic "setter" model – first applied to presidential–congressional

---

[11] Rhonda Holman (writing for the editorial board), "Buckle Up – Seat Belt the Best Tool for Curbing Fatalities," *Wichita Eagle*, October 2, 2002, p. 8A.

[12] "Governor Signs Final Spending Bill, Vetoes 22 Budget Items," *Chanute Tribune* (Kansas), May 26, 2001.

bargaining by Kiewiet and McCubbins (1988) and to state politics by Alt and Lowry (1994, 2000) – in which the first player to move can dictate the terms of a deal because an impasse reverts to the status quo policy. The best analogy for interbranch bargaining over the state budget, though, is the family of "alternating offers" games introduced by Osborne and Rubinstein (1990) and applied to state politics by Kousser (2005) and Kousser and Phillips (2009), which impose costly penalties on each side when negotiations break down.

We draw on the logic of these formal games, guided by the testimony of those inside governor's offices, to provide hints about how the strategic interaction unfolds between governors and the legislators they attempt to cajole. This yields predictions about what governors will ask for, what they will get, and which weapons will be most effective in helping them achieve their lawmaking goals.

1.3. How We Explore the Powers of Governors

We evaluate the predictions of our bargaining models using new sources of data and several methodological approaches. Much of our analysis relies on two data sets created expressly for this project. These data sets track, for a large sample of governors, the outcomes of interbranch negotiations over the budget as well as policy bills. We use these data to generate baseline measures of gubernatorial bargaining success and to estimate regression models of the determinants of outcomes. To these analyses, we add several case studies in which some shock brings about variation in a governor's formal or informal powers. In each, we consider whether the change in executive power results in a corresponding change in the governor's bargaining success and whether it alters the size, content, and scope of the governor's agenda. These detailed case studies allow us to more carefully isolate the causal impact of many of the variables we theorize will affect the governor's ability to shepherd her agenda through the lawmaking process. Throughout the volume, we supplement our empirical analyses with qualitative insights provided by political insiders and journalists who cover state politics.

1.3.1. *Two New Data Sets*

Our first data set tracks the fates of the proposals – both policy and budgetary – that governors make in their annual State of the State addresses. These speeches are delivered near the start of the legislative session and provide a venue, common to all states, for governors to lay their most important requests of legislators. According to Kevin Eckery, former communications director to California's Republican governor Pete Wilson, "the State of the State was meant to tee up the budget and create the agenda that you wanted to talk about. It is a combination of a wish list, a valedictory address for the year previous, a policy to-do list, and an attempt to form an agenda."[13] By tracking the success or failure of the specific proposals governors make in these speeches, we develop a systematic approach to measuring the success of state chief executives.

Our data set goes well beyond the efforts of prior scholarship. The legislative success of governors has been analyzed in comparative case studies (Lipson 1939), in a small sample of states (Moorehouse 1998), through success rates reported by governors and their staff (Rosenthal 1990), and quantified from journalistic sources for a single year (Ferguson 2003; Fording et al. 2002). None of these efforts, however, has produced a large, multiyear representative sample of gubernatorial proposals tracked by outside observers. Taking advantage of new digital search engines for statehouse journalism and online legislative archives, our three-year data collection effort yielded a comprehensive record of gubernatorial success, and failure, of the proposals contained in 52 State of the State addresses given in 2001 and 2006. The 28 states from which they are drawn capture the geographic, partisan, and institutional diversity that makes analysis of state government and politics so fruitful.

In each state, we begin by summarizing the discrete proposals made by a governor, separating policy bills from budget items to see whether outcomes and dynamics differ in these two realms. For all of the 1,088 budget and policy proposals, we then use journalistic coverage and legislative histories to see how the legislature treated the request and then determine whether the final disposition represented a victory, a defeat, or a compromise for the governor. We add richness to this data set by using the qualitative judgments of experts to measure the potential significance of a proposal and rely on the experts to record the ideological direction in which the proposal sought to move policy.

Our second data set allows us to gauge the outcome of negotiations over the size of the state budget. It takes advantage of the set of two yearly reports produced by the National Association of State Budget Officers (NASBO). The NASBO spring report tells us what governors asked for in their propose budgets. The fall report shows what was included in the

---

[13] Interview with Kevin Eckery, communications director to Gov. Pete Wilson, conducted by Thad Kousser in Sacramento, May 5, 2009.

enacted budget, that is, the budget that the governor signed into law at the conclusion of interbranch negotiations. Using this information, we can see how much of what governors ask for ends up in the final deal. For every dollar that the governor proposes to shrink or increase the size of state government, how many cents does the legislature deliver? This empirical strategy is very similar to the techniques used by scholars such as Kiewiet and McCubbins (1988) and Canes-Wrone (2001) to gauge presidential budgeting power. We collect gubernatorial proposals and final budget outcomes from the NASBO reports for a total of 21 fiscal years – 1989 to 2009. To both data sets, we add information about a host of economic, political, and institutional factors that may help account for variation in gubernatorial success.

1.3.2. *Natural Experimental Case Studies*

We also look in depth at a series of "natural experimental" case studies. Many books take the commendable approach of supplementing statistical analysis of a large number of observations with a close focus on a few cases, allowing their authors to trace causal processes and elucidate their broad themes, while grounding their analyses in the firm particulars of a few countries, states, organizations, or leaders. Scholars generally pick these carefully, often selecting cases that vary in the key explanatory factors that drive their theories, as suggested in King et al. (1994) and Brady and Collier (2004). For many projects, this is sufficient. In a study of gubernatorial success, however, it may be misleading to select cases in which governors' institutional or persuasive powers merely vary. The weapons governors take into battle with legislators are not simply given to them. They can be earned, as in the case of popularity, or bestowed on governors for nonrandom reasons, as in the case of veto powers. In the language of social scientific inquiry, they are "endogenous," created by causal forces that are often within a governor's control rather than imposed by outside events or authorities. Because variation in these sorts of factors can result from the actions of governors themselves, their effects may be difficult to judge through traditional case studies.

    An age-old method that has seen a recent revival (Dunning 2005; Political Analysis 2009) is the use of natural experiments to isolate the effects of these sorts of endogenous factors. Scholars following this approach look out at the real world that they are studying to find patterns that mimic an experimental laboratory, in which a random process creates the variation in a casual factor that one wishes to study. Natural experiments will rarely be driven by truly random variation, as laboratory experiments can be, but it is crucial that their variation be caused by "exogenous" forces such as outside events or authorities. In a chapter from his book *Guns, Germs, and Steel*, Diamond (1999) studies a "Natural Experiment of History," in which two genetically similar Pacific Islander communities migrated to islands with different environments, by tracking their histories to see how environmental factors shape the development of civilizations while holding genetics constant. Posner (2004) uses the location of the Zambia–Malawi border, imposed by a river, as a natural experimental treatment that shapes relationships between two tribes living in different concentrations on either side of the river. All these works rely on externally imposed variation in a causal factor, which is often, in other cases, endogenous.

Our natural experiments look for cases in which outside forces bring variation in a governor's powers, to avoid the causal complexities that would plague us if we selected cases in which these powers varied due purely to the actions of governors themselves. Consider, for example, the effects of popularity on a governor's ability to move a legislative agenda. One way to study this would be to select a case in which one governor's approval ratings fluctuated widely over the course of a few years and see how this correlated with proposal passage rates. The complication is that a governor's popularity can be endogenous, the product of actions and policy positions. In California, Gov. Arnold Schwarzenegger's popularity reached its peak in late 2004. Buoyed by his 65 percent approval rating,[14] the Republican used his 2005 State of the State address to launch an ambitious, conservative-leaning agenda, betting that his personal popularity would allow him to carry through a set of proposals that took on some of the state's most powerful interests. Schwarzenegger's aggressive agenda immediately incurred the wrath of – and a barrage of negative advertisements from – unions and the teachers' lobby, and his popularity tanked. Legislators were unresponsive, and when Schwarzenegger took the measures directly to voters through a special election in the fall, they rejected his slate of propositions. But what is the moral of this story? Did Schwarzenegger's agenda fail because he became unpopular, or did he become unpopular because he backed a losing agenda? With his popularity so closely tied to the substance of his State of the State agenda, it is difficult to separate cause and effect in this case.

[14] Governor Schwarzenegger reached this approval rating throughout much of 2004, according to Mark DiCamillo and Mervyn Field, "Schwarzenegger Continues to Get High Marks," Field Poll Release No. 2137, San Francisco, CA: The Field Poll.

The terrible tragedy of Hurricane Katrina provides a better way to study the impact of popularity on gubernatorial success. Before the storm, when they delivered their 2005 State of the State addresses, Louisiana's Democratic governor Kathleen Blanco was much more popular in her state than Mississippi's Republican governor Haley Barbour was in his. Her approval ratings stood at 55 percent, his at 37 percent, and this gap remained throughout each state's legislative session.[15] After the sessions closed and the storm hit in September 2005, their courses radically reversed. Barbour became a hero in his Gulf State with his calming, well-organized leadership after the storm, while Blanco lost support in hers as she struggled to lead a state that was flooded into chaos.

By the time the governors presented their 2006 State of the State addresses, Barbour's approval rating had climbed to 55 percent, while Blanco's had fallen to 38 percent, almost the mirror image of their ratings before the storm. While one can debate whether this switch revealed the ability of each governor to lead in crisis, or simply reflected differences in the severity of damage in the states or their partisan ties to the federal government, it is clear that it had nothing to do with the ambition or scope of their State of the State proposals. The natural experiment of Hurricane Katrina provides variation in popularity caused by forces that have nothing to do with Blanco's and Barbour's policy proposals, allowing us to gauge the effect of approval ratings on legislative cooperation by looking closely at the success of their 2005 and 2006 State of the State proposals.

We look at a series of other natural experiments as well. To explore the effects of the line-item veto, we take advantage of an Iowa Supreme Court decision from June 2004 that contracted the veto powers granted to governors in Iowa. In *Rants v. Vilsack*, the court narrowed the definition of what constitutes an appropriations bill, eliminating the ability of Hawkeye state governors to line-item veto language from legislation that primarily addresses policy concerns. The decision created exogenous variation in line-item veto power as the judicial branch stepped in to reshape the balance of power between the executive and legislative branches. Fortuitously, political control of the governorship and the legislature remained constant in Iowa before and after this shift, holding constant the preferences of each branch and isolating the impact of the institutional change. We also study how Republican governor Bob

---

[15] All of the Louisiana and Mississippi approval figures are taken from polls conducted by Survey USA.

Taft's record in the legislature changed when his popularity dramatically declined as a result of a homegrown political scandal, and how the balance of power between the branches shifted after a ballot proposition radically trnasformed California's legislature into a highly professional body. While they vary in the strength of their research designs, all these case studies seek to draw on the dual advantages of a close examination of governors guided by the logic of a natural experiment.

1.3.3. *Interviews and Qualitative Evidence*

Our approach to these analyses and the intuition behind our hypotheses are informed, in part, by a series of interviews with executive branch insiders that we conducted between spring 2009 and spring 2010. We interviewed several governors, their chiefs of staff and other senior advisors, the budget directors who helped them assemble state spending plans, and the communications directors and speechwriters who helped to pen their State of the State addresses. Although some of our interviews are drawn from Ohio, Kansas, Maryland, and Oregon, most come from California, where we had the privilege of interviewing members of three gubernatorial administrations spanning two decades. Speaking to so many officials from a single state allowed us to discuss the ways in which very different governors chose to operate in a similar institutional environment but under varying political conditions. Speaking with officials across several states provided us with insights about how differing institutional environments shape the strategies of chief executives.

Our interviews were conducted either in person or over the telephone, and all interviewees were asked a fairly similar set of questions. Without exception, the insiders with whom we spoke were forthcoming about their experiences in public service and happy to share their thoughts about the motivations of governors and the set of factors that shapes the outcomes of interbranch negotiations. We report, throughout the volume, the quotations, anecdotes, and insights gathered during these conversations.[16]

These interviews reflect our approach to political research. Scholars who seek to model the strategies and goals of political elites can, we believe, benefit from interviewing these individuals. Such conversations can help researchers choose plausible assumptions and pick the "right" models to apply to a given strategic interaction. Our conversations with

---

[16] All interviewees were told that their quotations and anecdotes may appear in the volume and were given the opportunity to review our notes.

state political insiders led us to adjust some of our assumptions regarding the goals of governors and the approaches they take to pursue these. Perhaps most important, interviews helped us realize that negotiations over the budget and policy bills have a very different logic.

In addition to interviews, our research is informed by statehouse journalism. To code the outcomes of proposals made in State of the State addresses, we read hundreds of newspaper articles detailing the dynamics of interbranch bargaining over individual policy or budgetary proposals. These articles, most of which were written by reporters who have spent years covering the statehouse, provide impressive detail concerning the legislative history of proposals and the circumstances leading to their passage or defeat. We relied on the rich qualitative information and expert judgments contained in newspaper coverage to further confirm our intuition about negotiations between governors and legislatures. Where useful – often to provide real world examples of our arguments – we report anecdotes gleaned from these articles.

1.4. Unveiling the Hidden Powers of American Governors

The questions we are addressing in this volume are not new. For more than 70 years, scholars have been asking whether state chief executives have the formal and informal power to be the "chief legislator" (Lipson 1939; Bernick and Wiggins 1991), the "legislator in chief" (Beyle 1983; Rosenthal 1990; Gross 1991; Ferguson 2003), or the "party leader" in governing (Morehouse 1998). Our investigation, by distinguishing between budget and policy negotiations, by using more direct measures of gubernatorial preferences, and by using more sophisticated statistical techniques, reveals powers of governors and nuances of this power that are hidden in prior investigations. Indeed, we show that at first glance, statistical patterns can often leave the powers of governors hidden, and we show how more accurate measures or more appropriate techniques can tell a more complete story. We discover that many of the findings of past scholarly studies of governors deserve a closer look. In this section, we highlight three of the ways our investigations reveal the hidden powers of governors.

1.4.1. *The Puzzle of Weak Governors: Revisiting the Determinants of State Policy*
In quantitative studies of state spending levels and policy outcomes, governors are usually reduced to mere bystanders (Dawson and Robinson

1963; Dye 1966; Hofferbert 1966; Winters 1976; Dye 1984; Brown 1995; Smith 1997; Garand 1988; Besley and Case 2003). Most existing work shows that states with Democratic governors do not spend more, or enact more liberal policies in politically contested programs like health care or welfare, than states with Republican governors. In the few models in which governors do appear to exert some control, the effect runs in a counterintuitive direction, with states led by Democrats spending less than those with a GOP governor (Clingermayer and Wood 1995; Rogers and Rogers 2000). All in all, according to most statistical analyses, governors' preferences do not appear to be reflected in either the size of the budget or in some of the most important state policy realms.

Can a George Pataki really be no different than a Mario (or Andrew) Cuomo? Can capturing the biggest prize in state politics be irrelevant to state governments' preeminent functions? In other words, can governors be as weak as these quantitative studies portray them, or are their powers somehow hidden? We argue that governors do play a key role in shaping state fiscal and policy choices, a role that is revealed when one recognizes important realities of state politics.

Most existing efforts to empirically evaluate gubernatorial power have relied on tests that are simply too blunt to fully flesh out executive influence. These studies rely exclusively on measures of party control as a proxy for gubernatorial preferences, gaining their causal traction from the assumption that Democrats always and everywhere want to expand government or move policy in the liberal direction. This ignores the unique opportunity that governors have to adapt to their states' political environments. Unlike presidents, governors do not have to carry their party's national banner. Unlike senators, they do not have to go to Washington, D.C., to vote on their party's national agenda, under pressure to toe their party's line. Governors are much freer to set their own paths. Because of this, Republican governors can win office in Hawaii and Democrats can survive in Alaska, but only by edging toward the middle.[17] Governors possess both the means and the motivation to be relative centrists, and this moderation will make their party affiliations less predictive of their policy goals. This, in turn, can leave their powers hidden in models that assume that the fiscal or policy preferences held by governors from the two parties will sharply diverge. Governors are forced to be more

---

[17] As Jacobson's (2006) work shows, public opinion about governors is much less polarized along party lines than opinion about senators or presidents, indicating that they do fit their states quite well.

pragmatic. "I don't think governors are driven primarily by ideology," former Maryland governor Parris Glendening told us. "There are too many day-to-day challenges in running a state. You have to get things done."[18] Instead of relying on party labels to judge gubernatorial preference, we measure what governors want directly, using their proposed budgets (from NASBO reports) and their State of the State addresses.

Using the new measures and methods, we find striking evidence of gubernatorial strength. Doing so brings quantitative models into line with the qualitative literature on governors, while it opens to the door to new lines of inquiry into the determinants of gubernatorial power.

1.4.2. *Policy versus Budget Games: The Empirical Implications of a Theoretical Distinction*

A central argument of this book is that governors play very different strategic games with legislators when they propose changes to the state budget, on one hand, or to state policy, on the other. These games should be different in both their outcomes and their dynamics. Chief executives will have a better chance of succeeding in the fiscal realm, we argue, because a budget is a moving vehicle that both branches have a huge stake in passing every year. In budget bargaining, patience is paramount, with factors such as the length of the legislature's session and the time remaining in a governor's term shaping outcomes. In the policy realm, by contrast, governors will have a hard time forcing legislative action, especially if lawmakers can live with existing laws. Here, governors will succeed when they have many legislative allies or when their power to persuade lawmakers is highest: when they are popular or in their first terms. Different factors should play different roles in these two divergent paths to the negotiating table.

These are theoretical distinctions, but they have clear empirical implications for the study of governors. Research that combines budget and policy proposals into a single quantitative model may obscure the effects of gubernatorial powers. Prior work on State of the State addresses has lumped together all types of gubernatorial pitches and often yielded weak or puzzling findings. In our empirical analysis, as we report at the end of Chapter 4, we would have missed many important dynamics if we had not treated the policy and budget games as separate. The impact of a governor's time remaining in office, the number of legislative allies, and

---

[18] Interview with Gov. Parris Glendening of Maryland, conducted by telephone by Thad Kousser and Justin Phillips, July 13, 2010.

the length of legislative sessions would have remained hidden, appearing insignificant in a model that pooled together the factors determining policy and budget success. The effect of popularity on policy success would have seemed much weaker than it truly is. It was only by testing the separate effects of these factors on policy and budget negotiations – an empirical choice guided by theory – that the importance of a governor's key powers became clear.

1.4.3. Can Governors Cash In Their Political Capital? First and Second Glances at Popularity

A first glance comparing the legislative success of popular and unpopular governors seems to show that political capital carries little to no currency in statehouses. Judged by her legislative batting average, Louisiana governor Kathleen Blanco's performance surprisingly improved when her popularity sunk in the wake of Hurricane Katrina. When Ohio governor Bob Taft's approval ratings dropped to historic lows after his administration became mired in an economic slowdown and ethics scandal, the legislature passed nearly every one of the bills that he proposed. Indeed, in our data set of State of the State proposals, summary statistics reveal only small differences in the batting averages of popular and unpopular governors, and prior research has found no evidence that popular governors are better able to move their legislative proposals (Ferguson 2003). Could it be that popularity does not translate into political success?

Our theoretical models of interbranch bargaining as well as our interviews with governors and their advisors provide us with an explanation of this puzzling pattern: governors' agendas (particularly their policy proposals) are endogenous to their political capital. Popular governors often anticipate that their proposals will receive a friendly reception in the legislature, and they aim high. These governors should often (though not always) propose more policy bills and ask for bills that are more ambitious in scope and closer to their own ideological liking than to the preferences of the legislature. Unpopular governors come more humbly to their State of the State addresses, frequently asking for bills that they can pass without possessing much in the way of political capital.

Recognizing this strategic logic changes how we evaluate the effectiveness of political capital. We trace the links between gubernatorial popularity and the ambition of proposals, showing that popular governors do often ask for more. In a second glance at gubernatorial success, we look not at raw batting averages but at measures that hold constant what a governor requests, thus asking whether a governor with higher approval ratings is better able to move a given set of proposals. In both our natural experiments and in our large-scale data analyses, we find this to be the case. Popularity matters, but in a subtle way that remains hidden when one looks only at raw batting averages and if one does not take into consideration the ambitiousness of a governor's proposals.

1.5. Organization of the Book

Before diving into these puzzles, we begin with a chapter that lays out our basic theories about the roots of executive power in the states. It begins by drawing a clear distinction between the ways governors bargain over policy bills and the ways they negotiate over budgets. For each process, we consider the obstacles that governors must overcome and the weapons they have for doing so. To discipline our thinking, we apply the framework of rational choice models but always illustrate our logic with the testimony of gubernatorial insiders and examples from the real world of state politics. This exercise generates explicit predictions about how the legislative and budget bargaining games should unfold in statehouses around the nation.

The next set of chapters explore these predictions broadly by introducing and analyzing our new data sets. In Chapter 3, we consider the public agendas of state chief executives. We begin with a sample of State of the State addresses, from which we identify over 1,000 individual proposals. For each proposal, we code whether it is a budgetary or policy item and make qualitative judgments about its significance and the ideological direction in which it will (if passed) move the status quo. Doing so allows us to construct measures of the content, ideological orientation, and scale of public agendas. Using these measures, we document the extent to which agendas vary across governors. We also consider the factors that shape agenda formation, including the governor's political circumstances, her partisanship, and the liberalness of her state's electorate. By examining what governors ask for, we are able to evaluate much of the intuition that underlies our models of both the policy and budget games.

In Chapter 4 we ask the critical questions, What do governors get? and When are governors most successful in their negotiations with legislatures? To do this, we track the outcomes of the proposals that we identified in our sample of State of the State addresses. For each, we ask whether legislators eventually passed what the governor proposed, either in its original form or in a half-a-loaf compromise, or whether the proposal died somewhere in the legislative process. Using these data, we present baseline measures of gubernatorial success. These answer important questions about the frequency with which governors successfully shepherd their proposals through the legislative process and the extent to which bargaining success varies across governors. We then employ regression analysis to systematically evaluate the predictions of our bargaining models, testing whether and how the determinants of gubernatorial success vary across the budget and policy games. The regression results not only tell us which factors meaningfully shape bargaining outcomes but also allow us to estimate the magnitude of their effects.

Chapter 5 explores these same questions by looking at negotiations over the size of state government. Here, we draw on our model of budget bargaining to argue that governors play a key role in shaping the size of the public sector, contrasting our model with models that predict executive weakness. To evaluate the strength of governors, we construct a data set comparing the budgets that governors signed at the end of negotiations to their original proposals. Using these data, we ask, for every dollar that the governor proposes to shrink or increase total spending (or taxes), how many cents does the legislature deliver? We also test our expectation that chief executives will do best when negotiating with relatively impatient legislatures.

In the remainder of the book, we narrow our focus, conducting in-depth investigations of three factors that may shape gubernatorial power: popularity, the line-item veto, and the professionalism of the legislature. These chapters rely on natural experiments and case studies to help untangle causality in ways that are not possible using large data sets that include dozens of governors and many states. In Chapter 6, we use two events – Hurricane Katrina in the Gulf States and the coingate scandal that plagued Gov. Taft in Ohio – to study how popularity shapes gubernatorial performance. For both, we match governors with control cases and measure the success of chief executives over time. Each of these case studies is designed to investigate the value of political capital by looking at how much governors get from legislatures before and after wide swings in their personal popularity, when these swings have nothing to do with the policies that they propose. Importantly, we consider not only how changing popularity affects gubernatorial success but also how it shapes agenda formation.

In Chapter 7 we consider the line-item veto, a tool that allows chief executives to nullify individual expenditures in appropriations bills. In particular, we ask whether governors with this power are able to shrink the size of government (as proponents of this institution contend) and whether the item veto can be used as a positive power, helping governors secure the adoption of their budgetary and policy proposals. To answer these questions, we turn to the eyewitness testimony of those who have used the line-item veto as well as legislators who have seen it used against them. We also rely on our new data sets, reestimating regression models from Chapters 4 and 5, but this time using statistical matching techniques and including measures of governors' line-item veto powers. The chapter concludes with a detailed case study, observing whether and how executive power shifted after the Iowa Supreme Court restricted the line-item powers granted to the governor.

Chapter 8 uses the passage of Proposition 1-a, which radically transformed the California legislature from a citizen house into a professional body, to study the effects of legislative professionalization on gubernatorial success. Our focus on California allows us to study the link between legislative professionalism and executive power by tracking how Golden State governors perform, first in negotiations with a citizen body and later when they face off with the nation's most professionalized legislature. Tracking gubernatorial success over the course of California's legislative evolution brings time series evidence to bear on a question that our other analyses examine only with cross-sectional data. Looking at one state over time also allows us to hold constant many factors that we were unable to address in our prior empirical analyses. Our concluding chapter summarizes our key results, puts the record of American governors in the broader context of the success of presidents and prime ministers, and lays out a research agenda that uses governors as part of the comparative study of chief executives.

Our book begins by noting the formal weakness of presidents and governors in America's separation-of-powers system. We show, however, through formal models of interbranch negotiations as well as our empirical analyses and case studies, that governors can often be the "legislator in chief." By distinguishing between budget and policy negotiations, by using direct measures of gubernatorial preferences, and by using a series of natural experiments, and case studies we are able to uncover evidence of gubernatorial power that was missed in prior scholarly work. Along the way, we find that the power of chief executives often depends more on each governor's political circumstances and resources than on the formal powers delegated by the state constitution. Capturing the governorship does not guarantee success; policy victories come most often when chief executives are popular, when they have allies in the legislature, and when they are in their first terms. Failures come when governors care a great deal about position taking and when they overwhelm lawmakers with an ambitious agenda. The institutional powers that matter most for executive power are those of the legislature: governors do much better when bargaining with citizen lawmakers than with professional legislators.

Just as Neustadt (1960) observed about American presidents, our nation's governors rely on their informal powers to persuade more than on the formal privileges of office. Because of this, it makes less sense to talk about strong-governor and weak-governor states than it does to speak of individual governors as being potent or feeble. One governor's failure does not doom his successors to a similar fate. Indeed, a chief executive's ability to move his agenda may wax and wane over the course of his governorship as his approval ratings rise and fall, as the number of his partisan allies in the legislature changes, and as his own ambitions evolve. Because institutional rules do not dictate bargaining outcomes, American governors have the opportunity to succeed, or fail, in any given state. It is the chief executives who realize this and adapt who win most often. By taking seriously the institutional disadvantages that governors confront and the many ways that governors can overcome these disadvantages, we cast governors in a new, powerful light.

2

The Roots of Executive Power

During his eight years as New Mexico's governor, Gary Johnson competed in the Ironman Triathlon World Championship, won the America's Challenge Gas Balloon Race, played guitar with Van Halen's Sammy Hagar, and helped save a house when massive wildfires struck Los Alamos.[1] Yet, one accomplishment that consistently eluded him was convincing legislators in Santa Fe to pass the items on his legislative agendas. Session after session, many of Gov. Johnson's policy proposals went nowhere. From the start of his administration, Johnson, a Republican with a background in business, openly clashed with a legislature led by Democratic political veterans. When he entered office in 1995, Johnson admitted, "I have no expectations to get anything out of the Legislature. The bottom line is we do have different philosophies."[2] The governor quickly highlighted these differences by vetoing a record-setting 200 bills passed by legislators, who retaliated by burying the bills that he wanted. By the end of that first year, Republican state senator Skip Vernon observed, "This guy couldn't pass Mother's Day through the Legislature."[3]

Little changed over the course of Johnson's governorship. The fate of the ambitious policy agenda that he announced in his 2001 State of the State address was emblematic of his frequent frustrations. He

---

[1] David Miles, "8 Years in the Life of Gary Johnson," *Albuquerque Journal*, December 22, 2002, p. A14.

[2] Bill Hume, "Johnson Vetoes Will Grade Session," *Albuquerque Journal*, March 25, 2001, p. B2.

[3] Bill Hume, "Johnson Vetoes Will Grade Session," *Albuquerque Journal*, March 25, 2001, p. B2.

began his speech with a call for education vouchers that could be used in private schools. After Republican representative Dan Foley introduced the governor's proposal as HB84, the legislature wasted little time killing it. The bill was defeated by a 9–4 vote in the House Education Committee, which then unanimously moved to table it. "It was dead when we got there; now it's blue and starting to smell," said Rep. Foley.[4] Johnson's proposals to implement merit pay for teachers and to ease the process for establishing charter schools also died. The national media gave Johnson much attention when the Republican triathlete called for drug legalization and a medical marijuana program, but legislators gave him few victories.[5]

The governor's push for a major reorganization of the executive branch was even less successful, with his calls for constitutional amendments meeting open hostility from the legislative branch. When Johnson asked for a change that would allow governors to appoint the attorney general and the secretary of state, Democratic representative Dan Silva of Albuquerque asked, "Is this a dictatorship that he wants to set up?"[6] Silva's colleagues answered his rhetorical question by ignoring Johnson's requests. Of the 21 policy proposals that Gary Johnson made in his 2001 State of the State address, four eventually passed, and the other 17 died unceremonious deaths.

What is most surprising about Gov. Johnson's record of legislative failure, though, is how it stands in contrast to his history of success in budget negotiations. While his policy proposals made little progress, Johnson often exerted influence over the total size and critical details of the state's spending plan. New Mexico crafts its two-year budget during 30-day legislative sessions convened in January of even-numbered years. In 2000, a month was not long enough for Johnson and his legislative opponents to negotiate a budget deal. Both branches paid a political price for the delayed budget, seeing their approval drop noticably in public opinion polls.[7] But later that spring, Gov. Johnson used his power to call the state's citizen legislators back to Santa Fe for a special session. As the standoff dragged on, legislators groused, took political heat, and ultimately gave in to many of the governor's demands. One legislator opined that such meetings "certainly are not special. They are absolutely

[4] "School Vouchers Considered Dead," *Albuquerque Journal*, February 15, 2001.
[5] Steve Terrell and Mark Hummels, "Gaming Compacts OK'd, Most Drug Reforms Not," *Santa Fe New Mexico*, March 18, 2001.
[6] "House Kills Succession Measure," *Albuquerque Tribune*, February 28, 2001, p. A4.
[7] "Voters Unimpressed with Johnson, Lawmakers," *Albuquerque Journal*, March 19, 2000, p. A1.

routine and, in my opinion, very annoying."[8] The special session took
legislators away from their day jobs, cost the government $45,000 a day
to run, and generated much political controversy. One legislator said, "I
think it would behoove all of us to be out of here by Saturday. I can just
see a lot of really ugly newspaper stories if we're still in session on April
Fool's Day."[9] Perhaps because of the legislators' hurry, they gave in to
Johnson's major fiscal demands and passed a budget that was described
as a "political home run" for the governor.[10]

Juxtaposed against Johnson's many strikeouts with policy proposals,
this budget success presents a puzzle about the roots of executive power:
how can the same governor be successful in one realm while failing so
miserably in the other? Are these two types of negotiations fundamentally
different? Governor Johnson's story deserves systematic scrutiny and is
far from the only puzzling pattern to emerge from a look at gubernatorial
success and failure.

In Massachusetts, in 2006, Republican Mitt Romney gave a State of
the Commonwealth address meant to lay the foundation for his planned
2008 run for the presidency. One might have expected him to build a
working relationship with the state's Democratic legislators and pile up
policy successes to trumpet on the campaign trail. Instead, his far-reaching
speech was an invitation to gridlock. It included 18 proposals, many
of them taking up controversial issues such as state employee pension
reform, abstinence education, a state takeover of failing schools, and work
requirements for welfare recipients, reforms which Democratic legislators
routinely oppose. In fact, though at least one of them was a recycled proposal that Gov. Romney had made and been denied in the past, that did
not stop him from vowing to "propose, again, mandatory parental prepa-
ration classes for parents of kids in failing schools."[11] It was not a shock
to anyone in Boston's statehouse, then, that only three of Gov. Romney's
bills passed in anything near their original form. The real question is, why
would a governor who sought higher office choose the perilous path of
asking for bills that he knew the legislature would not pass?

Another puzzle emerged from our look at governors in 2001. Leaders
of two of the nation's mega-states, New York governor George Pataki

[8] "Only Thing Special about These Sessions Are Lessons," *Albuquerque Tribune*, April 4, 2000.
[9] Hummels, Mark. 2000. "They're back." *Santa Fe New Mexican*, March 28, 2000.
[10] "Vetoes Enact Tax Reduction," *Albuquerque Journal*, April 22, 2000.
[11] Quotation from Gov. Mitt Romney in his State of the Commonwealth address, delivered on January 18, 2006, in Boston, Massachusetts.

(Republican) and California governor Gray Davis (Democrat), led state-houses that appeared primed to pass budgets on time. Both governors negotiated with full-time legislatures that employed thousands of staffers, including expert budget analysts. Yet, the legislature's expertise and long sessions seemed to create a recipe for delay rather than deals. Governor Pataki's $83.6 billion budget allocated $6 billion of new spending to popular programs like increased school aid, more money for the state university system, and tax rebates to farmers and senior citizens.[12] Still, he could not convince lawmakers to agree to such apple-pie proposals. New York did not pass a final spending plan until October 25, well into its fiscal year.[13] Governor Davis did not reach a deal with lawmakers until 25 days past the July 1 start of California's fiscal year. The Golden State's budget was late, even though Davis's spending plan included a multi-billion-dollar boost for state schools that enjoyed broad bipartisan appeal.[14]

For observers of each state, these budget delays came as no shock. Between 1985 and 2005, 20 of New York's 21 budgets were adopted after the beginning of the fiscal year (McMahon 2005). In California, while Gray Davis's first two budgets were completed on time, this was the exception rather than the rule in a state where budgets were signed prior to the July 1 deadline in only four years from 1987 through 2009.[15] Yet, both these patterns should in some sense be surprising. Why do states with the nation's most professional legislatures miss their deadlines, even in relatively good fiscal times? Why is a governor's job harder when negotiating budgets with lawmakers for whom legislating is a full-time job?

Solving these puzzles requires a close look at the strategic nature of the games that governors play when they bargain with legislators. After conducting interviews with key players in these games, we used the tools of rational choice to turn their testimony about the goals that they pursue and the rules of statehouse bargaining into systematic predictions about the factors that can help make governors more or less successful. Some of

[12] Eric Durr, "Governor Unwraps Budget $83.6 Billion Plan Includes School Aid Increase," *Watertown Daily Times*, January 16, 2001.

[13] Jordan Rau, "New York Budget Gets $500M Boost," *Newsday* (Melville, NY), October 25, 2001.

[14] Joan Hansen, "Strings Still Attached to School Budget," *Orange County Register*, January 18, 2001.

[15] California Department of Finance, "Chart P-1: Historical Data Budget Act Dates and Veto Information," accessed at http://www.dof.ca.gov/budgeting/budget_faqs/information/documents/CHART-P1.pdf/ on October 1, 2010.

these predictions, which we test in the chapters to come, formalize what other scholars have already noted. Yet, our approach also leads us to set forth new contentions and some counterintuitive predictions, which are borne out in our empirical analysis. And our models help us better understand why Gary Johnson, Mitt Romney, George Pataki, and Gray Davis won and lost when they did, revealing the roots of executive power.

2.1. Two Different Games That Governors Play

Whenever governors want to see legislation passed through their state-houses, they have to overcome their formal exclusion from most parts of the lawmaking process. Legislators monopolize everything, from the introduction of bills to committee votes to floor debates. Yet, governors are not without potent tools. State chief executives, like presidents, command the stage of American politics more than any single legislator (Neustadt 1960; Kernell 1986; Rosenthal 1990; Beyle 2004). Their policy priorities and the proposals they make become news. Public events, particularly a State of the State address, focus legislators on the executive agenda and can pressure lawmakers into taking action. Governors can and do flaunt their veto pen, knowing that its use and even the threat of its use are critical to their influence over policy. They can leverage their control over the fates of bills that legislators covet into support for executive proposals, turning their negative power into a positive one. Even beyond their ability to sign and veto bills, state chief executives can offer plenty of invaluable favors to cooperative lawmakers. These tools provide an important counterbalance to the legislature's monopoly over the lawmaking process.

Our models of executive–legislative bargaining focus on these tools, the strategic choices a governor can make at the beginning of negotiations, and especially the potential endgame – that is, what happens if the governor and legislature fail to reach a deal. Savvy players realize that there are different endgames to negotiations over a governor's policy proposals, on one hand, and over the budget, on the other. When legislators refuse to pass a governor's policy bill, nothing too terrible happens. State law in that area remains at the status quo, where it has been all along. If legislators can live with the existing policy, then they can stonewall the governor's new bill or attempt to extract favors from the governor in exchange for passing it. The legislative monopoly truly matters in policy negotiations. Governors who have better tools to convince lawmakers to go along with their proposals will see more success than weaker executives, but ultimately, all are at the legislature's mercy.

The endgame is dramatically different when it comes to the budget. If negotiations collapse, a serious political calamity looms. In most states, unlike in Congress,[16] a budget that is delayed past the start of the fiscal year triggers an automatic shutdown of the government (Grooters and Eckl 1998).[17] In all states, it generates unfavorable press and puts serious political heat on the governor and legislators. Neither side can hold out in a stalemate for long. Public polls conducted in California,[18] New York,[19] and New Mexico[20] have all demonstrated that a late budget cuts deeply into the approval ratings of both branches. Looking ahead to this endgame usually brings legislators to the bargaining table before calamity can strike. Since legislators cannot live with the status quo if they refuse to pass a budget, their advantage over governors dissipates dramatically in this realm. Both sides have incentives to deal, and budget bargaining becomes a staring match that patient governors often win.

The insiders who negotiate budgets and policy bills understand the differing dynamics of these two games. "You've gotta have a budget,"

[16] Continuing resolutions, although frequent in federal budgeting (Fenno 1966; Meyers 1997; Patashnik 1999), are not common or important considerations in state budget negotiations. Only nine states permit some form of continuing resolution (note 17), and even these measures are labeled "minibudgets" (Connecticut), "interim budgets" (New York), or "stopgap funding" (Pennsylvania). None can become permanent, and the players in budget negotiations do not hope or fear that they will avoid crafting a new budget.

[17] Jennifer Grooters and Corina Eckl, "Table 6-4: Procedures When the Appropriates Act Is Not Passed by the Beginning of the Fiscal Year," accessed at http://www.ncsl.org/programs/fiscal/lbptabls/lbpct4.htm in June 2008.

[18] The time series of legislative and gubernatorial approval in California reported by the Field Poll reveals how severe these penalties can be. In the first two years of Gov. Gray Davis's administration, 1999 and 2000, the branches reached budget deals before the start of the new fiscal year. During Davis's last two years, 2002 and 2003, negotiations dragged into September and August, according to Wilson and Ebbert (2006, p. 276). In 1999 and 2000, the governor's and the legislature's approval ratings remained essentially constant over the summer. But the legislature's approval ratings dropped from 45% to 35% from July to September 2002 and from 31% to 19% from April to July 2003 (Field Poll 2004, 2). Davis's already low ratings edged downward as well in each of those summers (Field Poll 2003, p. 3).

[19] When the 2001 budget deal in New York was delayed, 84% of survey respondents were "very concerned" or "somewhat concerned" about the budget, and 63% blamed both Gov. Pataki and the state legislature (Quinnipiac 2001). In 2004, 81% of polled New Yorkers voiced concern over the state's late budget, and 46% said that it made them more willing to vote out incumbents (Caruso 2004).

[20] When New Mexico's budget was delayed in 2000, Gov. Gary Johnson and the legislative leaders all polled poorly and "New Mexico voters faulted Johnson and lawmakers almost equally for their failure to reach agreement during the session on a $3 billion budget," according to the *Albuquerque Journal*, "Voters Unimpressed with Johnson, Lawmakers," March 19, 2000, p. A1.

notes Gary Hart, a longtime California state senator who also observed negotiations from the executive branch as Gov. Gray Davis's education secretary. "The governor's [policy] bills, you don't need them. But you do need the budget."[21] In Maryland, Democratic governor Parris Glendening pointed out the paramount importance of the budget endgame in a state where lawmakers are required to pass a budget on the 83rd day of a 90-day session: "If that deadline is missed, by law, all other action must be suspended. Both the legislature and the governor would lose, and the public simply would not have tolerated it. The Maryland culture is that the legislature meets for 90 days, and the budget is passed on time."[22]

Insiders also point out that the budget can be the exception to the rule of legislative advantage. Asked whether it was easier to move budget proposals than policy bills, Ohio governor Bob Taft (Republican) answered definitively, "Oh, that's very true."[23] In Kansas, Burdett Loomis, an advisor to Democratic governor Kathleen Sebelius, remembers that "much of the governor's tenure was focused on the budget because the big policy changes coming from the legislature in a conservative direction, she would veto, and she figured out pretty quickly that they would kill her policy initiatives. So, she turned to the budget."[24] For Gov. Sebelius, all of the action was in budget negotiations because this was the only venue in which she could successfully pursue her most important legislative goals. Indeed, when asked if the governor had been able to secure any significant agenda items through the policy game, Loomis responded, "Any major change was done in the budget process. I'm trying to think of a major change done through the regular bill process, and I can't think of a single one."

In this chapter, we formalize the intuition that our interviews, along with existing academic work, provide about how governors negotiate with legislators to get what they want. We present two simplified games that governors play with legislators, one meant to capture fights over policy proposals, the other tailored to the budget. Both adapt models

[21] Interview with Gary Hart, former California state senator and education secretary, interview by telephone conducted by Thad Kousser, July 16, 2009.
[22] Interview with Gov. Parris Glendening of Maryland, conducted by telephone by Justin Phillips and Thad Kousser, July 13, 2010.
[23] Interview with Gov. Bob Taft of Ohio, conducted by telephone by Thad Kousser and Justin Phillips, October 1, 2009.
[24] Interview with Burdett Loomis, Director of Administrative Communication to Kansas governor Kathleen Sebelius, 2004–5, conducted by telephone by Thad Kousser, May 14, 2010.

from the game theory literature to our view of the roots of executive power and to the features of American state government.

Distinguishing between the policy and the budget game helps resolve the puzzle that began this chapter: Gary Johnson failed in his policy negotiations with New Mexico's legislature but succeeded in many of his budget battles because of the stronger bargaining position that governors have in the budget, especially when they are negotiating with legislatures that meet in short sessions. The policy game gives legislators a chance to refuse to pass executive proposals because they can live with the consequences. Governors need to use the sticks and carrots at their disposal to convince legislators to come to the bargaining table and to pass the bills they propose. The most successful governors at this game will be the ones with sweeter carrots and sharper sticks. By contrast, budget bargaining is a staring match, with neither side able to hold out forever but both hoping to beat the other branch. The most successful governors will be the ones who are more patient than the legislators at whom they stare across the table. Because of this, we contend, what governors bargain over (policy bills or the budget) often determines whether they will win.

Our primary point is that because these games end differently, they will be played differently from the start. This makes the strategic logic of game theory, which looks down a game tree at all possible final outcomes and works backward to see what moves players will make, a useful tool to apply here. Our models help to explain the puzzles that with which we began and produce clear empirical predictions, which we test and explore in greater depth throughout this book.

2.2. The Policy Game

We fit our substantive arguments about what governors want in the policy realm and how they go about passing their bills into the framework of a classic game that has been used by other scholars to simplify the complex process of executive–legislative bargaining. We adapt and extend Romer and Rosenthal's (1978) *setter model*. This model considers how two players negotiate when one has the exclusive power to set the terms of a deal, while the other has only the power to accept or reject the deal. The setter model mirrors negotiations where legislators can offer bills, which governors must then either sign or veto. Because of this close fit, Kiewiet and McCubbins (1988) and Cameron (2000) apply the setter model to

Congress, while Alt and Lowry (1994, 2000) adapt it to bargaining over the scale of state government. Building on these works, we take the basics of the setter model and add in what we see as the key strategic dynamics that unfold after governors publicly announce their policy agendas.

2.2.1. What Do Governors and Legislators Want?

We build our model of negotiations over policy proposals in a governor's public agenda from first principles, beginning with what motivates each player. By *public agenda*, we mean the proposals that governors make in high-profile announcements designed to draw press and voter attention to their ideas.[25] State of the State addresses are the primary sources of such announcements, though governors can use other forums to make them.

What do governors aim to gain when they make these public pronouncements? We assume that they care about the policies that they ultimately extract from legislators but also about what they are seen asking for. When a governor evaluates how satisfied she is with negotiations, she takes into consideration both the final policy outcome and whether the position that she took in her public agenda reflects her sincere preferences (i.e., her ideal outcome).

What sources of leverage do governors have at their disposal to achieve their aims? Our assumption is that they can credibly promise to do favors (i.e., make side payments) to legislators who cooperate by passing the bills that the governor proposes, though some governors are better positioned than others to help legislators. When a state chief executive includes a policy proposal in her public agenda, this elevates the stakes of negotiations because it conveys the implicit promise that she will dole out the carrots at her disposal (or withhold her punishing sticks) if legislators send the bill to her desk.

Legislators care about the side payments that governors can make, but of course, they, too, care about policy outcomes. Unlike governors, they cannot offer favors to get what they want out of the other branch. The source of their power is their exclusive ability to author and pass legislation, an agenda-setting advantage that allows them to decide whether they are better off taking the governor's approach to a policy question and earning the promised side payment or forgoing these favors to pass a bill that more closely reflects legislative priorities.

---

[25] What we exclude from this definition are bills that a governor might support but only pushes for in informal negotiations with legislators or agency-backed bills on which the governor stakes no public political capital.

We turn our intuitions about these motivations and powers, informed by our interviews, into formal assumptions. Abstracting the process of executive–legislative negotiations into its key features, we construct a model that provides predictions about when the branches will deadlock and when they will be able to reach a deal, and who will shape the details of that deal. Our first necessary simplification is to think of policy bargaining as a battle between two unitary actors, the governor and the legislature. Of course, neither branch always acts as one. Within the executive branch, opinionated cabinet officials, competing advisors, and the governor sometimes want different things, and legislatures can contain as many policy preferences as they have members. Yet, by the time a single policy proposal has made its way into the governor's public agenda, executive rivalries have been settled, and a pivotal legislator or bloc of legislators will emerge to guide the branch's response on this policy dimension. By assuming that there are only two players in this game, a governor and the legislature, we follow the approach of Kiewiet and McCubbins (1988), Alt and Lowry (1994, 2000), Cameron (2000), Kousser (2005), and many others.[26]

Our second abstraction of reality is to think of bargaining over a bill as taking place on a single, spatial dimension. This dimension can be represented by a line, with each player's preferred policy ("ideal points" denoted by G^* and L^*) indicated as a point on the line. Another point on the line, SQ, represents the location of the status quo, the existing policy such as criminal sentences of a given length, current school testing procedures, or the lack of a program to address some policy challenge. New proposals can move the status quo in any direction and by any amount.

2.2.2. *What Do Governors and Legislators Know?*

Since this is a game of complete information, both players know each other's preferences. Governors, should they choose to do so, have the

---

[26] Krehbiel's (1998) pivotal politics model makes the critical point that bargaining models should also consider the positions of legislators who control veto overrides and who can filibuster legislation in the Senate, while Cameron (2000) explores the importance of veto overrides. While filibusters and similar delaying tactics are rare in the states, veto overrides (and their anticipation by governors) do play a role in negotiations. Since their threshold to override a veto varies across states, we measure this potential for each state in our data set empirically and take it into account elsewhere in our model, while maintaining the simplifying assumption of a unitary legislature. Other models (Tsebelis and Money 1997; Sin and Lupia 2008) consider the formal implications of bicameralism, another important path for future consideration in models of state politics that we ignore here for the sake of tractability.

opportunity to vet their proposals with key legislators in advance of making them public. Alternatively, governors (and their advisors) may be able to predict the legislature's response based on their prior experiences. But governors, administrators, and legislators generally know pretty well where each other stands, even if they do not agree. If legislators cannot figure out exactly what a governor wants from her public prouncements, they will have plenty of opportunities to do so.

The branches also know each other's powers. To counter the legislature's formal power over the agenda, the governor possesses a collection of formal and informal powers that we conceptually combine into the ability to make a single side payment of value S to a legislature that passes her proposal intact. Representing the sticks and carrots at a governor's disposal, S can be measured on the same spatial scale that we use to gauge policy movements. Governors use it to pay off legislators for bending to their policy will, just as legislators on the floor make a side payment to committee members in Krehbiel's (1991) model of congressional organization. The value of S can vary across governors. This "power to persuade" (Neustadt 1960) depends on concrete, measurable factors, giving strong governors the ability to buy more policy concessions by offering a larger S than weaker governors can offer.

2.2.3. *The Power of the Veto Pen*

What are these carrots and sticks, and what separates strong from weak governors? One crucial source of leverage that governors can use to compel cooperation is their control over the bills that legislators want to pass in other policy realms. Gubernatorial advisors and legislators alike tell us that the best way for a governor to secure support for her own high-profile public proposals is to signal her support for other pieces of legislation that, though they may not seem as important to the state, are just as critical to the careers and policy goals of legislators. Former California state senator Pat Johnston, who served in key committee roles through four governors' administrations, observes that "this is a bill driven process, so that's how we measure success here. Legislators, lobbyists, everyone focuses on getting bills passed and getting them signed by the governor, so a governor is able to use that concern to get some support for the governor's own agenda."[27] In New York, two close observers of Albany politics note that "bills are the currency of the legislature, and passing bills into law is the primary measure of a legislator's achievement. Any

[27] Interview with former California state senator Pat Johnson, conducted by Thad Kousser in Sacramento, June 22, 2009.

doubts? Check the achievements claimed in the biographies legislators write about themselves" (Feldman and Benjamin 1988, p. 280).

Because a governor can sign or veto any legislator's bills, she possesses a negative power that she may, even without making an implicit quid pro quo offer, turn into positive support for her own bills in the legislature. "How does a governor get something out of the legislature?" asks Bill Whalen, chief speechwriter to California governor Pete Wilson from 1995 to 1999. "First, a governor has the veto, so he can say 'I want this. You may not, but do you want your bill? Here's what will happen if you don't work with me.'"[28] Wilson's communications director, Dan Schnur, summarizes this transaction with, "It is the power to veto legislation that gives a governor the power to get legislation."[29] In their national look at the powers of governors, Beyle and Ferguson (2008, p. 216) write that "the governor can offer support on a member's 'pet legislation' in exchange for that member's support for the governor's initiatives." The veto is the key to the governor's leverage in this exchange.

Although all governors in the United States possess the veto, this power is not perfectly constant across governors.[30] Because vetoes may be overridden, governors will have a stronger bargaining position generally when their party controls enough seats in the legislature to prevent a veto override. A governor whose party holds an override-proof majority will also be in a stronger bargaining position if she resides in one of the 44 states that grant the governor line-item veto authority over spending provisions. Governors who can credibly threaten to veto a key legislator's bill or line out that legislator's favored spending will be better positioned to compel cooperation on their own policy proposals. Larry Thomas, who advised Republican governor George Deukmejian in California, concludes, "I think what matters most is the partisan mix between the legislature and the governor. If the governor has even a minority of Republicans, but he still has enough to sustain a veto, then this helps."[31]

---

[28] Interview with Bill Whalen, chief speechwriter to Gov. Peter Wilson, conducted by Thad Kousser, Palo Alto, California, May 21, 2010.

[29] Interview with Dan Schnur, communications director to Gov. Pete Wilson, conducted by telephone by Thad Kousser, July 7, 2009.

[30] North Carolina was the last state to grant its governor veto power, doing so in 1996. Currently, governors in 44 states possess some form of the line-item veto, although the specifics of this authority vary in the important ways that we will discuss in Chapter 7 (Council of State Governments 2010, pp. 201–2).

[31] Interview with Larry Thomas, press secretary and campaign manager to California governor George Deukmejian, conducted by telephone by Thad Kousser and Justin Phillips, June 30, 2009.

2.2.4. *The Power of Small Favors*

A second set of powers that governors can use to extract what they want out of legislatures resides in their ability to do all of the invaluable little favors that make legislators want to work with them. When governors attend fund-raisers for legislators, travel to their districts to campaign for them, consult them about commission appointments and state-funded local projects, or simply socialize and take pictures with legislators, they are building the goodwill that can turn into support for executive proposals.

Rosenthal (1990, p. 13) terms these the *powers of provision*, quoting an Alabama political observer who stated that "any legislator who says he needs nothing from the Governor's office is either lying or stupid." Governors can dole out small but important favors that provide concrete benefits to lawmakers in their districts. Pete Wilson aide Dan Schnur observes that "if you can sign at least some of their bills, work out the amendments necessary to get them signed, show them some support by giving them a signing ceremony instead of a signing statement, they will be more likely to cooperate with you on your priorities."[32] California governor Gray Davis explains that "it's important to give public recognition to legislators. They work hard on their bills, so when you want to sign one you can do one of two things. You can sign the bill and send out a press statement, or you can go down and do a press event in their district. If you go to Fresno, really make an effort, a legislator likes that."[33]

Governors elsewhere need not even exert this much effort to hand out a valuable carrot to legislators. "Often in Maryland, they send identical Senate and House bills, and a key question becomes 'Which bill gets signed by the governor?'" reports Gov. Parris Glendening. "They all wanted to go back to their district to say it passed and it was my bill, so we'd make a determination on these – about 20% of bills – of whose we'd sign, and this can help, strengthen your relationship with that legislator."[34] As Gov. Glendening's quotation makes clear, governors can dole out these small favors selectively, using them to reward or withholding them to punish legislators. Bill Hauck, who served as chief of staff to two

---

[32] Interview with Dan Schnur, communications director to Gov. Pete Wilson, conducted by telephone by Thad Kousser, July 7, 2009.

[33] Interview with Gov. Gray Davis of California, conducted by Thad Kousser, Los Angeles, California, May 28, 2010.

[34] Interview with Gov. Parris Glendening of Maryland, conducted by telephone by Justin Phillips and Thad Kousser, July 13, 2010.

California Assembly Speakers and as deputy chief of staff to Gov. Pete Wilson, recalls that "every legislator has needs, and while you don't want to indulge them to any great extent, you pick and choose."[35]

2.2.5. *Powers Erode over Time*

All governors can offer favors small and large or make veto threats. The importance that legislators will attach to these favors – and thus the governor's prospects of winning legislative game – depends on both the magnitude of what a governor can promise and how long she can promise it. At the beginning of an administration, governors and legislators alike foresee a long relationship in which the governor will have plenty of time to repay legislators who cast tough votes in favor of her bill. This is part of the mechanism by which governors can expect a honeymoon period during their first year in office.[36] By contrast, when a governor is nearing the end of her term in office and is viewed as a potential lame duck, she will have dramatically less time to follow through on her offer to make it up to legislators, leaving her with a smaller side payment to offer.

"For any governor in any state, and for the president, you are never as powerful as you are on the day of your inauguration," remarks Gov. Gray Davis. "You start at the peak of your power, and then it just goes downhill from there."[37] Prior academic study of governors also finds this dynamic at play. Margaret Ferguson's analysis of gubernatorial success in the 1993–4 session found that "executive success wanes over time. . . . This supports the traditional 'bank-account' theory of chief executive clout" (Ferguson 2003, p. 172). Put in the terms of our formal model, the value of side payment S that a governor can offer to cooperative legislators declines as she moves from the beginning toward the end of her administration.

2.2.6. *Power Grows with Popularity*

The size of the side payment that governors can offer to legislators should also be shaped by their approval ratings. Popular governors can make more potent payments, we contend. A governor with high approval ratings is going to be a bigger draw at a fund-raiser or campaign rally.

---

[35] Interview with Bill Hauck, former chief of staff to assembly speakers Willie Brown and Bob Moretti and deputy chief of staff to Gov. Pete Wilson, conducted by telephone by Thad Kousser and Justin Phillips, June 25, 2009.

[36] Another mechanism that may drive any honeymoon effect is that newer governors are often more popular, a factor that we hold constant in our empirical analysis.

[37] Interview with Gov. Gray Davis of California, conducted by Thad Kousser, Los Angeles, California, May 28, 2010.

Pictures with popular governors will appear on legislative campaign materials, while members will run against a governor – even one of their own party – who is unpopular. "I think if a governor has strong popularity ratings, he's got a bigger bully pulpit," concludes Ohio governor Bob Taft, who saw his popularity rise and fall over the course of his administration. "If a governor is strong and popular, whether or not he's going to use the electoral power that gives him, legislators still think that he might use that either for or against them in their reelection."[38]

The potency of the punishments that a governor can impose also depends on her popularity. It was possible for Arnold Schwarzenegger to campaign against six vulnerable Democrats in the lead-up to California's 2004 election, when his 65 percent approval helped convince them to veer right in their voting patterns (Kousser et al. 2007). By 2010, with his popularity dipping to 22 percent,[39] he stayed off the campaign trail and did not wield as much influence with legislators. Finally, popular governors can more credibly threaten to veto bills that legislators favor, promising to take the heat for doing so unless legislators go along with executive bills. In our view, the way that popularity inflates the value of these sorts of favors is the tangible path of "political capital" linking approval ratings to policy achievement. Popularity can sweeten a governor's carrots and sharpen her sticks, changing the value of the S that she can offer.

The testimony of those close to governors supports this assumption. According to Deukmejian aide Larry Thomas, "the higher the approval ratings, that is a time for a governor to aggressively pursue his agenda and have a legislature that is a little off balance, a little fearful of how popular the governor is, a little concerned about how the governor will exercise his power. That gives a governor an easier road. As that erodes, the legislature becomes less responsive to a governor, less willing to do what he says."[40] Phil Trounstine, former communications director to California governor Gray Davis, and now co-editor and publisher of calbazz.com, puts it in similar terms: "As long as he [the governor] is popular, he can help

---

[38] Interview with Gov. Bob Taft of Ohio, conducted by telephone by Thad Kousser and Justin Phillips, October 1, 2009.

[39] Mark DiCamillo and Mervyn Field, "Schwarzenegger and the State Legislature Both Get Very Poor Job Ratings," Field Poll Release No. 2346, July 14, 2010.

[40] Interview with Larry Thomas, press secretary and campaign manager to California governor George Deukmejian, conducted by telephone by Thad Kousser and Justin Phillips, June 30, 2009.

legislators by helping them get reelected, raise money, sign their bills, help allies get jobs and appointments. As he loses popularity, he can't deliver money, he can't deliver voters, isn't getting the same kind of respect in the media. Popularity breeds influence, and a lack of popularity breeds a decline in influence."[41]

2.2.7. *The Implicit Stakes of a High-Profile Policy Proposal*

When a governor elevates a proposal by including it in her public agenda, we assume that she is promising to pay legislators a fixed value of S if they pass the bill and nothing if legislators pass a different version or do nothing.[42] Longtime California legislator Pat Johnson observes that "when he [the governor] announces a proposal, that elevates its importance." Larry Thomas spoke similarly of the items in Gov. Deukmejian's State of the State address. If a proposal was in the speech, "It was what he wanted and what he was willing to put his prestige on the line for."[43]

While it may vary from strong to weak governors, S is constant across all of the proposals that a governor makes in her speech. Because doing small favors or restraining her veto pen does not hurt a governor, paying the cost of S does not factor into a governor's utility calculation for each proposal. However, since the game that we describe here is played many times simultaneously with the many proposals contained in a governor's public agenda, we assume that the governor has a fixed pot of favors to draw from and that making many proposals can deplete the value of S in each game. In each game, though, paying S is akin to anteing up in

[41] Interview with Phil Trounstine, former communications director to Gov. Gray Davis, conducted by telephone by Thad Kousser, July 8, 2009.

[42] The rationale behind the way that the payment of S is structured – with the legislature receiving all of S if it passes the governor's proposal in a close approximation of its original form but nothing if lawmakers send the governor a compromise more to their own liking – is that the State of the State or other public announcement serve as a clear focal point for where the governor has staked her political capital. We assume that governors and legislators may bargain over the details of policy informally but do not have the opportunity to negotiate over how much in favors the governor might pay for a specific compromise on every item in the governor's agenda. One possible extension of the model could loosen this assumption, allowing legislators to extract policy concessions from the governor in exchange for a smaller payment of favors, which would give legislators half-a-loaf of favors when they pass a bill that gives half-a-loaf of policy to the governor. We do not explore that extension formally here.

[43] Interview with Larry Thomas, press secretary and campaign manager to California governor George Deukmejian, conducted by telephone by Thad Kousser and Justin Phillips, June 30, 2009.

a poker game: governors put the offer of this side payment on the table every time they include an item in their public agenda.

How does a governor judge whether she won at the end of the game? We assume that she cares about policy and budgetary matters but also about whether she took a position, in her public agenda, that reflects her "sincere preferences." A governor's sincere preferences (at least as we conceive of them) may be intrinsic and thus reflect her long-held political ideology or governing philosophy. Alternatively, and perhaps more cynically, these preferences may be induced by the demands of voters, key interest groups, or campaign contributors. Regardless of their origins, governors receive some benefit from signaling these preferences in their public agendas. In this way, a governor resembles Mayhew's (1974) position-taking members of Congress. In our model, the governor's utility is the sum of her spatial policy payoff and a potential bonus that she receives if she asked for her ideal outcome in her public pronouncements. The policy payoff can be calculated as the spatial distance between the final outcome, x_F, and the governor's ideal policy, G^*. Making the standard assumption that governors have "tent utility," that one increment of policy movement away from their ideal has the same impact on their utility no matter which direction it goes and where on the spatial policy dimension it occurs, we can calculate the governor's policy payoff as $-|x - G^*|$. A governor's utility declines the farther the final bill gets from her ideal. Governors add to this a "position-taking bonus" of value B that they receive if and only if their proposal (x_G) reflects their sincere position (when $x_G = G^*$). The governor receives this benefit even if the proposal does not become law.

2.2.8. *The Payoff of Position Taking*

Including a position-taking bonus in our model reflects what we often heard from those involved in crafting State of the State addresses, who reminded us that it served both as a chance for governors to make proposals to which legislators would be receptive and for them to outline and signal their political philosophies, no matter what lawmakers might think. Sometimes, governors play to the audience in the legislative chambers in front of them, and sometimes they pitch their proposals to the state's voters, to their key allies, and even to a national audience. Considering how this public payoff can affect a governor's strategies can also explain some curious patterns in the governor's behavior. When the value of B is larger than what a governor could hope to gain by making a more modest proposal that is acceptable to the legislature, she will simply ask for what she wants, even knowing she has no hope of getting it.[44] "We called it the 80/20 rule," remembers Bill Whalen. "In your State of the State, you'd hope that 80 percent of what you ask for gets in play, and that 20 percent of it passes ... some of it is a wish list of items designed to appeal to your base. You know they will be dead on arrival."[45] Kevin Eckery, another Gov. Wilson aide, noted that "even if he couldn't accomplish it, the governor wasn't going to let the bastards stop him from talking about it."[46]

2.2.9. *The Legislature's Goals and Tactics*

What determines the legislature's utility? We assume that lawmakers care both about the spatial location of the final policy outcome and about whether they receive the side payment S for passing the governor's proposal in its original form. Assuming that they evaluate policies just like governors do, though from the vantage point of their own ideal law, the policy portion of the legislature's payoff is $-|x - L^*|$. Since we arbitrarily locate L^* at 0 on the line, this can be simplified to $-|x|$. Legislators can add to this the side payment of value S that they receive if and only if the bill that they pass (x_L) matches up with the executive proposal (when $x_L = x_G$). If the side payment is large enough, legislators will pass a governor's bill even when they know they could pass a bill more to their liking and force the governor to sign it (but, in doing so, forgo the side payment). In some cases, legislators will have an incentive to grudgingly pass a bill that makes them worse off than status quo in policy terms to stay in a governor's good graces and gain the side payment.

The structure of our game follows naturally from way that a State of the State address or another public announcement by the governor begins interbranch negotiations. The governor begins by making a proposal,[47]

---

[44] This is the formal rationale in our model for why governors sometimes lose, instead of always pitching a proposal that legislators will accept. Other formal models use incomplete information (Cameron 2000) or uncertainty about legislative preferences and vote-buying resources (Saiegh 2011) as rationales for bargaining failures. While we do not dispute that these mechanisms could play a role in the states, and encourage further empirical research to see whether state-by-state variations in proxies for these concepts predict gubernatorial performance, they are outside of our model.

[45] Interview with Bill Whalen, chief speechwriter to Gov. Peter Wilson, conducted by Thad Kousser, Palo Alto, California, May 21, 2010.

[46] Interview with Kevin Eckery, communications director to Gov. Pete Wilson, conducted by Thad Kousser, Sacramento, California, May 5, 2009.

[47] Another possible option the governor has is to introduce nothing in a particular policy area. Of course, because we do not get to observe these roads not traveled in a State of the State speech, we cannot analyze the effects of this decision.

either a sincere one, in which she asks for her ideal policy, or a more strategic, modest proposal that will be more amenable to the legislature. (Another way to think about a governor's choice between a sincere or a strategic proposal is that she can decide to be uncompromising – asking for her ideal public position, whether or not it reflects what is in her heart of hearts – or to make a proposal intended to be accommodating to the legislature. This phrasing, uncompromising vs. accommodating is analogous to the sincere vs. strategic dichotomy. We opt to use the latter dichotomy, however, because it is more common to the bargaining literature.) The legislature can choose to completely ignore the governor's proposal – ending the game right then and there and leaving policy at the status quo – or respond either by passing the governor's bill, x_G, or by sending a proposal of its own, x_L. Then, the governor decides whether to sign or veto the bill, resulting in a final policy outcome x. We do not consider the potential for a veto override, which will only occur when the legislature completely hijacks a governor's proposal and takes policy in the opposite direction.[48] This is a single-stage game,[49] and the extensive form of the game is depicted in Figure A.1. To summarize its relationship to past models, we take the basic setter game of Romer and Rosenthal (1978), as it is applied to interbranch bargaining in Cameron's (2000, pp. 90–94) most basic model, and add the following features: (1) a first stage, in which governors float their proposals; (2) the promise of side payment for the legislature if it passes the executive proposal; and (3) a position-taking bonus for governors who propose their ideal policy.

2.2.10. *The Logic That Drives the Game*

Using these assumptions, we build a game that predicts a unique policy outcome given the positions of each player and existing policy as well as the relative sizes of the side payment that the governor can offer to a cooperative legislature and the position-taking bonus that she can earn with a sincere proposal. In the appendix to this chapter, we characterize the subgame perfect Nash equilibrium.

In plain language, that means we obtain our predictions by assuming that each branch plays its best possible move at any point in the game,

---

[48] An override will only occur if the legislature disagrees so strongly with the governor's proposal that it goes its own way with a bill that makes the governor worse off than the status quo, sends it to her desk for a certain veto, then overrides it. In our view, this now ceases to be a governor's bill: it is an expression of the legislature's will that it is free to make – given its monopoly over the power to craft bills – whether or not the governor takes up the issue in her State of the State.

[49] Cameron (2000) introduces a multistage model of sequential veto bargaining to explore when presidents may attempt to veto bills to bend legislators to their will.

looking toward the endgame and maximizing its utility. This imposes some discipline about how we must think about bargaining, guiding us to start from the last move, considering the rational choice that each player will make at every stage of the game. When the legislature puts a bill on the governor's desk, the governor looks ahead to maximize her utility, not behind her at what might have been. She cannot carry a grudge about the process that got it there or compare it to her ideal policy. She must compare it to the status quo. If the bill would make her better off than she is under existing policy, she will sign it. Knowing this, legislators can take advantage of their agenda-setting ability to send the governor a bill that is just barely acceptable to her – anything that makes her at least as well off as the status quo – if that shifts the bill much closer to the legislature's ideal policy. Or, legislators can pass the governor's bill intact and accept her side payment. Their third option is simply to do nothing, if they will be better off under the status quo. When they do choose to pass a bill, lawmakers will weigh the value of the side payment against the policy gains that they could extract by passing a proposal amended to their liking.

Anticipating the legislature's decision calculus, a governor may chose to pitch her initial proposal somewhat toward the legislative ideal, hoping that an attractive proposal coupled with a side payment will be enough incentive to convince the legislature not to go its own way or to ignore the proposal entirely. Or, if the governor concludes that her cause is fruitless – either because her weakness keeps the side payment small or because there is a large ideological gulf between the branches – she will make a sincere demand for her ideal policy to collect the position-taking bonus, knowing that it will fail.

The appendix compares these utility calculations explicitly to derive a prediction about how play will unfold and what the final result will be – a gubernatorial victory, a compromise forced by the legislature, or a failed proposal – under different bargaining situations. Each situation represents different relative values of G^*, L^*, SQ, S, and B. Examining how the predicted outcome will change when one of these variables shifts, holding all others constant, yields the comparative static results that drive our empirical hypotheses. We can see, for instance, how the game will change when a governor can offer a larger side payment or when the branches' policy desires grow further apart. Here, we summarize the main theoretical predictions of the model:

1. Governors often must pitch their proposals strategically to convince legislators to pass them intact, or even to address the proposal at

all. What governors ask for will depend as much on the bargaining position in which they find themselves as it will on their political philosophies.[50] Sometimes, they will be free to demand what they want, but in many situations, they will be forced to propose what they think they can get.

2. When the governor wants to move policy a different direction from the status quo than the legislature does, but cannot make a large enough side payment to persuade legislators to budge very far, she will be best off proposing her ideal policy and then watching it die.

3. When both branches agree on the direction that policy should move, but disagree over the amount, some bill changing the status quo will be passed and signed into law.

4. If the governor wants to move policy in the same direction as the legislature, but can only offer a small side payment, the legislature will dictate the terms of the deal. In this situation, the governor again asks for exactly what she wants, while legislators pass a bill that reflects their branch's ideal policy.

5. If both branches agree on the direction that policy should move, but the legislature favors a more extreme policy shift, there will be numerous opportunities for a deal. Depending on the exact spatial alignment and on the governor's desire to take a popular position, the governor may get everything she wants, she may propose and sign a compromise bill, or she may ask for her most preferred outcome but sign the legislature's ideal bill.

6. Stronger governors who can offer a larger side payment are less likely to see their proposals fail and less likely to be forced into compromise with the legislature.

7. When a governor faces a legislature that is further away from her ideological scale, she will be less likely to secure passage of her proposal.

To provide a more concrete sense of what drives these general findings, in Figure 2.1 and the following discussion, we look at what can happen in policy areas where the governor and legislature want to move in different directions from the status quo (the case described in point 2). We consider

---

[50] Bill Whalen, chief speechwriter to California governor Pete Wilson, made an observation that fits closely with this theoretical prediction: "What a governor asks for in a State of the State is as much a function of the times in which he lives as it is a reflection of who he is as a person." Interview conducted by Thad Kousser, Palo Alto, California, May 21, 2010.

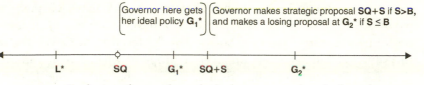

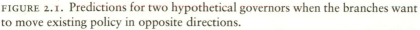

FIGURE 2.1. Predictions for two hypothetical governors when the branches want to move existing policy in opposite directions.

the predicted outcomes under two different situations: when a governor is just on the other side of the status quo from the legislature (G_1^*) and when the governor is located at a more extreme position relative to the legislature (G_2^*). A governor at the first location wants a policy that is between the status quo and $SQ + S$, the furthest point that she could convince the legislature to move toward by offering a side payment S. Any governor located in this policy space can convince the legislature to pass her ideal policy. She will propose a bill located at G_1^* in her State of the State, and for the legislature, passing it intact will be its best move. The legislature cannot propose any bill that it favors located to the left of SQ because it makes the governor worse off, thus guaranteeing her veto. If the legislature ignores the governor's request entirely, policy stays at the status quo, and legislators gain nothing. By passing the governor's bill, the legislature earns a side payment that more than compensates for its policy losses because the rightward policy shift is smaller than S by definition for any bill in the $(SQ, SQ + S)$ interval. The governor knows that she can "buy" her ideal policy from the legislature in exchange for S and thus proposes it. For strong governors who are able to offer a larger S, this interval is larger, giving them more opportunities to propose successful bills.

Now, consider the dilemma of a governor located at G_2^*. She cannot convince the legislature to pass her ideal policy because the value of the side payment she can offer is not enough to make up for the policy loss that the legislature would suffer (because her ideal is located to the right of $SQ + S$). However, she can make a strategic proposal at $SQ + S$, which the legislature then passes to curry her favor.[51] But in doing so, she would be giving up the position-taking bonus B that would come if she asked for her ideal policy, knowing full well that the legislature would reject

---

[51] Arbitrarily, we assume that legislators pass a governor's proposal (and that governors sign the legislature's bill) when it makes them indifferent between doing so and taking another course of action. The results would not fall apart, though, if we were to change this assumption: governors (or the legislature) could sweeten the deal by some tiny value to make their opponent just a bit better off in cooperating with them.

it and pass nothing. To resolve her dilemma, she calculates whether the payoff she gets by moving policy from SQ to $SQ + S$ (this payoff turns out to be S) is larger than the bonus that she forgoes, B. Governors in this situation will make the compromise proposal when $S > B$, and this proposal will become law. But when $S < B$ (or, arbitrarily, if they happen to be equal), the position-taking incentive is greater than the incentive to offer a policy compromise, and the governor makes a proposal located at G_2^* in her State of the State. It fails in the legislature, as she knew it would. Policy stays at the status quo, but the governor's utility rises because she made her point.

It is important to note that, again, we see stronger governors having a better chance at making a successful proposal. Holding B constant, a governor who can offer a larger side payment S is more likely to satisfy the $S > B$ condition that leads her to make a successful proposal, albeit one that is not her perfect policy. Stronger governors who meet this condition know they can buy larger policy concessions from the legislature, so they make a strategic, modest policy proposal, which passes. Weaker governors cannot get legislators to move as far, so their best play is to ask for their ideal and watch it die. Whenever governors find themselves wanting to move policy in a different direction than the legislature prefers, their chances of success are higher when the S that they can deliver is larger.

The strategic calculus that this model sets up for governors who want to move policy in a different direction than the legislature can help explain the patterns of introductions and passage that we observe in cases of divided government. In the face of policy disagreement, governors have to estimate their own power to get things done and compare it with the payoff they will receive from fighting the good fight but losing. Consider the case of Illinois governor George Ryan, a Republican negotiating with a Republican senate but a lower house that was firmly under the control of powerful Democratic speaker Mike Madigan. By 2001, after his approval ratings had collapsed to 31 percent, Ryan was out of political capital with lawmakers. Recognizing that most of his policies would be at odds with the house's priorities, and that he did not have the power to bend them to his will, Gov. Ryan asked for his policy wish list. He delivered a State of the State containing 10 ambitious proposals, asking for annual student testing, the elimination of red tape from the education bureaucracy, universal preschool, reform of the state's tollway system, a major ethics bill, and a consolidation of bonding authority that would have taken power away from 16 local authorities. All of these failed, handing Gov. Ryan victories only on two less ambitious proposals and a compromise bill to conform state law with a U.S. Supreme Court decision. Facing dim prospects, Gov. Ryan asked for a lot and saw little success.

In 2010, when his popularity with the public and standing with the legislature had fallen dramatically after a series of bruising budget fights, California governor Arnold Schwarzenegger went a similar route with some of his legislative proposals. Statehouse journalists characterized his final State of the State address as "an ambitious wish list," reporting that "California legislators quickly dismiss some of his key proposals for practical or ideological reasons."[52] Another governor in his lame duck term, Oklahoma's Frank Keating took a similar approach with Democratic legislators. He began his legislative agenda with a call for worker's compensation reform, which Senate Judiciary Committee chair Brad Henry quickly announced would not be granted a hearing,[53] and passed only 22 percent of his proposals that year.

What all these cases show is that during divided government (or when there is a great deal of ideological distance between the branches), chief executives who are in weak bargaining positions – due either to a short time remaining in office, low popularity, or soured relations with legislators – often make sincere, ambitious proposals, and fail. By contrast, New Hampshire's Democratic governor, John Lynch, faced a legislature in which Republicans controlled 65 percent of the seats in 2006. But serving in his first term, and with his approval ratings at 69 percent, he was able to secure the passage of two-thirds of his public agenda.

In our appendix, we explore what will happen when governors and legislators both want to move policy in the same direction, though by different amounts. In all subsets of this situation, some bill changing the status quo and making both branches better off will pass and be signed into law. The final outcomes may be at the governor's ideal, the legislature's ideal, or some other point, but we never see complete failure. This points out the importance of ideological agreement to a governor's prospects. Since the model predicts that a complete failure will occur only when governors and legislators disagree on the right direction to move on a particular issue, a governor can expect to be more successful in general when the faction controlling the legislature has policy preferences that are closer to hers. This suggests an empirical prediction about how the level of

[52] Michael Rothfeld, "In State of the State Address, Arnold Schwarzenegger Unveils an Ambitious Wish List," *Los Angeles Times*, January 7, 2010.
[53] "Worker's Comp Bill Won't Be Considered," *Daily Oklahoman*, February 21, 2001.

ideological agreement between the branches should affect gubernatorial success.

Hypothesis 1: A governor negotiating with a legislature located closer to her on the ideological spectrum should have a greater chance of passing a policy proposal in her public agenda, all else equal.

Empirically, we measure this ideological distance between the branches by either the share of seats held by members of the governor's party (averaged across both legislative houses) or by the presence of divided government. While the partisanship of lawmakers and governors may not be a perfect proxy for ideological proximity, this is the same sort of rough metric used by governors and their advisers. When asked why Kansas governor Kathleen Sebelius did not expect to win on many of her legislative proposals, her communications aide Burdett Loomis replied, "Because she was down almost 2–1 in both houses."[54]

Another consistent pattern is that stronger governors will be more likely to get their way. We have shown in Figure 2.1 that when governors disagree with legislators about which way to move policy, stronger governors are less likely to propose a sure-to-fail bill. In the appendix, we show that when the branches both want to move policy in the same direction, governors who can offer larger side payments are better able to tempt legislators into passing gubernatorial proposals rather than countering with a legislative alternative. The ability to offer a larger S leads to fewer half-a-loaf compromises and thus a greater chance of complete success. The empirical prediction that follows is that each of the three factors that, according to our interviews, should determine a governor's value of S will affect her chances of success.

Hypothesis 2: A governor who can credibly threaten to veto a legislator's bill without being overridden should have a greater chance of passing a policy proposal in her public agenda, all else equal.

Hypothesis 3: A governor serving in her first term should have a greater chance of passing a policy proposal in her public agenda, all else equal.

Hypothesis 4: A governor with higher approval ratings should have a greater chance of passing a policy proposal in her public agenda, all else equal.

Our model also highlights the importance of B in the $S > B$ calculus that governors use to determine when to make a sincere but hopeless

---

[54] Interview with Burdett Loomis, Director of Administrative Communication to Kansas governor Kathleen Sebelius, 2004–5, conducted by telephone by Thad Kousser, May 14, 2010.

proposal and when to pitch a safer, more strategic bill. A larger position-taking bonus makes it more likely that the political gains from position taking will outweigh the policy gains from making a proposal that legislators will accept. Thus, a higher B leads to more dead-on-arrival proposals.

While a variety of circumstances may shape the size of the B term, one of these ought to be presidential ambitions. Governor Mitt Romney's State of the State address in 2006 illustrates this point. Recall that in his speech, aimed more at the White House than at the Massachusetts statehouse, Gov. Romney called on the Democrat-dominated legislature to pass proposals that he knew they would not like. The motivation behind his approach was not lost on statehouse observers. Covering his abstinence education proposal, one journalist wrote that "Romney, who is considering a possible presidential bid and looking for the support of social conservatives, made yesterday's announcement at Boston Latin School, which brought in the program three years ago and where it has sparked controversy among some parents."[55] Those commenting on the stringent welfare-to-work requirements that he proposed "hinted that Romney's urgency may have more to do with welfare reform being a hot issue for the 2008 presidential race, with which Romney continues to flirt."[56] None of this national position taking, though, did him any good in Boston; legislators there passed only 18 percent of his proposals. We expect that this pattern will be repeated across the country for governors with presidential ambitions.

Hypothesis 5: A governor who seeks the presidency – and thus places a higher value on the public position that she takes on an issue – should have a lower chance of passing a policy proposal in her public agenda, all else equal.

Each of these hypotheses is driven by an exogenous factor, a measure of preferences or power that governors and legislators both know at the beginning of the legislative session, when the governor is finalizing her public agenda. But the model also points out the endogenous nature of what governors propose and the importance of what they ask for in determining what they get. How should we treat the nature of a gubernatorial proposal – its scale, the direction in which it seeks to move

[55] Andrea Estes and Tracy Jan, "State Widens Teaching of Abstinence," *Boston Globe*, April 21, 2006, p. A1.
[56] Kimberly Atkins, "Gov to Pols: Big Bucks Riding on Welfare Bill," *Boston Herald*, March 16, 2006.

policy, and whether it fits with the legislature's preferences – in our empirical analysis? A close examination of our model shows that it does not make consistent predictions about what governors propose when they are stronger or weaker. When the branches are ideologically proximate, stronger governors ask for items more to their liking. Yet, if the governor is at the extremes relative to the legislature, a higher S means that she will ask for less.[57] Because we cannot be certain of which situation occurs empirically for every bill, we do not know how a governor's strength will affect what she asks for on that bill. But we do know that this strategic choice of what she asks for determines what she will get, making it important to control for the nature of each proposal (i.e., its distance from the status quo) when analyzing its chances of success.

Finally, because this game predicts what will happen with a single bill, it is appropriate to test it at the level of gubernatorial proposals rather than by gauging success on a governor's entire agenda. Because we gather bill-specific data for our regression analysis, we take this approach. Still, one of our substantive assumptions about side payments – that their value can be depleted if a governor proposes bill after bill after bill – does yield a testable prediction about how the total size of a governor's agenda affects the prospects of each bill in that package. Asking for many bills requires governors to ante up a potential payment of S over and over again. There should be some limit on the number of times that they can do this before they begin to erode the bank account of their political capital. At some point, they will be overdrawn, leading to a prediction that a governor who calls for a lengthier agenda will face poorer prospects for each item on that agenda. This prediction is consistent with what others have seen looking at governors. Using a slightly different measure of the scope of a governor's agenda, Ferguson (2003, p. 161) finds evidence in the 1993–4 session for the hypothesis that "leaders possess a limited amount of political capital, and to be successful, they must pick priorities carefully, focusing on only a few key issues (Freguson 2002, p. 161)." In a few states, Rosenthal (1990, p. 97) observes an inverse relationship between the size of a governor's agenda and its success. We posit that this link should hold true across many states and eras.

Hypothesis 6: A governor whose public agenda contains more items should have a lower chance of passing each individual policy proposal on that agenda, all else equal.

---

[57] If the governor's S was small, then she would not hesitate to engage in position taking and ask for her true policy preferences.

2.3. The Budget Game

Budget negotiations between governors and legislatures unfold much differently. The need to pass a spending plan every year or biennium brings the legislature to the bargaining table. With legislators unable to set the terms of a deal, governors should generally have more influence over the size of the budget and its critical details. We base our argument in strategic logic and interviews, but this is also a point that Alan Rosenthal's (1990, p. 8) close observation of governors led him to make: "Probably the governor's greatest power of initiative is in the domain of budgeting." This is an area of relative strength for American executives. Additionally, because the bargaining dynamics of a budget standoff are so different from negotiations over policy bills, different factors should determine a governor's level of power. With both sides at the table, what matters most is who can stay at the table longest, who can win the staring match of a budget stalemate. In this contest, "blinking" means signing or passing a proposal that closely reflects the demands of the other branch. Whoever is most eager for a get-out-of-town budget will have to yield concessions to get it. As a consequence, governors who are the most patient, relative to the legislators they face, will win the budget game.

We make a straightforward application of the "divide the dollar" models outlined in Rubinstein (1982, 1985) and Osborne and Rubinstein (1990), which we describe more formally in Kousser (2005, chap. 6) and Kousser and Phillips (2009). As a consequence, this section presents a much briefer summary of the logic that drives this game and the empirical hypotheses that it suggests. Like the policy game, it is highly simplified, lacking the detailed discussion of the appropriations process contained in many descriptive analyses of state budgeting (cf. National Association of State Budget Officers 2002; Garand and Baudoin 2004; Rosenthal 2004). Yet, this abstraction is useful for conveying the logic of our argument in a simple, direct manner.

At the heart of budget bargaining is the give and take between governors and legislative leaders that occurs at the end of a session or when the deadline to pass a budget approaches. Everything else – from the governor's release of her budget plan in January through the introduction of budget bills and the legislative hearings held on them – is just a skirmish. Those exercises give each branch an important opportunity to stake out their values and spell out their wish lists, impressing constituents and courting interest groups. They convey the ideal divisions of the budget dollar that governors and legislators seek. Yet, they do not represent moves in our budget game. In the legislative game, what a governor proposes at the outset of the session is critical because if legislators are not tempted by it, they will not come to the bargaining table. With the budget, legislators must eventually come to the table, freeing the governor to make a public proposal in January that sincerely reflects her budget priorities.

Like all states, the key bargaining over the budget in California takes place late in the legislative session. Tom Hayes, who served as budget director for Gov. Pete Wilson, described for us the typical process. At the start of the legislative session, the governor would lay out his initial budget proposals, all of which closely reflected his fiscal priorities and governing philosophy. According to Hayes, the governor did not place a high priority on getting his proposals into the preliminary budget bills that were crafted in legislative committees. Instead, he waited for the negotiations between the "Big Five," the governor and the top Democratic and Republican leaders from the assembly and senate. These negotiations typically take place behind closed doors as the deadline for a new budget approaches. Hayes also told us that it is in this setting where the most contentious budgetary issues are resolved and where the proverbial dollar is divided among the key players. Since the consequential strategic bargaining in California, as in most states, takes place late in the session, while January proposals and legislative reactions are often dismissed as opening acts of "Kabuki theater."

Consequently, we treat a governor's initial budgetary proposals as statements about how she would like to divide the figurative dollar of a budget,[58] while the real bargaining begins much later. In the most natural application, the game begins with the legislature proposing how to divide the dollar. Because this bargaining takes place informally rather than through the legislative process, the governor could also begin negotiations. Yet, since Kousser and Phillips (2009) demonstrate that the logic of the game would be the same and the division of the dollar would remain largely unchanged if the governor moved first, we proceed with the legislature moving first by sending the governor a budget proposal. This offer generally comes on the eve of the end of the legislative session or the fiscal year, meaning that any delay in reaching a final agreement

---

[58] "Dividing the dollar" is a flexible analogy that can be used to describe any bargaining situation in which gains by one side must be accompanied by sacrifices from the other party. In the context of budgeting, a division of the dollar could mean moving the overall level of state spending closer to what the governor prefers than what legislators favor or funding a program desired by the governor (and thus leaving less money to fund programs favored by the legislature).

will be costly to both branches. Faced with this offer, the governor either accepts and signs the budget sent to her or delays agreement and sends the game into its next stage. The governor begins the second stage with a counteroffer, but even if the legislature immediately accepts it, the agreement has been delayed one round, and both sides receive a payoff that is discounted; that is, they suffer political and even personal costs for failing to pass the budget on time and would have been happier to have made the same deal before the deadline. Of course, by holding out longer, a governor might extract a better deal than she was first offered by the legislature, which is where strategic calculations come into play. When they make these calculations, both sides know each others' discount factors, which depend on how patient each branch can afford to be.

In formal terms, the discount factor is denoted by δ. The division of the dollar is represented as an offer of (X_L, X_G), and X_L can fall anywhere in the interval $[0, 1]$, with the legislature offering the governor something between nothing that she wants ($X_G = 0$) and everything she asked for ($X_G = 1$). Rounds of play are numbered as $T = 0, 1, 2, \dots$. Rounds of alternating offers continue until one player accepts the other's proposal. For every round that a bargain is delayed, the utility a player receives from his portion of the dollar is equal to that portion multiplied by δ. Assuming that this discount factor remains constant from round to round, we designate the value of an agreement in round t to the governor as $X_G \delta^t$.

What does this mean for the deals that governors will be able to extract out of legislatures? Suppose, a governor is intent on winning a tax cut. If she is very patient, with a δ set at 0.9, she will be indifferent between winning a tax cut of $90 million in an on-time budget or one of $100 million if it is delayed one round (since the utility of a delayed $100 million is 0.9 * $100 million = $90 million). Legislators can take advantage of their chance to make the first move by extracting a small concession. Yet, if the governor is much less patient, with $\delta = 0.6$, legislators can turn the power to move first into a real advantage, proposing a mere $60 million tax cut because they know the governor fears a budget stalemate. Of course, legislators also worry about this sort of gridlock and discount the value of future deals just like the governor does. Consequently, if legislators make a proposal that gives the governor too little of what she wants in the first round, she will make a tough counteroffer and dare legislators either to accept it in the second round or to incur further delays (and discounting) by sending the game into a third round. Legislators who look toward the endgame can predict this. Seeking to avoid such a dead end, they will sacrifice some of what they want early in the process, making the governor a fair first offer that she can accept. When both branches know that they will suffer if the budget is late, the rational play will be to compromise early.

Driven by this logic of making early concessions to avoid a stalemate, the budget game yields a unique subgame perfect equilibrium.[59] The proof behind this prediction is outlined by Osborne and Rubinstein (1990, p. 45) and traced out for the state politics application by Kousser (2005, pp. 233–7) and Kousser and Phillips (2009). If both players face the same discount factor, the game will end in the first round as the legislature proposes an offer that gives lawmakers a "first mover" advantage, which the governor accepts to avoid delay. As a quick calculation of the payoffs demonstrates, the first mover's advantage that accrues to the branch making the initial offer is small when both players are relatively patient and not tremendously large even when they are in a hurry to pass a budget. When both branches discount payoffs that are delayed one round by a factor of 0.9, the first mover receives 53 cents of the dollar, and the other branch gets 47 cents. Even when the discount factor equals 0.7, the division of the dollar is still a fairly equitable 59 cents to 41 cents.

The implication for executive power is that, in the budget game, governors will not face a severe bargaining disadvantage because they lack the formal power to move first. Both branches bargain in the shadow of a late budget and the political penalties it can bring. Legislators know they must secure the governor's signature to get what they want out of the budget. They cannot simply ignore her requests because they cannot afford to live without a budget deal. This grants governors leverage that they lack when they pitch the bills they want to legislators. In contrast with the policy game, governors can expect to get something out of budget negotiations no matter how much they disagree with legislators or how weak they are politically because of the nature of the process. Both branches fear the potential endgame of a budget stalemate, a shared dread that puts governors in a stronger bargaining position.

---

[59] Since the Nash prediction is quite vague in this case – any division of the dollar can be reached in the first round in equilibrium because players can make threats that are not credible – Osborne and Rubinstein (1990) employed Selten's (1975) notion of a subgame perfect equilibrium, which requires that best responses be played at every point in the game that begins a subgame (see Morrow 1994). Subgame perfection generally refines the set of acceptable equilibrium strategies and, in this case, generates a unique prediction.

That is why governors like Gary Johnson can do better in the budget than in their policy proposals, and why there is much give-and-take between the branches in this realm. That does not mean that governors dictate the terms of budget bargaining, only that it fits with the "alternating offers" dynamic of Rubinstein's game. Ohio governor Bob Taft asked if there are logrolls on the budget, and made it clear that the fiscal plan reflected both his and the legislature's priorities. "We had our items that we wanted to be in the budget, and they had their items. You had to work with the legislative leadership, and if it was something very important to them, I needed their support for things I wanted in my budget, so there was give and take in that relationship. As long as it wasn't horrible public policy."[60] The timing of the budget – its place on the annual (or biennial) "must-do" list in every state, and the incentives to complete it on time – are what drives this dynamic.

Hypothesis 7: A governor's chance of passing a proposal will be greater if it is a budget proposal rather than a policy bill.

2.3.1. *Which Governors Perform Best in Budget Bargaining?*

A given governor should do better in the budget than in policy negotiations, but which sorts of governors will perform better than others in fiscal bargaining? In a staring match model of budget negotiations, the final division of the dollar is driven by patience. This directs our attention to the factors that determine the relative patience – and thus the relative power – of the two branches. While the basic model assumes that governors and legislators possess the same patience level, this assumption may not always hold true. Governors could be more patient than the legislators with whom they bargain, signified by $G > L$ (or perhaps even less patient). The formalized extension of the basic Rubinstein model that is applied to states in Kousser (2005, pp. 160–1) and Kousser and Phillips (2009) spells out the implications for budget bargaining when governors can outwait legislators. It shows that if the governor's advantage in patience is large, it will swamp the advantage that the legislature obtains by moving first.

To get a sense of how this changes outcomes, go back to our example where both branches had a discount factor of $\delta = 0.9$. In this case, the legislature captured 53 cents of the dollar, while the governor took 47

---

[60] Interview with Gov. Bob Taft of Ohio, conducted by telephone by Thad Kousser and Justin Phillips, October 1, 2009.

cents. If we keep the governor's patience level high but make the legislature less patient, with a discount factor of $\delta = 0.7$, this slight shift has a dramatic effect: legislators would control 27 cents and the governor 73 cents of the dollar, even when the legislature moves first. Governors who are a bit more patient than legislators can, under this model, reap large rewards in budget bargaining. What, then, determines patience levels?

2.3.2. *Governors Can Wait to Secure Their Legacies*

In our model of the policy game, we made the argument that a governor's ability to deliver carrots and sticks to legislators erodes over the course of her time in office. In budget negotiations, though, governors on their way out of the door should wield significant power. In their legacy years – when they negotiate their last budget before leaving office and executive term limits make them ineligible to run again – governors will be at their most patient. With nothing to lose in the short term from a delayed budget, and everything to gain in their legacies, they can stubbornly dig in until legislators give them what they want. Lacking any fear of electoral punishment, governors will be free to stall, while many of the lawmakers with whom they negotiate will be eager to pass a budget on time and turn their attention to campaigns. This dynamic delivered California's Republican governor Arnold Schwarzenegger his biggest budget victories in his final year in office. Negotiating with Democratic leaders who were not inclined to help out the unpopular governor, Schwarzenegger demanded severe spending cuts, pension reforms, and a ballot measure to enact a constitutional spending cap in summer 2010. Then, he simply waited. With a 22 percent approval rating,[61] Schwarzenegger could not rely on his political capital to pressure legislators, but he knew that as summer turned into fall, legislators eager to resolve what became the state's longest budget standoff would eventually cut a deal. After locking down their chambers for 20 hours in early October, legislators emerged with a deal that included pension reform, a spending cap, and no new taxes. Celebrating these victories, Gov. Schwarzenegger recalled, "I have been fighting to fix California's broken budget and pension systems since I came into office."[62] Because of the dynamics of budget bargaining, he was not able to win them until he was about to leave office. In contrast,

---

[61] Mark DiCamillo and Mervyn Field, "Schwarzenegger and the State Legislature Both Get Very Poor Job Ratings," Field Poll Release No. 2346, July 14, 2010.

[62] Shane Goldmacher, "Legislators Sweat the Small Stuff," *Los Angeles Times*, October 9, 2010.

when governors are bargaining over policy, their powers should erode over time and be at their nadir as their terms draw to a close.

Hypothesis 8: A governor serving in her legacy year should have a greater chance of passing a budget proposal, all else equal.

2.3.3. *Governors Can Outwait Part-Time Legislatures*

Governors should also have an advantage in patience when they negotiate with part-time citizen legislatures compared with governors of states with more professionalized statehouses. The rationale here is that, in addition to political costs that both branches pay when there is budgetary gridlock, lawmakers serving in a less professionalized legislature face private costs of delay. These costs will decrease the legislature's patience and advantage the governor.

As Squire and Hamm (2005) document, the range of legislative professionalism across the American states is astonishing, meaning that different governors sit across the bargaining table with very different sorts of opponents. Some highly professionalized chambers resemble the U.S. House of Representatives: they meet in lengthy sessions, their members are well paid, and the legislature employs numerous nonelected staff. In states such as New York, California, and Michigan, there are few, if any, restrictions on the number of days the legislature may meet; as a result, lawmakers are in session much of the year. Furthermore, legislators serving in these chambers receive annual salaries in excess of $75,000 as well as generous per diems (Council of State Governments 2005). These lawmakers can therefore treat legislative service as a career and do not need second jobs, even though the session length makes holding a second job close to impossible. Most state legislatures, however, are notably less professionalized. In these chambers, the number of days that legislators are allowed to meet is often constitutionally restricted. On average, regular sessions are limited to approximately 90 calendar days per year; in extreme cases, sessions are constrained to no more than 60 or 90 days biennially. Compensation for service in most chambers is also low or nonexistent. To support themselves and their families, legislators in citizen chambers usually hold second jobs to which they must return soon after the legislative session.

As a result, members of a part-time body face high opportunity costs when they fail to reach agreement on a budget with the governor. In the absence of such an agreement, legislators are usually forced into what may be a time-consuming special session and are prevented from pursuing their private careers or personal lives. The prospect of leaving their day jobs to resolve budget conflicts should make members impatient. Governors, however, pay much lower private costs when they veto a budget at the end of a session. They may force a special session, stalling whatever private, travel, or governing plans they might have,[63] but because all governors are paid well to do their job full time, they can endure round after round of negotiations. They will be more patient and can reap the bargaining rewards of this patience. We therefore expect professional chambers to be able to match the governor's endurance, whereas part-time bodies will be vulnerable to threats of a veto and extended negotiations and give in to governors early.

Participants in gubernatorial negotiations with the less professional legislatures point out the paramount importance of this dynamic. A senior advisor to Oregon governor John Kitzhaber, a Democrat, remarks that "as session goes on, the wait is in our favor."[64] Remembering his battles with Maryland's hybrid citizen-professional legislature to pass a budget in time for the 83rd day of session, Gov. Parris Glendening concludes, "A governor's power grows as we get to the 83rd day, no question about it."[65] This asymmetry in patience explains why Gary Johnson was able to extract so many concessions from New Mexico's citizen legislators when he called them back into a special session after they had returned home to their jobs as real estate agents, professors, ranchers, and lawyers.

It also helps to solve one of the puzzles that began this chapter, which asked why states like New York and California could not pass budgets on time. Legislators in those full-time bodies can afford to hold out in budget standoffs longer than their colleagues in part-time bodies because they face only political and not personal costs when budgets are late. These states are emblematic of a larger pattern. In 2007, five of the six states in which a budget standoff dragged on past the beginning of the next fiscal year – California, Illinois, Michigan, Pennsylvania, and Wisconsin – had professional legislatures that typically met at least

---

[63] Legislatures in 30 states have the authority to call their own special sessions (Council of State Governments 2000), but they are often forced to do so by a governor's veto. Although special sessions are not often called to resolve legislative–executive conflicts, the threat of a special session is not unimportant. Delayed bargains are off the equilibrium path of Rubinstein's basic model, but they are weapons that do not need to be unsheathed to be powerful.

[64] Interview with senior advisor to Oregon governor John Kitzhaber, conducted by Thad Kousser, Salem, Oregon, July 8, 2001.

[65] Interview with Gov. Parris Glendening of Maryland, conducted by telephone by Justin Phillips and Thad Kousser, July 13, 2010.

20 months in a two-year biennium.[66] The patience of those legislators should turn into bargaining power, while governors will have the upper hand in negotiations with part-time legislatures.

Hypothesis 9: A governor negotiating with legislators who serve in shorter sessions should have a greater chance of passing a budget proposal in her agenda, all else equal.

Finally, the divide-the-dollar framework of our model has an implication for the link between the scale of a governor's agenda and the predicted success of each item in it. There are only so many cents to go around in this zero sum game, so a governor winning a figurative amount in concessions from the legislature must determine how to allocate this across her agenda. If she has enough power to get, say, five items in negotiations with the legislature, she will have to pick and choose which ones to press for. That will make the success rate for a governor who asks for five things to start off with higher than the rate of a governor who asked for 10. This produces a hypothesis that parallels a prediction of the policy game.

Hypothesis 10: A governor whose public agenda contains more items should have a lower chance of passing each individual budget proposal in that agenda, all else equal.

2.4. Can Governors Accomplish Their Policy Goals through the Budget?

Because governors have a built-in advantage in budget negotiations, why not attempt to achieve all of their legislative goals through this process? If they often lose at the policy game, why not simply change the game? Our interviews taught us that governors and their advisors do recognize the strategic advantages of the budgeting process. In some instances, they seek to shift their proposals toward it. Yet, legal and procedural constraints prevent them from freely moving any policy idea into the budget, forcing them to play the difficult game of policy negotiations.

The testimony of top advisors to California governors shows that they perceived the advantages of the budget process, and sometimes even sought to blur the lines between budget and policy, but saw the limits of this approach. "The budget is a governor's point of leverage," says Tim

---

[66] Personal communication between the authors and Arturo Perez of the National Conference of State Legislatures.

Gage, who served as budget director to Democratic governor Gray Davis. "The budget has become the vehicle for lots of policy proposals; they are introduced to the legislature in the context of the budget, or in budget trailer bills. Pushing policy through the budget is a practice that has gone on as long as I've been involved in the processes . . . it's an opportunity for the governor to advance those proposals. That being said, the legislature sometimes pushes back and runs those bills through the normal committee hearing process."[67] "If the Governor's team could put his policy ideas into the budget conversation, we'd have more leverage," explains Joe Rodota, cabinet secretary to Republican governor Pete Wilson.[68]

However, Maryland governor Parris Glendening makes the critical point that, precisely because the budget must move every year, any achievement gained through budgeting is more vulnerable to being undone in the near future than is a policy victory. "Well, the budget is easier," Glendening allows, "but it is harder to get major substantive changes out of the budget process. You can push an amendment through one year, but the committee chairs pay pretty close attention and they can change things the next year."[69]

A final constraint on this strategy is a legal one, though its application is far from universal. In Ohio in 2001, the 226-page bill enacting the state's corrections budget contained a single sentence that took away collective bargaining rights from employees of the Ohio School Facilities Commission. In our conceptual framework, this was a policy proposal snuck into budget language (though we do not know whether the proposal originated in the governor's office or the legislature). To the Supreme Court of Ohio, this was a violation of the state's single-subject rule. The court rejected the argument that the policy shift belonged in a budget bill because it had fiscal implications. "Such a notion, however, renders the one-subject rule meaningless," the Court wrote, "because virtually any statute arguably impacts the state budget, even if only tenuously."[70]

---

[67] Interview with Tim Gage, Director of Finance to California governor Gray Davis, conducted by telephone by Thad Kousser, July 9, 2009.

[68] Interview with Joe Rodota, cabinet secretary to California governor Pete Wilson, conducted by telephone by Thad Kousser, July 16, 2009.

[69] Interview with Gov. Parris Glendening of Maryland, conducted by telephone by Justin Phillips and Thad Kousser, July 13, 2010.

[70] Opinion of Chief Justice Thomas J. Moyer, quoted in Ohio Office of Public Information, "Court Hold Collective Bargaining Amendment in Appropriations Bill Violates Single-Subject Rule," accessed at http://www.sconet.state.oh.us/PIO/summaries/2004/1215/031010.asp in July 2011.

While Ohio's decision does not affect other states, it puts yet one more obstacle in the way of governors who try to win by changing the game. If they attempt to shift their policy proposals into the budget process, governors risk running afoul of the committee chairs who jealously guard their legislative turf, of future lawmakers who can make annual changes through the budget, and of courts seeking to keep regulatory and fiscal legislation distinct.

2.5. Conclusion

This chapter presents two contrasting theories of the logics that drive bargaining when governors ask for policy bills, on one hand, and budget concessions, on the other. The models diverge because of the different endgames of each process. Because legislators can get away with burying a governor's policy bills but are unable to survive without passing a state budget, governors should have a better chance of success with their budget demands. Yet, this first-order hypothesis, that what governors bargain over determines what they get, is not our only empirical forecast. The two models also make separating predictions about what factors will – and what factors will not – determine the success of gubernatorial proposals made through each process.

In budget negotiations, it is the twin predictors of patience – whether a governor is in her legacy year and the legislative session length – that drive the outcomes of our staring match model. By contrast, governors will do better at the policy game when their party controls more seats in the legislature and when they have more political capital because they are popular or because they are serving in their first term. Their policy bills should fare worse when their presidential ambitions cause them to care more about signaling their policy preferences than about asking for what legislators are likely to give them. In both types of negotiations, governors who include more items in their agendas will have a lower chance of passing each one.

It is also important to ask what factors should be irrelevant, according to our models, in determining a governor's power through each process. Governors who are more popular or who serve in their first terms should not do any better in budget bargaining because it is their patience rather than side payments that allows them to win a fiscal staring match. Perhaps most surprisingly, our model predicts that governors do not need to have more allies in the legislature to do well in the budget. Controlling a committee or access to the floor is less vital because the legislative

TABLE 2.1. *Predicted Effects on Chances of Success for a Governor's Proposal*

	Policy bills	Budgetary proposals
Legislative session length	none	−
Governor's legacy year	−	+
Legislative seat share (governor's party)	+	none
First-term governor	+	none
Public approval	+	none
Presidential ambitions	−	none
Total number of proposals	−	−
Proposal is a budget item		+

majority cannot ignore the budget in the way that they ignored Kansas governor Kathleen Sebelius's policy bills. The necessity of passing a state spending plan brings them to the table whether they are the governor's partisan allies or not, and even a Democratic governor in a red state like Kansas can succeed through the budget. In the policy game, patience should not matter, as scholars examining the setter model have shown formally.[71] The implication for state politics is that citizen lawmakers should be just as likely to reject a governor's policy bills as their full-time counterparts are because all American legislatures possess a monopoly over the legislative process.[72]

In Table 2.1 we summarize the factors that should systematically shape the fates of governors' policy and budgetary agendas. Of course, all the predictions contained in this table are about the general patterns that should appear in an analysis of the fate of scores of executive proposals. None are deterministic, iron laws. Some governors succeed against all odds, passing legislative items through an unfriendly legislature even though their popularity is low and their time in office is running out. Other governors can fail even when they possess every systematic advantage. Because politics is an intensely personal art, the persuasive skills of governors still have much to do with their levels of success. When he governed California, Ronald Reagan turned his star power into political

---

[71] Primo's (2002) formal investigation of Romer and Rosenthal's (1978) setter model finds that, even when it is extended to multiple stages of bargaining, discount rates do not factor into the equilibrium, concluding that "impatience and time preferences may not be key features of political bargaining" (Primo 2002, p. 421).

[72] This prediction runs contrary to Ferguson's (2003, p. 173) finding on legislative professionalism and executive success; her work finds that "professional legislatures actually bolster the legislative success of the governor."

capital that often bought him success with a Democratic legislature. "Reagan had Tuesday morning legislative time, any legislator could get 5 minutes for whatever they wanted," recalls his personal aide, Sal Russo. "Some would come and talk about their legislation, some would bring their sister-in-law who loved his movies, some would bring the Cucumber Queen from their district, and some wanted to come and tell him a joke. . . . I think legislators saw him for the decent man he was and felt like they got a fair shake out of him. So they wanted to give him a fair shake back, and that's an important currency with the legislature."[73] After following Reagan's path from Hollywood to Sacramento, Gov. Arnold Schwarzenegger famously erected a smoking tent in the courtyard of his capitol office in Sacramento, and invitations to it became a prize for state legislators. Schwarzenegger credited it for his early bipartisan success so much that in a visit to Washington in 2007, he advised President Bush to build one himself, saying, "People come in there, Democrats and Republicans, and they take off their jackets and rip off their ties, and they sit down and smoke a stogie, and they talk, and they schmooze. . . . To the President, I say: Get yourself a smoking tent."[74] Late in his administration, however, Schwarzenegger gave up his personal ties to legislators, and with it much of the goodwill to support his agenda. "I remember the day when all the Republican caucus wore nametags," says one veteran lawmaker, "because they had never met the governor and they wanted him to know who they were."[75] These personal, idiosyncratic factors no doubt play an important role in determining whether a governor succeeds in the legislature. Governors who make use of smoking tents may do better than our model would predict, while those who require name tags will underperform.

Another caveat is that there may be other important systematic influences on gubernatorial success that are not featured in our models and that do not appear in Table 2.1. We do not presume that we have captured every dynamic at work in a statehouse. For instance, in an extension of the budget bargaining model, Kousser (2005, chap. 6) shows how legislative term limits can strengthen a governor's hand, a finding that is clear in many empirical investigations, including analyses of budgets (Kousser

---

[73] Interview with Sal Russo, personal aide to Gov. Ronald Reagan and deputy chief of staff to Gov. George Deukmejian, conducted by telephone by Thad Kousser, July 20, 2009.

[74] Marc Sandalow, "Follow California's Lead, Governor Tells DC," *San Francisco Chronicle*, February 27, 2007.

[75] Remarks by former state senator Sheila James Kuehl at the "Rebooting California" conference, Loyola Law School, Los Angeles, September 24, 2010.

2005); qualitative case studies (Powell 2007); and surveys of legislators (Carey et al. 2006), legislative leaders (Peery and Little 2003), and lobbyists (Thompson and Moncrief 2003). Governors might be less powerful in states where legislative leaders hold more power over their houses, a factor that is also linked to professionalism (Clucas 2007). Even though we have included some of the factors that make up Beyle's (1983, 2004) index of gubernatorial power in our models, others, such as a governor's appointment powers or the presence of separately elected state-level officials, might help determine their influence. Our theory does not contain the entire catalog of potential gubernatorial powers. Because the research designs that we present in the rest of this book focus on testing the hypotheses presented in this chapter, we cannot exhaustively test every potential power. We control for some of these important factors, where appropriate, and leave the investigation of other promising hypotheses for future research.

We also recognize that our model will not perfectly predict gubernatorial success because some governors will not play the strategic game perfectly, and others will not play the one we have in mind. The real political world often veers off the equilibrium path, as players lack the perfect information and calculations to play games perfectly. A governor might overshoot, sending proposals to the legislature that are too ambitious or attempting to hold out for a budget victory that she is not patient enough to win. This is why statehouse reporters use the term *political miscalculation* so frequently, and such mistakes can lead to gubernatorial defeats that our model fails to predict. Governors may also be following their own strategic logics rather than ours. We do not presume that our assumptions about their motivations and tactics apply to every governor across the nation in every era. No abstract model will be able to capture the full range of executive strategies.

All these important, hard-to-measure factors will play a role in determining when governors win or lose. Yet, underlying the fluctuations in success that they bring, we argue, are basic patterns that link party control, political dynamics, and the institutional features of statehouses to the fate of executive proposals. Working through the logic of strategic bargaining in the specific context of state politics provides clear hypotheses about the causal patterns that should shine through once random variation in personal charisma and persuasive powers washes out. If the predictions hold true, we will have answers for the puzzles that began this chapter. If governors across the country meet with more success on the budget items contained in their agendas than they do on their policy proposals, this will explain why New Mexico's Gary Johnson could win fiscal concessions but not pass his bills. If bill passage rates fall whenever a governor aspires to the Oval Office, this will show why Mitt Romney saw so many failures when he launched a legislative agenda designed to take him from Boston to Washington, D.C. And we will have a better understanding of why states like New York and California have chronic budget delays (and why their budgets have a stronger legislative imprint) if full-time legislatures across the country are more likely to stymie a governor's fiscal proposals when they wait patiently during the budget staring match. By empirically investigating patterns in gubernatorial success, we will see whether the theories presented in this chapter teach important lessons about the roots of executive power.

2.6. Appendix

In the main text, we introduced the form of the policy game, described the players, and summarized the intuition behind the main findings. In Figure 2.2, we present the game in extensive form and include the payoffs for the governor and the legislature. We also define the variables that we use as shorthand for spatial locations, offers, and payments.

The players make offers over a single dimension and have utility functions that are the sum of tent spatial utility[76] plus any side payment or position-taking bonus. Arbitrarily, we assume that legislators pass a governor's proposal (and that the governor signs the legislature's bill) when it makes them indifferent between doing so and taking another course of action. When a governor is indifferent between the outcome that will occur if she makes a sincere proposal of a bill at her ideal and the utility from making a strategic proposal that the legislature can accept, she makes the sincere proposal. These arbitrary assumptions do not strongly affect the results. In Proposition 1, we characterize the subgame perfect Nash equilibrium that gives predicted outcomes for different spatial arrangements of players and relative values of S and B.

Proposition 1. A subgame perfect equilibrium to the complete information policy game is as follows:

when $G^* \in (\infty, L^* - S)$ and $S \leq B$, gov proposes $x_G = G^*$, leg passes $x_L = L^*$, gov signs L^*

---

[76] One increment of policy movement away from the governor's ideal has the same impact on her utility no matter which direction it goes and where on the spatial policy dimension it occurs.

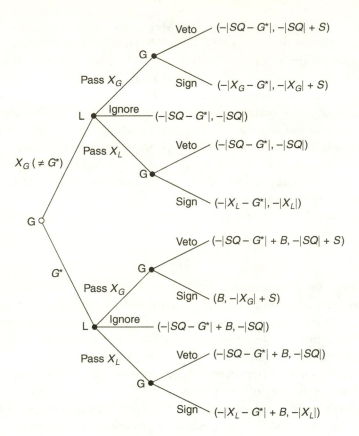

Notation:

SQ is the status quo policy
*G** is the governor's ideal policy
*L** is the legislature's ideal policy
X is any bill
X_G is the governor's proposed bill
X_L is the legislature's responding bill
S is the side payment offered by the governor to the legislature if X_G is passed
B is the position-taking bonus that the governor receives if $X_G = G^*$
$U_G(X) = -|G^* - X|$ is the spatial component of a governor's utility
$U_L(X) = -|L^* - X|$ is the spatial component of the legislature's utility

FIGURE 2.2. Policy game in extensive form, with definitions of variables.

when $G^* \in (\infty, L^* - S)$ and $S > B$, gov proposes $x_G = L^* - S$, leg passes $x_L = L^* - S$, gov signs $L^* - S$

when $G^* \in [L^* - S, L^*]$, gov proposes $x_G = G^*$, leg passes $x_L = G^*$, gov signs G^*

when $G^* \in (L^*, 1/2 SQ]$ and $S \geq G^*$, gov proposes $x_G = G^*$, leg passes $x_L = G^*$, gov signs G^*

when $G^* \in (L^*, 1/2SQ]$ and $S < G^*$ and $S > B$, gov proposes $x_G = L^* + S$, leg passes $x_L = L^* + S$, gov signs $L^* + S$

when $G^* \in (L^*, 1/2SQ]$ and $S < G^*$ and $S \leq B$, gov proposes $x_G = G^*$, leg passes $x_L = L^*$, gov signs L^*

when $G^* \in [1/2SQ, SQ)$ and $S \geq SQ - G^*$, gov proposes $x_G = G^*$, leg passes $x_L = G^*$, gov signs G^*

when $G^* \in [1/2SQ, SQ)$ and $S < SQ - G^*$ and $B \geq S - 2G^* + SQ$, gov proposes $x_G = G^*$, leg passes $x_L = 2G^* - SQ$, gov signs $2G^* - SQ$

when $G^* \in [1/2SQ, SQ)$ and $S < SQ - G^*$ and $B < S - 2G^* + SQ$, gov proposes $x_G = L^* + S$, leg passes $x_L = L^* + S$, gov signs $L^* + S$

when $G^* \in [SQ, SQ + S]$, gov proposes $x_g = G^*$, leg passes $x_L = G^*$, gov signs G^*

when $G^* \in (SQ + S, \infty)$ and $S > B$, gov proposes $x_G = SQ + S$, leg passes $x_L = SQ + S$, gov signs $SQ + S$

when $G^* \in (SQ + S, \infty)$ and $S \leq B$, gov proposes $x_G = G^*$, leg ignores, policy remains at SQ

To show how these predictions occur in equilibrium, we separately analyze the interaction between the players for three unique different spatial arrangements: (1) when both branches wish to move policy in the same direction but the governor favors a more extreme departure from the status quo than the legislature does ($G^* < L^* < SQ$); (2) when both branches wish to move policy in the same direction but the governor favors a less extreme departure from the status quo than the legislature does ($L^* < G^* < SQ$); and (3) when the players want to move policy in different directions ($L^* < SQ < G^*$), which we address in the main text. We do not address the symmetric and thus redundant cases in which $G^* < SQ < L^*$ or $SQ < L^* < G^*$.

Figure 2.3 illustrates the first case, where a governor desires an extreme policy shift. In this situation, a governor will never veto a bill because either x_G or x_L will be to the left of SQ and thus make the governor better off. Knowing this, the legislature can always pass a bill at its ideal policy $x_L = L^*$ and see it signed into law. But the legislature will be willing to be bought into policy to the left of L^* for a side payment S so long as that payment exceeds the policy loss, $-|x_G|$ (or simply x_G, because $G^* < L^*$). A governor with an ideal point like G_3^*, located to the left of $L^* - S$, has the opportunity to make a strategic proposal for a bill at $x_G = L^* - S$. The legislature will pass this proposal if it prefers it to the utility it gains from passing its ideal or is at least indifferent. The legislature compares

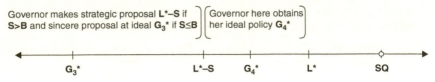

FIGURE 2.3. Predictions for two hypothetical governors, when the governor favors a more extreme departure from the status quo than the legislature does.

the utility of passing the governor's proposal ($x_G = L^* - S$) and receiving a side payment (S) to passing its ideal policy $x_L = L^*$. The legislature will pass $x_G = L^* - S$ if and only if:

$$U_L(x_G) \geq U_L(x_L)$$

$$-|L^* - x_g| + S \geq -|L^* - x_L|$$

$$-|L^* - (L^* - S)| + S \geq -|L^* - L^*|$$

$$-|S| + S \geq 0 \text{ because } L^* = 0$$

$$-S + S \geq 0 \text{ because } S > 0$$

$$0 \geq 0$$

Since this condition is met, the legislature will pass the governor's strategic proposal, and the governor knows it. Will the governor make this strategic proposal at $L^* - S$, or will she instead make a sincere proposal of $x_G = G_3^*$? The governor knows that if she makes a sincere proposal, the legislature will instead counter with $x_L = L^*$, because $G_3^* < L^* - S$, making the policy costs to the legislature for passing $x_G = G_3^*$ greater than the side payment S. Thus, the governor does not maximize her spatial payoff but receives a position-taking bonus that may be enough to compensate. She compares her total payoffs and will make sincere proposal $x_G = G_3^*$ if and only if:

$$U_G(L^*) + B \geq U_G(L^* - S)$$

$$-|G_3^* - L| + B \geq -|G_3^* - (L^* - S)|$$

$$-|G_a^*| + B \geq -|G_a^* + S| \text{ because } L^* = 0$$

$$G_a^* + B \geq G_a^* + S \text{ because } G_a^* < 0 \text{ and } G_a^* + S < 0$$

$$B \geq S$$

In plain language, a governor will make the sincere proposal – knowing that it will not pass the legislature in its original form and that she will be forced to sign a compromise measure at the legislature's ideal – when the position-taking benefit B outweighs the policy cost to her equal to S. By contrast, a governor will make a strategic proposal of $x_G = L^* - S$ when $B < S$. In this case, the legislature will pass x_G in its original form. What does this tell us about what to expect from stronger and weaker governors? Holding constant the locations of G_3^*, L^*, and SQ, as well as the value of B, a stronger governor able to offer a side payment $S > B$ will make a more modest, strategic proposal than a weaker governor but see it pass into law. A weaker governor for whom S does not outweigh B will make a more extreme proposal but will see it fail and be forced to sign a compromise bill more to the legislature's liking. By similar reasoning, a governor who cares more about her public positions (and thus has a larger B, all other factors equal) is more likely to satisfy the $B \geq S$ condition, leading to a sincere proposal and a compromise at the end of negotiations.

Our second spatial arrangement, when $L^* < G^* < SQ$, can be further divided into two regions: when the governor is closer to the legislature's ideal point than to the status quo and when the governor is closer to the status quo. In the first region, both branches will do quite well, but the legislature knows that if it passes a bill at its ideal policy, the governor will have to sign it because it will make her better off than the status quo. That gives the legislature leverage and the opportunity to choose whether to pass its ideal policy or to allow itself to be "bought off" by an executive side payment and pass the governor's ideal policy. When is it in the legislature's interest to pass L^*? It will do so when the spatial loss it would have to incur by passing G^* outweighs the value of the side payment S that the governor offers for passing her ideal policy. Because we arbitrarily set $L^* = 0$, the spatial loss of a movement from L^* to G^* is G^* itself. The legislature will thus pass L^* whenever $G^* > S$, and the governor will sign it because it makes her better off than the status quo. More formally, the legislature will pass L^* if and only if:

$$U_L(L^*) > U_L(G^*)$$
$$-|L^* - L^*| > -|L^* - G^*| + S$$
$$-|0| > -|-G^*| + S$$
$$0 > -G^* + S$$
$$G^* > S$$

When, instead, S is larger than or equal to G^*, meaning that the governor's side payment is enough to make up for the legislature's spatial policy loss, lawmakers will pass G^*, which the governor happily signs.

Can the governor do better here by making a strategic proposal? In the case where she gets her ideal policy, no. But when $G^* > S$, the governor might be able to do better than being forced to sign L^*. The governor could propose a policy at $L^* + S$, making the legislature indifferent between passing that bill and passing its own ideal (and, because of our tiebreaking rules, the legislature would thus pass the governor's proposal). Yet, for the governor, the cost of making this strategic offer and winning a policy gain of S is that she loses the position-taking bonus B. She will do this only when the policy gain is greater than the position-taking loss, then, if and only if $S > B$. Under these conditions, the governor proposes $L^* + S$, the legislature passes the bill, and the governor signs it.

The calculations become more complex – but the logic is similar – in the second region of the $L^* < G^* < SQ$ spatial arrangement, when the governor is closer to the status quo. Here, the governor can credibly threaten to veto L^* and, in fact, will veto anything to the left of $2G^* - SQ$ (the point that makes her indifferent between signing the legislature's bill or reverting to the status quo). Proposing a bill at that point will be the legislature's best play from a policy standpoint, but it might prefer to pass a bill at the governor's ideal point and reap the side payment as a reward. Again, the legislature compares these two plays and will pass G^* if and only if:

$$U_L(G^*) + \geq U_L(2G^* - SQ)$$
$$-|-G^*| + S \geq -|2G^* - SQ|$$
$$-G^* + S \geq -2G^* + SQ$$
$$S \geq -G^* + SQ$$
$$S \geq SQ - G^*$$

When, instead, the side payment is not large enough to make up for the legislature's policy loss (when $S < SQ - G^*$), the legislature will stick with its best policy outcome by passing a bill at $2G^* - SQ$, which the governor grudgingly signs. Again, can the governor do better here by making a strategic proposal? The governor might be able to do better than being forced to sign $2G^* - SQ$ by giving up the position-taking bonus B in exchange for the policy gains that would come from proposing $L^* + S$, which the legislature would then accept. She will do this only when the policy gain is greater than the position-taking loss, then, if and only if the gain of moving from $2G^* - SQ$ to $L^* + S$ outweighs B. Because both positions are to the right of zero (where L^* is located), the policy gain is $L^* + S - (2G^* - SQ) = L^* + S - 2G^* + SQ = S - 2G^* + SQ$. Therefore, when $S - 2G^* + SQ > B$, the governor proposes $L^* + S$, the legislature passes the bill, and the governor signs it.

Now consider the case of a governor with an ideal point like G_4^*, which is located in the $[L^* - S, L^*]$ interval. She will be able to propose her ideal policy, $x_G = G_4^*$, and get it. We have already demonstrated that the legislature will pass $x_G = L^* - S$ in its original form, so any bill located in the $[L^* - S, L^*]$ interval, and thus closer to the legislature's ideal, is an even better deal, making the legislature strictly better off than countering by passing its ideal policy. Because the governor knows that her sincere proposal $x_G = G_4^*$ will become law, there is no reason to make a strategic offer closer to the legislature's ideal. She proposes $x_G = G_4^*$, receives her position-taking bonus, and it becomes law. What this shows is that both branches can be very happy when they want to move policy in the same direction and are ideologically proximate. Looking across many potential policy areas, and holding SQ, B, and S constant, we are more likely to see successful gubernatorial proposals more often when the distance between L^* and G^* is smaller. Also note that for stronger governors possessing a larger S, the $[L^* - S, L^*]$ interval is larger. When this is the case, holding the locations of G^*, L^*, and SQ constant, G^* is more likely to be located in the $[L^* - S, L^*]$ interval, where she asks for and gets her ideal. Here, stronger governors are more likely to make sincere proposals, a comparative static prediction that moves in the opposite direction it moved in the case of the more extreme governor G_4^*, located far beyond the $[L^* - S, L^*]$ interval. This highlights the complicated relationship between a governor's strength and whether she asks for her ideal or makes a more strategic proposal. Still, the consistent pattern here and in the cases addressed in the main text is that stronger governors have more opportunities to make proposals that will pass in their original form.

3

What Do Governors Propose?

Each January, governors in nearly all states stand before a joint meeting of the legislature and deliver what has become known as a State of the State address.[1] These speeches, like the president's State of the Union address, are highly anticipated and choreographed events. The process of drafting the governor's comments begins weeks in advance, and debate within the administration over the content of the speech is spirited. For the governor, the State of the State not only kicks off the legislative session but is almost always her highest-profile speech of the year. This address receives front-page coverage in state newspapers, serves as the lead story on local news broadcasts, and is sometimes even carried live by local television stations. The State of the State is a crucial opportunity for the governor to speak directly to the lawmakers seated in front of her (whose votes will decide the fate of her legislative agenda) as well as to the voters and party activists who helped put her in office. Simply put, "the most precious rhetorical real estate of the year is a sentence in the State of the State address."[2]

These speeches are, of course, part political theater. Governors use the State of the State to highlight their political and legislative triumphs from the prior year and to praise the strength and character of their constituents. Like the State of the Union, these speeches are peppered with

[1] In a handful of states, the governor does not deliver her State of the State address until February or even March. In states with biennial legislative sessions, the governor only delivers an address once every two years.

[2] Interview with Dan Schnur, former communications director to California governor Pete Wilson, interviewed by Thad Kousser, July 7, 2009.

applause lines designed to bring lawmakers to their feet and to appeal to voters watching from home. To help convey an important point, many governors tell the story of an accomplished audience member who has been invited to watch from the balcony, while others bring props – a school bag, a veto pen, or even a revolutionary war musket. The primary objective of the speech, however, is to lay out a road map for the upcoming legislative session. As political scientist Alan Rosenthal notes, the State of the State is "the vehicle that announces to all what policies and programs the governor will pursue and gives the legislature its first strong indication of what the governor has in mind" (Rosenthal 1990, p. 7). Indeed, these speeches are as close as most governors ever come to submitting a formal legislative plan to lawmakers or the public.

Here, and throughout the book, we use State of the State addresses as a means of determining the governor's public agenda. These speeches do not, of course, contain everything a governor will want during the forthcoming legislative session. For practical reasons, a State of the State is usually limited to 30 or 40 minutes, meaning that the governor may not be able to include all of her proposals. Furthermore, her agenda will occasionally evolve throughout the legislative session. Some items may fall by the wayside due to changing circumstances, while others may be added as new issues become salient. However, in our interviews, lawmakers, staffers, and former governors universally indicated that these addresses contain the most significant legislative and budgetary proposals, making them reasonable proxies for a governor's public agenda. Existing research has arrived at a similar conclusion (Herzik 1991; Crew 1992; Fording et al. 2001; Ferguson 2003).

In this chapter, we consider the public agendas of state chief executives. We begin with a sample of State of the State addresses from which we identify over 1,000 individual proposals. For each proposal, we code whether it is a budgetary or policy item and make qualitative judgments about its significance and the ideological direction in which it will (if passed) move the status quo. Doing so allows us to construct measures of the content, ideological orientation, and scale of public agendas. Using these measures, we document the extent to which agendas vary across governors. We also use these data to consider the factors that shape agenda formation, including the governor's political circumstances, her partisanship, and the liberalness of her state's electorate. By examining what governors ask for, we are able to evaluate much of the intuition that underlies our models of both the policy and budget game.

3.1. Coding State of the State Addresses

Due to the onerous nature of tracking gubernatorial proposals, we limited our data collection to a nonrandom sample of governors in 28 states over two legislative sessions – 2001 and 2006. This sample of states was designed to maximize geographic, partisan, and institutional variation. We successfully coded State of the State addresses for all but four of the selected state years. During 2006, the governors of three of these states – North Carolina, North Dakota, and Texas – did not deliver an address. In North Dakota and Texas, this is because the legislature only meets biennially, whereas in North Carolina, the governor traditionally only delivers a State of the State during odd-numbered years. Massachusetts (2001) was excluded because its electronic legislative database only contains bills from more recent sessions, making it difficult to confirm the outcome of several agenda items. The states included in our analysis are mapped in Figure 3.1. Ultimately, our final data set consists of 52 state years with 48 unique governors – 23 Democrats and 25 Republicans. Importantly, these governors confronted a variety of strategic circumstances. Some bargained with citizen legislatures, and others faced highly professionalized chambers; many approached the bargaining table with a great deal of political capital, while others did not.

From State of the State addresses, we carefully identified individual agenda items, distinguishing between budgetary and policy proposals.[3] We define budgetary proposals as those that are exclusively fiscal in nature. These usually address tax rates, spending on *existing* government programs, or rainy day funds (those funds that allow state governments to set aside revenue to cover future budget deficits). Such proposals can be dealt with in annual or biennial negotiations over the budget bills that keep government running. Bargaining over these items takes place in the context of the budget game, where governors should enjoy a great deal of leverage over the legislature.

We treat agenda items that are not exclusively fiscal in nature as policy proposals. These ask the legislature to make changes in statutory or constitutional law, create a new government program, or make substantive changes to the design of an existing program. Policy proposals usually must be moved as stand-alone bills and not as part of the budget, even though they often have fiscal implications. Bargaining over bills

---

[3] Each address was read and coded by at least one paid research assistant and one of the authors of this volume.

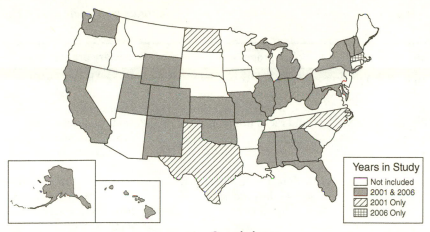

FIGURE 3.1. Sampled states.

like these takes place in the context of the policy game, where governors are often disadvantaged relative to the legislature. As we noted in Chapter 2, governors might prefer (for strategic reasons) to move some of their policy proposals into budget bills and thus negotiate over them in the budget game. The ability of chief executives to do so, however, is seriously constrained by the reluctance of the legislature to play along, by the impermanence of budget language and, in some states, by constitutional single-subject rules that prohibit these strategies. Indeed, we find very few instances in which governors are able to successfully move policy items through the budget process.[4]

Examples of typical budgetary and policy proposals are shown in Table 3.1. Three of the listed items, each of which addresses public education, are especially useful for illustrating the distinction between proposal types (these items are identified in the table using boldface). In 2006, Gov. Bill Owens (Republican) proposed increasing the amount of the tuition voucher offered to Colorado high school graduates who attend a state college or university. Because the voucher, known as the College Opportunity Fund, was an existing state program, the governor's

---

[4] Ultimately, the coding of agenda items into policy and budgetary proposals is based on our understanding of each proposal, as informed by media coverage of the legislative session and corresponding bills found in state legislative databases. Inevitably, there is some "noise" in our coding since the distinction between the two types of proposals is not always prefectly clean. However, we believe that coding errors are infrequent and, because they introduce random error into an independent variable, bias against finding empirical evidence that confirms our hypotheses.

TABLE 3.1. *Examples of policy and budgetary proposals from State of the State addresses*

Governors	Policy proposals	Budgetary proposals
Pataki (R-NY), 2001	Expand the state DNA database to include all convicted criminals	End the Alternative Minimum Tax on businesses
Glendening (D-MD), 2001	End racial profiling by police	Provide $45 million to expand community parks and playgrounds over the next 3 years
Easely (D-NC), 2001	**Adopt a state lottery and use the proceeds for education**	Invest more in the Teaching Fellows program, which helps recruit science and math teachers
Bush (R-FL), 2006	**Pay math and science teachers more for working in underperforming districts**	Invest $12 million to expand shelter capacity for an additional 100,000 people by the 2007 hurricane season
Owens (R-CO), 2006	Require proof of citizenship before allowing someone to register to vote	**Raise the tuition voucher offered to high school graduates to $2,580**
Lynch (D-NH), 2006	Reduce mercury emissions from power plants by requiring scrubber technology	Place a significant portion of the budget surplus in the state's rainy day fund

proposal could be moved as part of the budget.[5] No additional legislation authorizing the program and establishing its procedures was required. As a result, we code this agenda item as a budgetary proposal. Indeed, the spending increase was included in the executive budget submitted to the legislature and passed in full (a clear win for the governor).

While the tuition voucher is coded as a budgetary proposal, the two other education items are coded as policy proposals. In 2001, Gov. Mike Easley of North Carolina (Democrat) called on lawmakers to create a state lottery and dedicate its proceeds to hiring new teachers and reducing classroom sizes. Despite its obvious fiscal implications, efforts to enact a lottery could not be handled exclusively through the budget process. A bill was needed not only to authorize a lottery (since no such authorization existed) but also to design a commission to oversee it; determine

[5] Governor Owens asked the legislature to increase the vouchers from $2,400 to $2,580. This was included in the state budget, HB 1385.

the powers, compensation, and method of selecting commissioners; and establish the permitted games. Four lottery bills were introduced in the legislature, though all were eventually blocked in committee.[6] In 2006, Gov. Jeb Bush of Florida (Republican) called on lawmakers to pay math and science teachers more to work at low-performing schools. Like the proposal of his counterpart in North Carolina, Gov. Bush's plan necessitated legislation outside of the budget process. In particular, he needed the legislature to give local school boards the authority to create salary incentives. Unlike Gov. Easley, Gov. Bush was successful at securing the required statutory changes, all of which were approved by lawmakers as part of a larger education reform bill.[7]

We also code two additional features of each agenda item. The first of these is a proposal's overall ideological orientation. Agenda items that would move the status quo in a leftward direction are coded as liberal. Examples of liberal items include efforts to adopt new regulations on business activity, increase social services expenditures, strengthen abortion rights, or grow the economy through publicly funded investments. Proposals that would move the status quo in a rightward direction are coded as being conservative. Examples of conservative agenda items include efforts to cut taxes, roll back regulations on business, increase the sentences for convicted criminals, and adopt merit pay for public school teachers. Proposals that do not move policy in a clear ideological direction are coded as being neutral.

Second, we code the significance of each proposal using a scale ranging from 1 to 5. A score of 1 signifies an agenda item that we anticipate will have a very minor impact if enacted, whereas a 5 signifies the sort of change that would be highly consequential. An example of an agenda item coded as 1 is a proposal by Gov. Knowles (Democrat of Alaska) for his state to contribute $500,000 to the Special Olympics. While the adoption of a proposal such as this may be socially desirable, it represents a very minor change in the annual state budget. An agenda item that was assigned a score of 5 is a proposal by Gov. Bush of Florida to amend the state constitution to allow for the use of school vouchers. Several weeks before the governor's State of the State address, the Florida Supreme Court struck down a plan to use tax dollars to pay for students to attend private schools. The governor's proposed amendment would have

---

[6] "What Legislators Did and Didn't Do This Year," *Winston Salem Journal*, December 7, 2001, p. A17. The four bills introduced were HB1, HB511, HB 1218, and SB 986.

[7] Governor Bush's proposal was passed as HB 7087, also known as the governor's A++ education reform.

reversed the court's decision. Overall, 80 percent of the agenda items in our data set were given a significance score of 2 or 3, and as one might expect, a very small number (just 1.8%) were assigned a value of 5.

To verify the accuracy of our coding of the ideological orientation and scale of agenda items, we relied on outside experts. Specifically, we selected random samples of proposals and sent them to scholars, journalists, and practitioners of state politics, being sure to remove all references that would allow expert coders to identify the state or governor in question. We translated raw dollar figures into dollars per capita so that they would be proportional to the vastly different sizes of states. Working with these experts, we obtained a second coding for nearly all the agenda items from 2001. A comparison of our coding to that of experts indicates a reasonably high level of reliability.[8] The findings that we report subsequently and throughout this book remain unchanged if we replace our coding with those of the experts.

3.2. What Did Governors Ask For?

In total, our efforts identified 1,088 agenda items, for an average of nearly 21 per governor. Of these, we code 612 (or 56%) as policy proposals and 476 as budgetary. These numbers exclude agenda items that do not require action by the legislature. We also do not treat statements like "let's decrease our high school drop-out rate by 50 percent over the next decade" as proposals, unless they are accompanied in the speech by a more specific budgetary or policy recommendation.

The ideological distribution of the proposals in our sample differs across budgetary and policy items. A majority of the budgetary proposals are liberal, with governors of both parties often asking for increases in expenditures on public education as well as a variety of social service programs. The large share of liberal items may, in part, have been a function of prospering state economies. In both 2001 and 2006, the average unemployment rate among our sampled states was low by historical

---

[8] With respect to ideology, our codes are strongly correlated with those of the experts, and we shared the exact same code (liberal, neutral, or conservative) in 67% of cases. The correlation was lower, however, when it comes to the magnitude of the proposal ($r = .34$, but still clearly significant). Our coding only perfectly matched that of the experts for 33% of all agenda items. Of course, what we are really trying to separate are the big agenda items (4s and 5s, or 22% of cases) from the medium (3s, 26% of cases) and from the small ones (1s and 2s, 52% of cases). On these categories, we match up very well. We agree on the big proposals 75% of the time. We agree on what is a medium 53% of the time, and we agree on what is small 61% of the time.

standards (4.5%), and most states concluded the prior fiscal year with a budget surplus. The health of state budgets meant that additional public sector investments were not only feasible but that such investments could be funded with existing revenue streams and would not require tax increases. Among policy items, there was more balance, with roughly one-third of proposals falling into each ideological category.

Not surprisingly, there is a great deal of heterogeneity across governors in terms of the ambitiousness as well as the overall ideological orientation of their agendas. This is demonstrated in the appendix to this chapter, where we present basic descriptive statistics for the legislative agenda of each of our sampled chief executives (see Table 3.3). The best measure of ambitiousness is what we refer to as the *total scale* of the agenda. This is calculated by multiplying the number of items in a governor's agenda by their average scale (again, each proposal has been assigned a value ranging from 1 to 5, with higher values indicating a proposal that, if enacted, would have a larger impact). For the governors in our sample, total scale has an average of 57 but ranges from a low of 10 (for Democratic governor Howard Dean of Vermont) to a high of 115 (for Democratic governor Bill Richardson of New Mexico). Simply put, some governors offered quite modest agendas, while others proposed bold prescriptions for change. We observe similar variation in the liberalness of agendas. The share of proposals that are liberal ranges from a high of 100 percent (for Democratic governors Parris Glendening of Maryland and Rod Blagojevich of Illinois) to a low of 11 percent (for Republican governor Lisa Murkowski of Alaska).

Finally, we have coded the subject matter of gubernatorial agendas by categorizing each proposal into one of nine issue areas.[9] The results of this effort are presented as a stacked bar graph (Figure 3.2) in which

[9] Policy categories are defined in the following manner: (1) crime, proposals that address public safety, drug prevention and rehabilitation, corrections, sentencing, or victims rights and services; (2) development, proposals designed to grow, protect, or shape the state economy, including infrastructure investments, business incentives, tourism promotion, minimum wage and other labor laws, and the delivery of energy; (3) education, proposals that directly address either public or private education (early learning programs through higher education); (4) environment, proposals that address the environment, state parks and open spaces, or the use of natural resources; (5) health care, proposals that address the general cost and availability of health insurance, the delivery of health care, or disease prevention and awareness; (6) other, proposals that do not fit into one of the existing categories; (7) political reform, proposed changes in the constitution, fiscal rules, electoral rules, or the powers, responsibilities, and obligations of political actors; (8) social issues, proposals that are commonly linked with the so-called culture wars or morality policy (gay and lesbian rights, abortion, marriage, gaming, etc.); (9) social services, proposals

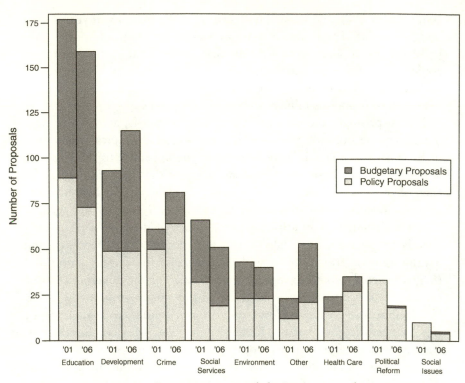

FIGURE 3.2. Governors' proposals by issue area and year.

each bar represents both an issue area and year, either 2001 or 2006. Bar heights are counts of proposals, with the lightly shaded region of each showing the number of policy items and the darkly shaded region showing the number of budgetary items. Issue areas are ordered from left to right along the x axis by their total number of proposals.

As Figure 3.2 demonstrates, public education featured quite prominently. In both years, education proposals constituted a plurality of agenda items (33% and 28%, respectively), with the typical State of the State address containing between six and seven education items. The amount of space dedicated to this issue is not surprising. Respondents to opinion polls consistently rank public education as one of their top public policy concerns. Agenda items pertaining to development and crime rank

that address redistributive (welfare-type) programs targeting the working poor, unemployed, elderly, or disabled, including Temporary Assistance for Needy Families (TANF,) Medicaid, State Children's Health Insurance Program (SCHIP), unemployment insurance, workers compensation, etc.

as the second and third most common. These issue areas, like education, are among the core responsibilities of state governments. In total, proposals dealing with education, development, or crime made up over 60 percent of the agenda items contained in governors' public agendas.[10]

We observe very few proposals that address controversial social issues, such as abortion, sex education, or gay and lesbian rights. Only 10 such proposals were made in 2001 and 5 in 2006. This may be unexpected to many readers given the important role that cultural issues have played in American politics over the past two decades. However, our observation is consistent with what we were told during interviews. Parris Glendening, former governor of Maryland, reported that "governors are, for the most part, concerned with the day-to-day challenges of running a state" and try to avoid polarizing fights over culture-war issues.[11] While such fights are sometimes unavoidable, governors tend not to put these issues on the agenda themselves.

Figure 3.2 also illustrates that governors are able to use the budgetary process to pursue change in a wide variety of issue areas. The only categories with few budgetary items were *political reform* and *social issues*. Here, governors tend to ask for changes in statutory or constitutional law that are difficult to move through budget bills. Even in these issue areas, however, governors are occasionally able to offer budgetary proposals. Our data set contains two excellent examples. Democratic governor Freudenthal, for instance, pursued political reform via the budget when he called on the state of Wyoming to begin assuming more responsibility for many of the critical activities of local government. His proposal did not ask the lawmakers for legislation altering the distribution of power or responsibilities between the state and its localities but rather proposed that the state dramatically increase its direct financial assistance to cities and counties. The best example of pursuing a social issue via the budget is Republican governor Mitt Romney's proposal to use Massachusetts state revenues to fund abstinence-only sex education programs, an important concern for religious conservatives.

[10] Across legislative sessions, we only observe relatively minor changes in the content of gubernatorial agendas. The most noteworthy change occurs in the "other" category and is due largely to a number of proposals dealing with natural disaster preparedness that appeared in State of the State addresses in 2006. These proposals were motivated by Hurricane Katrina, which hit New Orleans only a few months prior to the start of the 2006 legislative session.

[11] Interview with Gov. Parris Glendening of Maryland, conducted by telephone by Justin Phillips and Thad Kousser, July 13, 2010.

Of course, the content of agendas, just like their ambitiousness and ideological orientation, varies across governors. Our data reveal, for example, that state chief executives place differing emphasis on budgetary and
policy matters. For some, fiscal proposals dominated their agenda, while
for others, these concerns took a backseat to policy items. The same is
true for the issue areas shown in Figure 3.2. Though education proposals
constituted a plurality of agenda items for most governors, others focused
largely on health care, economic development, or crime. We observe some
of the most dramatic variation when it comes to political reform. In 24
of the state years in our sample, the governor did not offer a single
proposal targeting this issue area. For two of our governors, however,
political reform was crucial, constituting 33 percent of their total agenda
items. One of these governors was Republican John Engler of Michigan,
who proposed a series of reforms, ranging from enhancements to his
state's Taxpayers Bill of Rights to a constitutional amendment altering
the method by which justices are selected for the state supreme court.

3.3. Agendas and Bargaining Circumstances

Our theoretical model of the policy game indicates that a chief executive's
agenda will be endogenous to her political circumstances. Sometimes,
governors will need to pitch their agenda items strategically to convince
legislators to pass them intact or even to address them at all. Other times,
governors will ask for their ideal policy either knowing that they will
be able to secure its passage or because they know that their proposal
is likely to fail but they hope to score political points (a position-taking
bonus) simply by placing it on the agenda. Our model shows that a
governor's strength – her ability to offer side payments to lawmakers –
is an important determinant of whether she proposes her ideal policy or
some sort of compromise. The model does not, however, posit a consistent
effect of gubernatorial strength (the S term) but rather demonstrates that
its effect is contingent on the relative policy positions of the governor and
legislature, the location of the status quo, and even the value a governor
places on position taking. Under some configurations of these variables,
strong governors are likely to offer compromise proposals, while weak
governors are more likely to ask for items that reflect their true policy
preferences. Under other configurations, we expect the opposite.

Unfortunately, fully evaluating the nuanced predictions of our model
is impossible given existing data constraints. While we can reliably measure variables that shape a governor's strength – her popularity, ability

to sustain a veto, and length of time in office – it is not feasible to identify the policy preferences of the legislature and governor across all potential agenda items and all sampled states. Knowing the location of players' ideal points as well as the location of the status quo is crucial for predicting the types of policy proposals that will be made. Furthermore, because our model predicts what will happen on a single bill (what the governor will propose and how the legislature will react), it provides only limited guidance when it comes to anticipating the characteristics of the governor's overall agenda.

That being said, our interviews with political insiders and the data compiled from State of the State addresses confirm several of the basic insights of our model. First, state chief executives often look to the legislature when formulating their agendas. Bill Hauck, who has worked in both the legislative and executive branches in California, told us that agenda formation is, in part, about determining what the legislature will be receptive to – "you don't want to spend your life as governor making proposals that won't see the light of day."[12] Strategic behavior often entails modifying proposals by making them less liberal or conservative or by reducing their scale. It may even mean leaving some desired proposals out. During the process of developing their agendas, many governors actively seek the input of the legislature by consulting informally with the party leaders and committee chairs. Dan Schnur, who served as communications director to California governor Pete Wilson, explains that one step in building the governor's legislative agenda is "to reach out externally to legislators, both to vet the governor's proposals and to get their solutions as well. We worked with both caucuses. Not only does this improve the substantive product, but it also allows you to establish relationships, and to learn what will fly.... There are ideas that seem brilliant in December, but after a little quiet vetting, they turn out to be losers."[13] Former Republican governor Taft of Ohio told us, "There would be consultation with them [legislative leaders] and their staffs in developing the State of the State. It wouldn't be a tripartite meeting where they had veto power, but we had a relationship based on candor and trust."[14]

[12] Interview with Bill Hauck, former chief of staff to assembly speakers Willie Brown and Bob Moretti and deputy chief of staff to Gov. Pete Wilson, conducted by telephone by Thad Kousser and Justin Phillips, June 25, 2009.

[13] Interview with Dan Schnur, communications director to Gov. Pete Wilson, conducted by telephone by Thad Kousser, July 7, 2009.

[14] Interview with Gov. Bob Taft of Ohio, conducted by telephone by Thad Kousser and Justin Phillips, October 1, 2009.

This does not, however, mean that legislators are always consulted. Insiders were quick to tell us that on some issues, chief executives are willing to go it alone. Many of the policy and budgetary proposals in gubernatorial agendas are never vetted, including some that represent significant and potentially controversial changes to the status quo. In his 2001 State of the State address, Hawaii governor Ben Cayetano announced a proposal to send all A and B students to a state university for free. Prior to his address, he had not made his plan known to legislative leaders or University of Hawaii officials.[15] Similarly, Indiana governor Mitch Daniels included an unvetted proposal for a 25 cent increase in the tax on a pack of cigarettes. Newspaper coverage referred to this agenda item as a "surprise," especially for the governor's copartisans in the legislature, and commented that the line in the governor's speech containing the proposed tax hike was followed by a "notable and uncomfortable murmur that moved through the chamber."[16]

A second insight from our model of the policy game is that strong governors will not consistently offer bolder or more ambitious agendas than their weaker counterparts. Indeed, one might frequently expect the opposite, particularly if the branches of government are ideologically distant or want to move policy in the opposite direction. The logic behind what our model suggests is that stronger governors know they can buy larger policy concessions from the legislature (given their value of S), so they make strategic (i.e., compromise) policy proposals. These proposals, coupled with the promised side payment, induce the legislature to the bargaining table. Weaker governors, conversely, cannot get legislators to move as far, so their best play is to ask for their ideal policy, collect a position-taking bonus, and then watch their proposal die. If this process (which is shown in Figure 2.1) repeats itself across most of the issue areas that constitute a governor's agenda, we might observe weaker governors offering agendas that are more consistent with their ideology and possibly more ambitious overall.

This logic is supported by the actions of the chief executives in our sample. In Chapter 2, we briefly discuss the cases of two governors – Republicans Gary Johnson of New Mexico and George Ryan of Illinois – both of whom had very low political capital and were bargaining with legislatures in which the opposition party controlled at least one chamber.

---

[15] Jennifer Hiller, "Tuition Proposal," *Honolulu Advertiser*, February 1, 2001, p. 1A.
[16] Niki Kelly, "Cigarettes and Schools Top Agenda, Daniels Urges 25-cent-a-Pack Hike," *Journal Gazette*, January 12, 2006, p. 1A.

These men saw that they had little chance of success, and each offered a bold, ambitious agenda that was likely to be dead on arrival. In contrast, Gov. Kathleen Sebelius of Kansas, who was also bargaining with an ideological distant legislature, had a great deal of political capital – she was in her first term, she had an approval rating of 62 percent, and enough of the legislature's seats were in the hands of her fellow Democrats to make her veto threats credible. Instead of forwarding a bold agenda, Gov. Sebelius's State of the State contained mostly budgetary items and only three relatively modest policy proposals.

When asked about Gov. Sebelius's fairly modest set of agenda items, one of her communications directors noted that it simply was not worth the governor's effort to propose an extensive policy agenda because it was bound to fail. "It wasn't failing on the merits – she was very confident in both her political and her policy ability – but it was going to fail simply because Republicans in the legislature, particularly conservatives in the House, weren't going to hear the bills. So why would you work on them extensively? ... When you get swatted down a bunch of times, and you can get a lot done administratively or through the budget, you just say, well screw it, I'm not going to beat my head against a wall."[17] Governor Sebelius's policy proposals, which were all either ideologically neutral or conservative, were clearly designed to be acceptable to a legislature that was dominated by conservative Republicans. In taking this more modest approach, she was ultimately able to secure the full passage of each of her policy proposals.

Basic descriptive statistics from our data set confirm these patterns. During periods of divided government, it is chief executives with high amounts of political capital who are most likely to offer a compromise agenda. This is particularly evident when it comes to the ideological orientation of proposals. To help illustrate this, we create an index of gubernatorial strength in which one point is assigned for each of the determinants of a governor's political capital discussed in Chapter 2: being able to issue credible veto threats, having above average popularity, and serving in one's first term. We also assume that the governor's partisanship is a reasonable proxy for the types of policy she would ideally like to propose, with Democrats preferring, on average, to make liberal proposals and Republicans preferring conservative ones (an assumption that is validated in the following section). During divided government, we observe that a whopping 71 percent of the policy proposals of the

---

[17] Telephone interview with Burdett Loomis, conducted by Thad Kousser, May 14, 2010.

strongest governors (those who score a 3 on our index of political capital) are either ideologically neutral or consistent with the ideology of the opposition party. For governors with the lowest level of political capital – those with little incentive to compromise with an opposition legislature – this number falls quite noticeably to 43 percent.[18] We also observe governors with high levels of political capital offering less ambitious (i.e., smaller) agendas, though this difference is fairly minor (approximately 3 points in total scale). Though issues of sample size limit our ability to conduct a more sophisticated analysis, these descriptive statistics are broadly consistent with our theoretical model of agenda formation as well as our discussions with former governors and their advisors.[19]

A third insight from our model of the policy game has to do with the importance of the position-taking bonus (the B term). As the value of this bonus rises, it becomes more likely that the political gains from staking out a clear position outweigh the policy gains to be had by making a compromise proposal that the legislature will accept, even for those governors with the political capital to buy sizable concessions from lawmakers. This insight does not generate a clear prediction for most governors, however, because position taking can entail making either a moderate or ideological proposal (depending on the signal the governor wants to send) or may entail recommending either large or small changes to the status quo.[20] For example, both Gov. Romney of Massachusetts and Republican governor Frank Keating of Oklahoma wanted to signal their social conservatism in their State of the State addresses. Governor Romney did so by offering a relatively modest proposal to include abstinence in the state's sex education curriculum, while Gov. Keating went with a much bolder alternative, calling on lawmakers to strengthen the institution of marriage by removing mutual incompatibility as a legal grounds for divorce. Neither proposal was expected to be well received by the legislature, which (in both states) was controlled by Democrats. Though no meaningful legislative action was taken on these proposals (a clear indication that they

---

[18] When calculating these figures, we exclude governors with presidential ambitions. These individuals are likely to place a very high weight on position taking regardless of the type of legislature with which they are bargaining. Note that the differences in the ideological orientation of agendas that we observe here cannot be explained by the liberalness of state electorates.

[19] Our data set contains 20 governors who are bargaining with a legislature in which the opposition party controls at least one chamber. Of these, six score a 1 on our index of gubernatorial political capital, nine score a 2, and five score a 3.

[20] Additionally, the value of B may vary depending on the issue or bill.

lacked support), the governors' social conservatism was made clear to voters, lawmakers, and interest groups.

To demonstrate the potential effect of a large position-taking bonus on agenda formation, we consider the agendas of governors who should have a very large B term – those with clear presidential ambitions. In formulating her State of the State address, a presidential aspirant should receive political rewards by making proposals that signal her acceptability to the interest groups and voters who constitute her party's base.[21] This most likely means making proposals that are consistent with the ideological leaning of her party, regardless of the reception these proposals are likely to receive in her home-state legislature. If the B term is large enough (as we anticipate it will be for presidential aspirants), both weak and strong governors should prioritize position taking. It will be difficult for a governor to signal her acceptability to primary voters if her agenda is filled with policy compromises aimed at inducing home-state lawmakers to the bargaining table.

Among our sample of governors, we have identified five who were reported (in either state or national media) to be seriously considering a presidential campaign.[22] As expected, the agendas of these governors tended to be more consistent with their partisanship than those of governors without presidential aspirations; that is, Democrats were more likely to propose liberal items and Republicans were more likely to offer conservative ones. The difference, though, is a relatively modest 6 percentage points (and is not statistically meaningful). Ideally, we should make this comparison while also accounting for other features of the bargaining environment. We would expect to observe the largest effect of presidential ambitions on those governors who, absent any desires to run for the presidency, have an incentive to offer compromise proposals. Unfortunately, the small number of presidential aspirants in our sample prevents us from making this type of comparison and may account for the relatively small differences we observe here. Though not necessarily predicted by our model, we also observe that governors who are eying the White House offer more ambitious agendas. The average total scale of the policy agendas of presidential aspirants was 8 points higher than

[21] The individuals who participate in presidential primaries and caucus are, on average, more ideological (i.e., more liberal or conservative) than the typical voter in a general election.

[22] In 2001, these governors are Howard Dean (Vermont) and Gray Davis (California); in 2006, they are George Pataki (New York), Bill Richardson (New Mexico), and Mitt Romney (Massachusetts).

governors who were not. If we estimate a regression that controls for the partisanship of the governor, her political capital, and the partisanship of the legislature, this difference rises to a statistically significant 17 points.

Finally, while we expect governors' policy proposals to be endogenous to their bargaining circumstances, we do not have a similar expectation when it comes to budgetary items. Simply put, governors do not need to be strategic when formulating their fiscal agendas. With the budget, legislators must eventually come to the table, freeing the governor to make public proposals in January that reflect her budget priorities. Our interviews generally confirmed this intuition. Tim Gage, who, as director of finance, served as Gov. Gray Davis's chief budget advisor, explains that "the budget is mostly 'this is what I as governor want.' The extent to which a governor is willing to negotiate depends. It is rarely the case that the governor says I really want X, but the legislature will only give me Y, so I'll put Y in the budget. They pretty much start with what they want."[23] Indeed, we observe little evidence of strategic behavior when it comes to the formation of budgetary agendas. The share of budgetary proposals that are consistent with the governor's presumed ideology are very similar regardless of the governor's political capital or the partisanship of the legislature. Chapter 5, which uses a different data set to analyze negotiations over the size of the state budget, also finds that executive budgetary proposals are not meaningfully shaped by features of the bargaining environment. There is some weak evidence that governors who bargain with patient legislatures (i.e., those that meet in lengthy sessions) make fewer budgetary proposals, but this relationship does not quite reach statistical significance.[24] The only evidence that we observe with respect to strategic agenda formation in budgeting has to do with the position-taking bonus. Governors with presidential ambitions create budgetary agendas that are both more ideologically consistent with their partisanship and more ambitious than their counterparts who are not eyeing the White House.[25] This pattern is quite similar to what we observe in policy agendas. Ultimately, our interviews and data are broadly

[23] Interview with Tim Gage, director of finance to California governor Gray Davis, conducted by telephone by Thad Kousser, July 9, 2009.
[24] Regression models indicate that a governor who is bargaining with a legislature that meets in lengthy sessions will call for five fewer budget proposals than a governor that who is bargaining with a legislature that meets in sessions of average length.
[25] Fifty-nine percent of the budgetary items of governors with presidential ambitions are consistent with their partisanship. For all remaining governors, only 39% are consistent. The average total scale of the budgetary agenda is 28 for governors with presidential ambitions and 22 for all others.

consistent with our expectations that different logics drive bargaining over policy and fiscal issues.

3.4. Agendas and Gubernatorial Partisanship

Do Republican and Democratic governors propose different types of legislative agendas? In contemporary American politics, Democrats are much more likely to identify as liberal and to support government action as a means of improving social welfare, the environment, and the plight of minorities. In contrast, Republicans tend to identify as ideologically conservative and are generally suspicious of government power. While not all elected officials closely adhere to their partisan label, it seems reasonable to expect that Democratic governors will offer agendas that are more liberal (and potentially more ambitious) than their Republican counterparts. Similarly, Democrats and Republicans often prioritize different issues, a fact that may lead to partisan variation in the content of agendas. Of course, the incentive to bring lawmakers to the table by offering compromise proposals may have the effect of reducing partisan differences. Likewise, governors care about making proposals that appeal to voters. For Democrats serving in states with a conservative electorate and Republicans in states with a liberal electorate, this may entail formulating agendas that are more centrist than those of the copartisans elsewhere.

In Table 3.2, we consider whether there are partisan differences across several key characteristics of gubernatorial agendas. The first column of the table lists the characteristic of interest, the second and third columns report the mean values for Democratic and Republican governors, respectively, and the final column is the difference between these values, with asterisks indicating those differences that are statistically meaningful at either the 90 percent (*) or 95 percent level (**). We begin with measures of a governor's ambitiousness – the number of items in her State of the State address, their average and total scale, and the share that are policy proposals. The table reveals that the Republicans in our sample were slightly more ambitious than their Democratic counterparts. Though the average scale of agenda items was identical by partisan type, Republican State of the State addresses included more proposals. The result was that the *total scale* of Republican agendas averaged 12 more points than those of Democrats, a difference that is statistically meaningful. While the agendas of Democrats focused a bit more on policy items, this difference is minor.

TABLE 3.2. *Features of gubernatorial agendas by party*

	Democratic governors	Republican governors	Difference
The basics			
Average number of proposals	18.6	22.8	−4.2
Average scale (1–5)	2.8	2.8	0
Total scale	50.0	62.2	−12.2*
Share that are policy proposals	62.1%	56.2	5.9
Subject matter (share of the total agenda)			
Education	28.3%	34.5	−6.2*
Development	18.6%	21.2	−2.7
Crime	14.3%	11.5	2.8
Social services	10.7%	8.5	2.1
Environment	8.1%	6.5	1.6
Health care	9.1%	3.7	6.1*
Political reform	2.7%	7.2	−4.5**
Social issues	1.6%	1.0	0.6
Ideological orientation (share liberal)			
All proposals	57.6%	42.7	15.0**
Budget proposals	65.1%	57.0	8.1
Policy proposals	51.6%	30.1	21.6**

The middle section of Table 3.2 considers the content of gubernatorial agendas, reporting the average amount of agenda space dedicated to each of eight issue areas. In five of these, there are only small differences between Democrats and Republicans, none of which are meaningful. In the remaining three – education, health care, and political reform – there are statistically significant distinctions. Republican governors dedicated a larger share of agenda items to education and political reform, while Democrats were more likely to address health care. The absolute size of these differences was, however, fairly moderate, ranging from 4.5 percent (for political reform) to 6.2 percent (for education).

The largest partisan distinction that we observe is in the ideological orientation of agendas. On average, the share of liberal agenda items is 15 percentage points higher for Democratic governors than it is for their Republican counterparts, a difference that is statistically significant at the 95 percent level. This finding is consistent with the general ideological placement of the parties in contemporary American politics and indicates that even though Democratic and Republican governors focus on the same issue areas, the proposals they offer within each are often philosophically different. If we separately consider budgetary and policy agendas, we uncover an important caveat – the ideological distinction is greatest for policy proposals. The budgetary agendas of Democratic chief executives are only 8 percentage points more liberal than those of Republicans, while their policy agendas are nearly 22 points more liberal. Only the ideological difference in policy agendas is statistically meaningful.

An alternative approach to looking for partisan differences in legislative agendas is to see what happens following a change in the partisanship of a state's governor. If, for instance, a Democrat is replaced by a Republican, do the proposals included in the State of the State address become more conservative? Within our sample, we have 16 states that witnessed a change in executive partisanship between 2001 and 2006 – 10 moved from a Democratic to a Republican governor, and 6 moved in the opposite direction. Not surprisingly, these partisan changes were followed by sizable adjustments in the overall ideological orientation of the agenda. Following a switch to a Republican governor, the share of policy proposals that were liberal fell by an average of 31 percentage points. A similar, though smaller, change occurred in the budgetary agenda, where the proportion of liberal agenda items decreased by 8 points. When the switch occurred in the opposite direction – when a Republican governor was replaced by a Democrat – the share of liberal policy and budgetary proposals increased by 13 and 19 percentage points, respectively. Regression results reported in the appendix show that the correlation between partisan change and ideological change is statistically significant (at the 95% level) for both the total and policy agenda but falls short of significance in budgeting.

We are somewhat surprised by the relatively small partisan differences that we observe in the ideological orientation of budgetary items, especially given the ability of governors to make sincere proposals in the budget game. That being said, differences in the fiscal policy preferences of the Democratic and Republican governors included in our sample simply may not have been that large. Moreover, governors (and legislatures) face important institutional constraints when it comes to budgeting that may also have the effect of minimizing partisan differences. These include balanced budget requirements, tax and expenditure limitations (laws that restrain the growth of governmental budgets), and earmark mandates (which lock in state expenditures on certain activities).

Do chief executives also craft their agendas to fit the ideological tilt of the state electorate? As we noted earlier, the desire to formulate an agenda that appeals to voters may lead governors to offer agendas that differ from what one might ordinarily expect, particularly if they hold office in a state where their partisanship does not match the ideological orientation of the electorate. To consider this possibility, we rely on multivariate regression models, which allow us to consider the effect of voter liberalness while holding constant (or controlling for) the governor's partisanship. We measure the liberalness of the electorate using the share of a state's voters who cast their ballot for John Kerry in the 2004 presidential election.[26] For the sake of completeness, our models also control for the partisanship of the legislature and the state's fiscal health. The regression results are reported in full in the appendix to this chapter.

First, these regressions confirm our expectation – the liberalness of a governor's agenda is positively correlated with the liberalness of the state electorate, even after accounting for other potential influences. Simply put, Democratic governors in conservative states like Alabama, Kansas, and Wyoming, along with Republican governors in liberal places such as California, Massachusetts, and Vermont, craft agendas that are more moderate than one would expect given their partisan labels. Our regressions reveal that the correlation between voter liberalness and the ideological orientation of agenda items is most pronounced when it comes to policy proposals. Second, these results also confirm the finding presented in Table 3.2 that a governor's partisanship is a key predictor of the ideological orientation of her agenda. Indeed, the regressions go further by demonstrating that (even though the ideology of the electorate often matters) a governor's partisanship is the single *best* predictor of the ideological tilt of her overall agenda as well as the liberalness of her policy proposals.

Despite a strong correlation between a governor's partisanship and the liberalness of her legislative agenda, ideological purity is rare, even among governors whose partisanship matches the ideological orientation of their states' electorate. Nearly all gubernatorial agendas, even the portion dedicated to policy proposals, are composed of a mix of liberal, conservative, and neutral items.[27] To help illustrate the relative dearth of ideological purity, Figure 3.3 plots along the *y* axis the share of a governor's policy proposals that are liberal and, along the *x* axis, the share

---

[26] Presidential voting patterns, while not a direct measure of ideology, correlate strongly to a variety of more direct (but less readily available) measures of voter liberalness (Erikson et al. 2007).

[27] The proposals that run counter to a governor's partisan type are not usually minor or "throw-away" agenda items. The average scale of these proposals is nearly identical to the average scale of those items that are consistent with the governor's partisanship, 2.67 vs. 2.73 (on a 5-point scale).

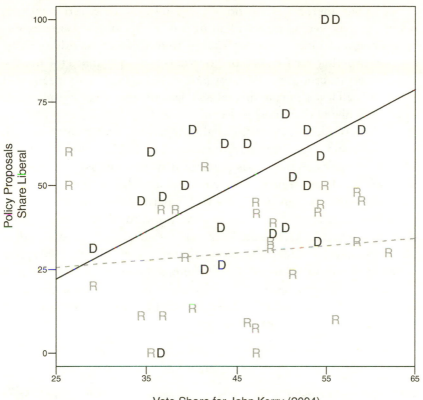

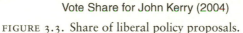

FIGURE 3.3. Share of liberal policy proposals.

of voters who cast their ballot for John Kerry. All governors in our data set are included, with Democrats identified using a "D" and Republicans an "R." The figure also includes two regression lines showing the relationship between the liberalness of a state's voters and the ideological orientation of its governor's policy proposals. The darker, solid line is for Democratic governors, and the lighter, dashed line is for Republicans. The steepness of these lines tells us how sensitive gubernatorial agendas are to the liberalness of voters, with a steeper line indicating a closer link between voter preferences and the direction of governors' proposals.

Figure 3.3 clearly demonstrates that the policy agendas of Democrats tend to be more liberal. This can be seen just by eyeballing the distribution of proposals – most Ds reside higher up on the *y* axis than do the Rs. Of the governors with policy agendas that were less than one-quarter liberal, all but one – Kathleen Sebelius of Kansas – were Republican. The opposite is true as one approaches the top of the y axis. Of the governors whose policy agendas were more than half liberal, all but two – Sonny Perdue of Georgia and Mike Leavitt of Utah – were Democrats. Additionally, the regression line for Democratic governors is always above the line for Republicans (except at the leftmost part of the x axis). This means that at virtually all levels of voter liberalness, Democratic policy agendas tend to be more liberal than those of Republicans.

The lack of ideological purity is also apparent. A large share of both Democratic and Republican governors are clustered between the 25 and 50 percent marks on the y axis (an area that we could label as the ideologically moderate region). Gubernatorial agendas do not seem to be particularly polarized by party, and within parties, there is a fair amount of ideological heterogeneity. The positive (upward) slope on the regression lines indicates (as we noted earlier) that governors adjust the ideological orientation of their agendas so that they more closely correspond to the preferences of the electorate. There is, however, a clear partisan difference in these regression lines – the slope for Democratic governors is much steeper, indicating that the agendas of Democrats (at least in our sample) are more sensitive to voter preferences.[28]

3.5. Conclusion

When governors stand at the speaker's rostrum and deliver their State of the State messages, what do they ask for? Our data show that governors tend to offer ambitious agendas, averaging nearly 21 proposals each. These agendas focus predominately on public education, economic development, and crime, rarely delving into the controversial social issues that often characterize partisan political conflict at the national level. While not all proposals in governors' public agendas represent significant changes to the status quo, many do. Within our sample of State of the State addresses, we observe chief executives offering up bold and newsworthy reforms, some of which went on to shape policy debates beyond the borders of the governor's home state. Our data also show that nearly all state chief executives pursue their legislative goals through both the budget and policy games, though their agendas appear to suggest a

---

[28] If the governor is a Democrat, a 10 percentage point increase in the Kerry vote translates into a policy agenda that is approximately 7 percentage points more liberal. For Republicans, it would only translate into a change of 2 percentage points.

preference for policy items. The tendency for governors to prefer playing the policy game, despite its inherent disadvantages, may reflect the twin realities that many goals cannot be achieved through budgeting alone and that budgetary victories may be more fleeting than victories in the policy game, given that the budget is revisited either annually or biennially.

Taken as a whole, the public agendas of most state chief executives are ideologically moderate. Though the agendas of Democrats are, on average, more liberal than those of their Republican counterparts, ideological purity is rare. Nearly all governors, regardless of party, offer a mix of liberal, conservative, and ideologically neutral proposals. Indeed, in our sample of 54 governors, only two proposed agendas consisted entirely of liberal items, and no governor delivered a State of the State that contained exclusively conservative proposals. Furthermore, within parties, there appears to be a fair amount of ideological heterogeneity. Some Republican governors, for example, delivered State of the State addresses filled largely with conservative proposals, while others offered agendas that were much more moderate and, in a few cases, agendas that were relatively liberal, even when compared to those of many Democrats.

These patterns suggest that governors enjoy and exercise a great deal of ideological flexibility. One perspective on this was offered by Gov. Parris Glendening of Maryland, who argues that the realities of running a state do not allow for ideological rigidity. Governors must ensure that the budget is balanced, that the state can adequately respond to its day-to-day challenges, and must be able to work with lawmakers from both parties and across the ideological spectrum. Our model of the policy game suggests a second, though not entirely inconsistent, explanation – to move a policy agenda (i.e., to bring the legislature to the bargaining table), the governor will sometimes have to start by offering a compromise position.

This chapter also provides important evidence about the forces that shape gubernatorial agendas. Obviously, partisanship is one of these. Despite the ideological flexibility of state chief executives, we find that a governor's partisanship remains by far the single best predictor of the ideological tilt of her overall agenda. The effect of partisanship is most pronounced when it comes to the formulation of a governor's policy proposals. Governors also appear to shape the ideological orientation of their agendas to fit the liberalness of their states' electorate. This suggests that some of the ideological flexibility that we observe is the result of governors trying to craft agendas that appeal to state voters.

Finally, our data indicate that the *policy* proposals of chief executives are endogenous to their bargaining circumstances. We find that whether governors offer compromise proposals or items that are closer to their ideal outcome often depends on the preferences of the legislature, the governor's own political capital, and even the value the governor places on position taking. The nuanced patterns in our data, while not necessarily what the existing literature would predict, are generally consistent with our theoretical model of the policy game. For example, we find that among chief executives bargaining with an opposition legislature, it is high-political-capital governors who offer more modest compromise agendas, while weaker governors tend to shoot for the moon. We also observe governors who place a high value on position taking (presidential aspirants in this case) making many proposals and offering agendas that are larger in scale and more consistent with their ideology. As expected, there is little evidence of strategic agenda formation when it comes to budgetary agendas.

3.6. Appendix

Table 3.3 presents descriptive statistics for the public agendas of the governors included in our sample. We begin with several measures of agenda size or ambitiousness. The first column is a count of the number of legislative proposals that appeared in the governors' State of the State address, the second is the average scale of all proposals (ranging from 1 to 5), the third is the total scale of the agenda (calculated by multiplying the number of items in a governor's agenda by his average scale), and the fourth column is the share of proposals that are budgetary. Next, we show the ideological orientation of the governor's agenda. The fifth column reports the share of all agenda items that would move the status quo in a liberal or leftward direction, while columns 6 and 7 report the share of budgetary and policy items that are liberal.

Table 3.4 reports the results of regression models that explore the relationship between gubernatorial partisanship and the ideological orientation of legislative agendas. In particular, these models consider what happens following a change in the partisanship of a state's governor. If, for instance, a Democrat is replaced by a Republican, do the proposals included in the State of the State address become more conservative? The dependent variable in the three regressions is operationalized as the share of proposals that were liberal in 2006, minus the share that were liberal in 2001. A positive value means that the agenda offered by the state's

TABLE 3.3. *Governors' legislative agendas (2001 and 2006)*

	Total proposals	Average scale	Total scale	Budgetary items (% of total)	Total agenda liberal (%)	Budget items liberal (%)	Legislative items liberal (%)
2001							
Siegelman (D-AL)	20	2.60	52	25	60	100	47
Knowles (D-AK)	28	2.82	79	46	61	62	60
Davis (D-CA)	23	2.96	68	26	65	83	59
Owens (R-CO)	24	3.04	73	17	50	75	45
Bush (R-FL)	13	2.38	31	77	54	70	0
Barnes (D-GA)	9	3.00	27	11	22	0	25
Cayetano (D-HI)	21	2.57	54	57	48	58	33
Ryan (R-IL)	13	3.38	44	23	62	100	50
O'Bannon (D-IN)	25	2.68	67	44	60	73	50
Graves (R-KS)	29	2.38	69	76	62	68	43
Glendening (D-MD)	11	2.91	32	18	100	100	100
Engler (R-MI)	18	2.89	52	6	22	0	24
Musgrove (D-MS)	8	3.00	24	63	75	80	67
Holden (D-MO)	15	2.60	39	47	67	71	63
Shaheen (D-NH)	10	3.20	32	30	80	100	71
Johnson (R-NM)	21	3.38	71	14	38	33	39
Pataki (R-NY)	37	2.86	106	32	46	42	48
Easley (D-NC)	11	2.73	30	27	73	100	63
Hoeven (R-ND)	12	2.08	25	83	58	70	0
Taft (R-OH)	29	2.31	67	69	55	65	33
Keating (R-OK)	22	2.91	64	59	27	38	11
Perry (R-TX)	27	2.81	76	22	56	100	43
Leavitt (R-UT)	15	2.67	40	67	73	80	60
Dean (D-VT)	3	3.33	10	0	67	NA	67
Locke (D-WA)	14	3.29	46	43	43	33	50
Wise (D-WV)	34	2.38	81	44	44	67	26
Geringer (R-WY)	38	2.71	103	34	37	69	20
2006							
Riley (R-AL)	20	2.95	59	55	25	36	11
Murkowski (R-AK)	9	2.78	25	44	11	25	0
Schwarzenegger (R-CA)	12	3.33	40	25	42	33	44
Owens (R-CO)	37	2.51	93	27	22	60	7
Bush (R-FL)	31	2.77	86	61	39	37	42
Perdue (R-GA)	22	2.59	57	59	64	69	56
Lingle (R-HI)	44	2.50	110	57	41	40	42
Blagojevich (D-IL)	10	3.10	31	20	100	100	100
Daniels (R-IN)	9	3.22	29	22	33	50	29
Sebelius (D-KS)	8	2.63	21	63	38	60	0
Ehrlich (R-MD)	33	2.36	78	70	67	91	10
Romney (R-MA)	24	3.21	77	17	29	25	30
Granholm (D-MI)	21	2.76	58	10	57	100	53
Barbour (R-MS)	18	2.67	48	17	28	100	13
Blunt (R-MO)	29	2.31	67	62	45	67	9
Lynch (D-NH)	23	2.70	62	30	35	29	38
Richardson (D-NM)	44	2.61	115	68	52	60	36
Pataki (R-NY)	28	2.82	79	46	39	46	33
Taft (R-OH)	18	2.72	49	11	39	100	31
Henry (D-OK)	27	2.44	66	59	48	50	45
Huntsman (R-UT)	12	3.00	36	83	33	30	50
Douglas (R-VT)	17	2.88	49	35	41	33	45
Gregoire (D-WA)	17	2.24	38	65	59	55	67
Manchin (D-WV)	10	3.00	30	20	30	0	38
Freudenthal (D-WY)	35	2.46	86	54	43	53	31

TABLE 3.4. *Partisan change and ideological change (2001–6)*

	All proposals (change in share liberal)	Budget proposals (change in share liberal)	Policy proposals (change in share liberal)
Partisan change	20.29**	11.43	23.98**
	(6.47)	(11.44)	(9.04)
Democratic seat share	.25	−.45	.12
	(.66)	(.75)	(.60)
Voter liberalness	.57	1.79	.33
	(.30)	(1.16)	(.92)
Intercept	−46.72	−62.35	−27.89
	(25.08)	(44.34)	(35.06)
N	24	24	24
Adjusted R^2	.26	.03	.17

Note: The units of analysis are states. All models are OLS regressions, and two-tailed tests are used: * < .10, ** < .05.

governor in 2006 was more liberal than the one offered by its governor in 2001. The key independent variable, *Partisan Change*, is a trichotomous measure that is coded 0 for no change, −1 for a Republican change, and 1 for a Democratic change. We also include variables that capture the share of legislative seats held by Democrats (*Democratic Seat Share*) and the overall liberalness of the state electorate (*Voter Liberalness*). This last variable is operationalized as the share of the state electorate that voted for John Kerry during the 2004 presidential election. We estimate three models, one for the total agenda and one each for the policy and budgetary agendas.

For the total agenda as well as the policy agenda, change in gubernatorial partisanship is a statistically significant predictor of change in the ideological orientation of proposals, even after controlling for the partisanship of the legislature and the liberalness of voters. Specifically, we find that switching from a Republican to a Democratic governor increases the liberal share of agenda items by just over 20 percentage points and increases the liberal share of policy items by 24 points. In budgeting, the coefficient on *Partisan Change* does not reach statistical significance, though it is still positive. It is worth keeping in mind that we are estimating our model with a fairly small sample of states – 24 in total, 16 of which experienced a partisan change in the executive branch. If our analysis included more states over a larger number of legislative sessions, we might very well find partisan effects in the budgetary agenda as well. In Chapter 5, which looks at the size of the executive budget proposal

TABLE 3.5. *Voter liberalness and the ideological orientation of gubernatorial agendas*

	All proposals (share liberal)	Budget proposals (share liberal)	Policy proposals (share liberal)
Democratic governor	13.70**	7.89	20.47**
	(4.74)	(8.13)	(5.72)
Democratic seat share	−.18	−.21	−.11
	(.18)	(.31)	(.22)
Voter liberalness	.49	.09	.74**
	(.30)	(.53)	(.36)
Budget surplus (lagged)	−.12	−.32	−.05
	(.12)	(.20)	(.14)
2001 dummy variable	11.74**	11.72	7.59
	(4.65)	(7.99)	(5.63)
Intercept	25.63	61.93	−.61
	(12.85)	(22.28)	(15.58)
N	52	52	52
Adjusted R^2	.24	.02	.25

Note: The units of analysis are gubernatorial agendas. All models are estimated using OLS. Two-tailed tests are used: * $< .10$, ** $< .05$.

for all 50 states over a 20-year period, we do observe differences in the budgets of Democrats and Republicans.

Table 3.5 considers the relationship between the liberalness of the state electorate and the ideological orientation of governors' agendas. Again, three models are estimated, one for the overall agenda and one each for the policy and budgetary agendas. Like the models reported in Table 3.4, we use the Kerry vote as our proxy for voter liberalness and the share of legislative seats in the hands of Democrats. To these we add the partisanship of the governor, a lagged measure of the state's budget surplus (this captures the state's overall fiscal health), and a dummy variable for the 2001 legislative session. Note that our results remain robust to the inclusion of variables that capture the size of state government (either the total budget or government spending per capita) as well as alternative measures of state fiscal health (such as the unemployment rate).

Across all models, we observe a positive correlation between the liberalness of the electorate and the liberalness of the governor's agenda. This correlation, however, is only statistically significant in the model for policy proposals (though it comes close to reaching significance in the model of the overall agenda). With respect to the policy agenda, a 10 percentage point increase in the Kerry vote equates to about a 7 point increase in the share of liberal proposals. These results also confirm that a governor's partisanship is a key predictor of the ideological orientation of her agenda. Indeed, across all models, the liberalness of the electorate is a less substantively meaningful predictor than the partisanship of the governor.

4

Gubernatorial Success

Many of the chief executives in our study proposed headline-grabbing education reforms in their State of the State addresses. These governors fought hard to move their reforms through the legislature, but not all emerged victorious. Democrat Roy Barnes, for instance, called on Georgia lawmakers to end the practice of "social promotion" in public schools by expanding use of high-stakes standardized testing.[1] Nearly two months to the day after announcing his proposal, Gov. Barnes was seated at a teacher's desk in front of a classroom full of third graders, signing his bill into law.[2] The governor's rapid success occurred despite strong opposition from black lawmakers and civil rights leaders, who feared that minority students would be disproportionately hurt. Republican governor Robert Ehrlich of Maryland also made public education a centerpiece of his State of the State, though he pursued his goals through the budget. Ehrlich called on lawmakers to make record financial investments in the state's primary and secondary schools as well as its colleges and universities. Ultimately, the governor secured much of what he originally asked for, even though he confronted a legislature controlled overwhelmingly by the opposition party. Indeed, his large education investments were initially dismissed by Democratic lawmakers, including an Appropriations Committee member who responded to the governor's proposal by

---

[1] Social promotion is the practice of advancing a failing student to the next grade level to keep him with his peers. The governor asked that all third, fifth, and eighth grade students be required to pass a standardized test before being advanced to the next grade level.
[2] James Salzer, "School Reform Signed," *Atlanta Journal-Constitution*, April 10, 2001, p. C1.

saying, "He's spending money like a drunken sailor, and I apologize to self-respecting drunken sailors out there."[3]

Though he fought just as hard for his education agenda, Gov. Gary Locke of Washington did not enjoy the success of governors Barnes or Ehrlich. In his address, Locke unveiled an overhaul of the state's education laws that, according to the *Seattle Times*, would "influence everything from what students eat to how teachers get paid."[4] Locke's proposals asked lawmakers to abolish the current education code and to design a new teacher compensation system based on knowledge, skill, and performance. While he secured early support from some of his copartisans in the legislature, Locke's proposals failed even to make it out of the House Education Committee. By summer, a local newspaper had already declared the governor's education proposals "dead and gone."[5]

Cases like these can help us test the hypotheses generated by our bargaining models. Our formulation of the policy game, for instance, predicts greater success for Gov. Barnes as opposed to Gov. Locke. When he proposed his education reforms, Barnes enjoyed a great deal of political capital – he was a popular first-term governor – and his party controlled nearly 60 percent of the seats in the legislature. Locke, conversely, was not in a particularly enviable bargaining position. He was a second-term governor, his popularity was beginning to decline, and though his copartisans controlled one chamber of the legislature, the other was in the hands of Republicans. Similarly, our models suggest that Gov. Ehrlich would outperform Locke. While Ehrlich also faced partisan obstacles, he made the strategic decision to pursue education reform through the budget process, capitalizing on the bargaining advantages enjoyed by chief executives in budgeting.

Of course, there are limits to the usefulness of such paired comparisons, particularly when one needs to evaluate the effects of multiple potential determinants of bargaining success. In the cases of education reform presented here, Gov. Locke may have done poorly relative to governors Barnes and Ehrlich because of his low political capital, compounded by his decision to play the policy as opposed to the budget game. Alternatively (or additionally), he may have done poorly because his education

3 Andrew A. Green, "Ehrlich Seeks 12% Increase in Budget – Proposal Includes No New Sales, Income Taxes," *The Sun*, January 18, 2006.
4 David Postman and Ralph Thomas, "Locke Insists on Solutions: Schools, Roads Head Second-Term Action List," *Seattle Times*, January 11, 2001, p. A9.
5 David Ammons, "Yet Another Legislative Session Will Begin Today," *The Columbian*, July 16, 2001.

proposals were larger in scope than those of the other governors, potentially making them very difficult to pass, *no matter* the bargaining circumstances. Unfortunately, there are just too many moving parts in these sorts of comparisons to draw much in the way of conclusions.

To overcome this obstacle, we track the outcomes of the over 1,000 policy and budgetary proposals that we identified in our sample of State of the State addresses, combining these into a single data set. For each, we ask whether legislators eventually passed what the governor proposed, either in its original form or in a half-a-loaf compromise, or whether the proposal died somewhere in the legislative process. These data form the core of a rich data set of case studies that allows us to simultaneously evaluate the effects of several potential determinants of gubernatorial bargaining success. In this chapter, we detail our data collection process, explaining how we track bargaining outcomes. Using these data, we present baseline measures of gubernatorial success. These answer important questions about the frequency with which governors successfully shepherd their proposals through the legislative process and the extent to which bargaining success varies across governors. We then employ regression analysis to systematically evaluate the predictions of our bargaining models, testing whether and how the determinants of gubernatorial success vary across the budget and policy games. The regression results not only tell us which factors meaningfully shape bargaining outcomes but also allow us to estimate the magnitude of their effects.

4.1. Tracking Gubernatorial Proposals

Before we can empirically evaluate our hypotheses, we need to know the final outcome of each of the 1,088 proposals that we identified in State of the State addresses. To track proposals, we take advantage of searchable archives of statehouse journalism as well as state legislative databases. These sources allow us to identify the bills that contain State of the State proposals, chart their legislative histories, and determine whether their final disposition represented for the governor a victory, a defeat, or a half-a-loaf compromise.

For each proposal, we began by searching for newspaper coverage using LexisNexis Academic and Newsbank. These sources provide electronic access to the archives of several major newspapers in each state. Journalistic coverage of the State of the State address and the proceeding legislative session were crucial for coding outcomes. First, newspaper stories helped us ascertain salient details of gubernatorial proposals. Within the structure of a State of the State address, a governor is unable to devote much time to presenting the particulars of each agenda item. Media coverage of the address and subsequent coverage concerning the progress of individual proposals enable us to fill in the blanks. Second, journalists also often provide informed, qualitative assessments as to how closely a particular bill matched the governor's original proposal. We augment these periodic assessments with wrap-up articles, which are published at the end of the legislative session and highlight the governor's significant legislative achievements and failures.

We supplement journalistic coverage with information from state legislative databases. These databases provide very detailed information about bills, including summaries, the full text, a list of sponsors, and the bill's legislative history. Histories tell us whether a particular bill was signed into law and, if not, where in the legislative process it died.

Ultimately, we were able to gather definitive information on the fates of nearly 90 percent of the proposals from our sampled State of the State addresses. Using this information, we code each proposal as a "pass," "compromise," or "failure." We code a proposal as having passed if a bill that closely resembles what the governor originally wanted is signed into law. Relatively minor deviations from the original proposal do not lead us to categorize the final outcome as a compromise. For instance, in 2006, Gov. Pataki of New York asked for a law requiring that all criminal offenders provide a sample to the state's DNA database. The bill that the legislature ultimately passed differed in minor ways from Pataki's proposal – it required that all felony offenders submit a DNA sample but only mandated that 17 types of misdemeanor offenders do so. Since the list of misdemeanor offences in the final bill is broad and includes the most common entry level convictions (such as petty larceny), we treat this proposal as a full pass.

A proposal is coded as a compromise if the enacted bill gives the governor only some of what she originally wanted – compromise bills all fall *meaningfully* short of the governor's initial proposal. For example, in 2006, Utah governor John Huntsman used his State of the State address to recommend a series of proposals aimed at reforming what he viewed as Utah's antiquated tax code. One of these reforms was the elimination of the sales tax on food, which had initially been adopted as a temporary fix for the state's frequent revenue shortfalls during the Great Depression. Unfortunately for the governor, Republicans in the state senate disagreed, and after a protracted negotiation, Huntsman was only able to get the legislature to agree to a reduction in the food tax from 4.75 to 2.75 percent. This outcome moved policy in the direction preferred by the governor but fell far short of what he called for in his State of the State address, making this a clear compromise. As is evident from these examples, determining whether an enacted bill is a pass or compromise requires a qualitative judgment on our part. Usually, however, the appropriate coding was relatively unambiguous, and our efforts were made easier by the assessments contained in local newspaper coverage.

Finally, a proposal was coded as a failure if a corresponding bill never reached the governor's desk or if we did not find any journalistic coverage of a proposal (after the State of the State address) or any corresponding bills in the legislative database. The assumption that the absence of information means a failure seems reasonable given the thorough nature of our searches. Moreover, that a nontrivial share of proposals in the State of the State address seem to go nowhere is consistent with our theoretical model, which predicts that governors will, at times, make dead-on-arrival proposals as a means of signaling their true policy preferences to voters and key constituencies. It is also consistent with our interviews of former governors and their staff, many of whom indicated that it is fairly common for items to be included in State of the State addresses that the governor knows in advance to be unpalatable for legislators. This assumption does not, however, have any effect on our substantive results.

4.2. Baseline Measures of Gubernatorial Success

How effective are governors at winning legislative approval for the proposals in their State of the State addresses? The answer to this question is a crucial first step in establishing the importance of governors as lawmakers. Are governors "legislators in chief," as some have claimed, or are their strategic disadvantages simply too much to overcome? Our data enable us to provide systematic insight into this question, telling us not only the share of gubernatorial proposals that become law but the amount of variation in bargaining success that exists across governors.

We begin with aggregate data on gubernatorial success.[6] Of the 1,088 proposals we identified in State of the State addresses, 41 percent eventually passed, 41 percent failed, and 18 percent ended in some form of half-a-loaf compromise. Combining the pass and compromise categories

[6] The measures of gubernatorial success reported here combine both budgetary and policy proposals.

reveals that state chief executives get at least some of what they want in approximately 6 out of every 10 proposals. If we exclude (from our data set) proposals about which we have no information, governors are modestly more successful bargainers.

Success does not appear to vary much by year or issue area. Governors secured either a full pass or a half-a-loaf compromise on 55 percent of their proposals in 2001 and on 63 percent in 2006. A difference of means test shows that this modest improvement between years is not statistically significant. Success is also fairly constant across each of the nine policy categories we identified in Chapter 3, with one clear exception – political reform. When governors propose changes to existing constitutional, fiscal, or electoral rules, they are usually ignored by the legislature. Indeed, only 27 percent of such proposals pass with another 6 percent ending in compromise. In each of the remaining categories, governors received at least some of what they wanted on a majority of agenda items.

Not surprisingly, if we disaggregate the data, we uncover wide variation in bargaining success across governors. Here, we report legislative achievement using two metrics. The first is a governor's *batting average*, which tells us the share of a governor's agenda that was adopted by the legislature and signed into law, counting compromises as half a success. The second metric is what we refer to as a governor's *impact score*. These scores are a function of the number of items passed as well as their policy significance. Neither batting averages nor impact scores tell the full story of executive achievement, but both provide an instructive look at how a governor fared during a legislative session, drawing on the same clear signs of success that statehouse reporters often use when they evaluate chief executives.

Figure 4.1 reports batting averages. The y axis lists (by year) all sampled governors in descending order from the highest to lowest average. The name of each governor is reported along with her partisan identification ("D" for Democrats and "R" for Republicans) and the postal abbreviation of her state. The x axis is the batting average, which has a possible range of 0 to 100 percent. In our sample, the mean was 52 percent, with governors distributed nearly throughout the full range of possible values. The governors with the highest batting averages are Barnes (2001) and Purdue (2006) of Georgia, both of whom won passage for nearly 90 percent of their proposals. At the other end of the spectrum are governors Pataki of New York (2001) and Romney of Massachusetts (2006), who had batting averages of 16 and 21 percent, respectively. Interestingly, no governor secured the passage of everything she asked for in her State of

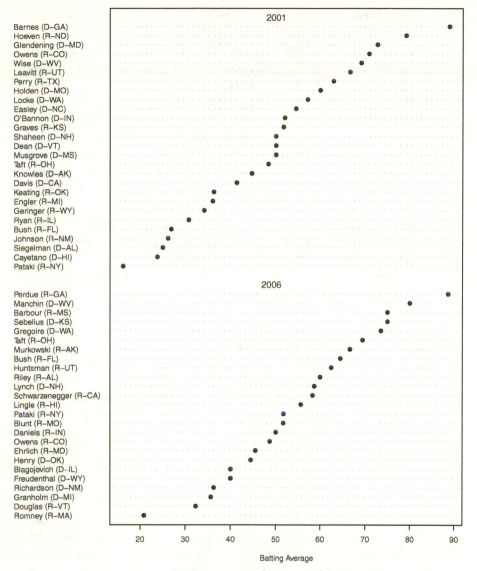

FIGURE 4.1. Batting averages, by year and governor.

the State address, and no governor was completely shut out. This means that even the most popular and strategically advantaged chief executives were defeated on some proposals and that those with the fewest carrots and sticks still had enough power to secure the adoption of at least a small portion of their agendas.

How do these batting averages compare with those reported elsewhere in the state politics literature? Unfortunately, there have been surprisingly few efforts to systematically quantify gubernatorial legislative achievement. Those that exist, however, tend to find higher levels of success than we do. Rosenthal (1990) reports batting averages for 10 governors from the late 1980s, 9 of which had a success rate between 75 and 95 percent. Fording et al. (2002) conduct a similar exercise for 37 governors in 1999, uncovering a mean batting average of 73 percent – again, well above the 52 percent in our sample. However, there are reasons to believe that the numbers reported in the existing literature are inflated. Rosenthal relies on the success rates reported by governors and their staff (who probably have an incentive to overstate their achievements or to ignore Rosenthal's inquiry if they were unsuccessful), while Fording et al. count half-a-loaf compromises as a full pass and remove from the denominator those proposals for which they lacked information.[7]

While batting averages nicely summarize the proportion of a governor's agenda that was enacted, they can obscure important aspects of gubernatorial success. As Alan Rosenthal (1990, p. 41) notes, "The governor's scoreboard or batting average standard is a deceptive one. It does not distinguish qualitative aspects of the measures proposed. The governor may have won the little ones, but lost the big ones." In other words, batting averages tell us nothing about the policy significance of the proposals that the governor was able to shepherd through the legislature. They also tell us nothing about the number of enacted proposals. A governor can receive a very high average by putting forth an agenda that consists of a handful of relatively minor proposals and getting the legislature to agree to most of them. This was the case with Kathleen Sebelius of Kansas (2006). Governor Sebelius offered only eight proposals in her State of the State address, most of which represented relatively uncontroversial or modest policy changes such as increasing prison sentences for sex offenders and exempting industrial machinery from local property taxes. Governor Sebelius had little trouble getting most of her agenda adopted and, at the end of the legislative session, had a batting average of 75 percent, the fifth highest in our sample. By this metric, she was quite a success. However, it is hard to argue that Gov. Sebelius was 3.5 times more successful than Gov. Romney of Massachusetts or twice as

---

[7] Ferguson (2003) and Ferguson and Barth (2002) conduct very thorough studies of gubernatorial success using data on governor's bills for all 50 states during the 1993–4 legislative sessions. Unfortunately, they do not report descriptive statistics for gubernatorial success.

successful as Democratic governor Granholm of Michigan. Though most of Romney's ambitious and controversial legislative agenda went down to defeat, he did manage to secure the passage of nearly as many proposals as Sebelius, including a major health care reform package aimed at providing health insurance coverage to all state residents. Granholm, who had a meager batting average of 35 percent, also secured as many full passes as Sebelius. These include proposals with a significant policy impact, such as a $2.25 increase in the hourly minimum wage and a bill creating a required core curriculum for all Michigan high school students.

Heeding these warnings, we also present impact scores – a novel and alternative quantification of gubernatorial achievement. These allow us to better encapsulate the ambition of a governor's enacted program by taking into account qualitative differences in successful proposals. These scores give governors points for each of their accomplishments, with more points assigned when they win bigger and more complete victories. Impact scores are calculated by totaling the number of gubernatorial proposals that the legislature passed, weighting each by its policy significance and whether or not the governor was forced to compromise. Remember, the policy significance of all proposals in our sample was coded using a scale ranging from 1 to 5 (see Chapter 3). If the significance of a proposal was coded a 4, full passage counts for 4 impact points. If the proposal reaches the governor's desk as a compromise, it counts for half as much as a full pass. When a proposal fails, it does not matter how ambitious it was; it counts for nothing. Because there is no denominator that divides accomplishments by the number of proposals, governors are not numerically penalized for pursuing lengthy agendas as they are with batting averages.

Figure 4.2 reports impact scores. All sampled governors are again listed in descending order from the highest to lowest batting average, though the y axis now shows impact scores. Again, we observe wide variation in gubernatorial achievement. While the mean impact score across all governors is 28, the range extends from a high of 61 for Republican governor Lingle of Hawaii (2006) to a low of 4.5 for Democratic governor Dean of Vermont (2001). The five most successful governors all had scores above 50. On average, each member of the "top five" secured the full passage of 18 proposals from his or her State of the State address as well as 7 compromises. The list of full passes for each of these governors includes at least one significant proposal (coded as a 4 or 5). The five least successful governors, conversely, all had impact scores below 15 and averaged fewer than three full passes and three compromises each.

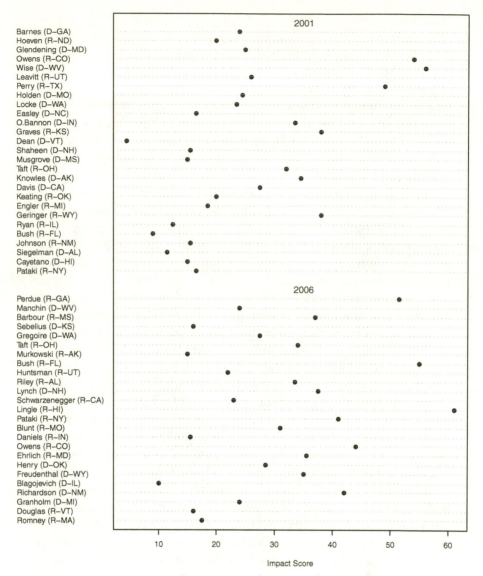

FIGURE 4.2. Impact scores, by year and governor.

Only one of these governors – Ryan of Illinois – secured the passage of a significant proposal.

A comparison of Figures 4.1 and 4.2 demonstrates that any ranking of governors by bargaining success is somewhat dependent on the measure used. The correlation between batting averages and impact scores, while a statistically meaningful .38, is far from perfect. Some governors who appeared to do quite well when we look only at batting averages perform poorly on their impact score, and vice versa. In 2006, Gov. Sebelius had one of the highest batting averages but one of the fifth lowest impact scores. Governor Lingle of Hawaii, conversely, finished the 2006 legislative session with a fairly pedestrian batting average of 50 percent but had the largest impact score of any chief executive included our sample. Overall, it seems reasonable to conclude that governors who scored well on both measures had a very successful legislative session, not only winning the passage of a sizable share of their agenda but also securing a set of accomplishments that should have a large impact on status quo policy. Likewise, it seems fair to conclude that governors who scored poorly on both measures were unsuccessful.

Overall, our data reveal that governors are often able to get at least some of what they want out of the legislative process. Whether the amount of gubernatorial achievement reported in Figures 4.1 and 4.2 makes governors "legislators in chief" is ultimately a subjective assessment. For us, the data indicate striking evidence of gubernatorial strength, especially in light of the inherent disadvantages that chief executives face in the American separation of powers system. To be sure, we find gubernatorial influence to be uneven – some governors appear to be much better than others when it comes to shepherding their proposals through the legislature. Exploring the determinants of this variation is our next task.

4.3. Determinants of Success

How do governors get what they want out of the legislature? Why are some chief executives so much more successful than others? The models that we developed in Chapter 2 argue that success will depend on the particular bargaining game that a governor is playing – the budget or policy game – and the resources that she can employ. A governor should do best when making budgetary proposals, particularly if she is more patient than the lawmakers with whom she is negotiating. When bargaining over policy proposals, however, her patience should matter little. Instead, success should depend on the ideological distance between the governor and the legislature as well as the governor's ability to make side payments to lawmakers.

To evaluate our hypotheses, we estimate regression models in which the units of analysis are individual agenda items, meaning that we have a total of 1,088 observations. Because our bargaining models predict what will happen with a single bill, it is appropriate to test our hypotheses at the level of individual gubernatorial proposals rather than by gauging success on a governor's entire agenda via batting averages or impact scores. The dependent variable in each model is coded 0 if the proposal failed, .5 for a compromise, and 1 if the governor secured a full pass. The regression results tell us whether a statistically significant correlation exists between each explanatory variable and gubernatorial success, holding constant (or "controlling for") all of the remaining variables in the model. In addition to telling us the statistical strength of this relationship, the regressions reveal the direction and size of the correlation.

As dictated by our hypotheses, the regression models capture the patience of players, the ideological distance between the branches, the ability of the governor to make side payments, and the size of the governor's total agenda. We also include a dichotomous variable (*Budget Proposal*) that indicates whether a proposal is budgetary. When we expect the effect of a variable (such as gubernatorial popularity) to differ in the budget and policy games, the variable is included in the regression model on its own and is also interacted with *Budget Proposal*.[8]

The regression models also control for other features of each agenda item that may affect its probability of passage. These include the proposal's significance, the ideological direction in which it would move the status quo, and its subject matter. Finally, we add a variable indicating whether the proposal was made in 2001 as well as a measure of state fiscal health. We often heard from our interviewees that it is easier for governors to move their legislative agendas when the state is not experiencing a budget deficit, a dynamic also observed in Ferguson's (2003) analysis.

We report in full the results of two regression models in Table 4.3, which appears in the appendix of this chapter. Both models are estimated as ordered logits and use standard errors clustered by state year.[9] The two models are identical, with one exception – the first does not include a measure of a governor's public approval. A problem with estimating the effects of gubernatorial approval is that the necessary data are somewhat sparse. We very rarely have data for governors in the first year of their

[8] The coefficient on the uninteracted variable tells us the relationship between the variable and gubernatorial success in passing policy proposals. To determine the effect of the variable in the budget game, one needs to add the coefficient on the uninteracted variable to the coefficient on the interaction term.

[9] In our analyses of negotiations over the size of government (see Chapter 5), we rely on multilevel models. We do not use such models here, given the difficulty of estimating ordered logits using a multilevel approach.

first term, nor do we have consistent data for many smaller states (particularly in 2001). Rather than drop all observations for which we have no approval data (approximately 18% of our sample), we simply estimate a first model that excludes this variable. Fortunately, there are only minor differences across models.[10]

In the following paragraphs, we discuss the explanatory variables employed in our empirical analysis, the manner in which each is operationalized, and our results. Since the regression coefficients reported in Table 4.3 are order log-odds coefficients (and not easy to substantively interpret), we use our regression results to generate predicted probabilities. These show how the likelihood of gubernatorial success changes when we alter the value of a single variable of interest, holding all others constant. Unless otherwise stated, our predicted probabilities are calculated by setting all of the continuous variables at their means and all dichotomous variables to zero. This essentially means that we assume a "typical" governor and a "typical" strategic environment. Table 4.1 concisely reports predicted probabilities for our key explanatory variables.

4.3.1. *Budgetary versus Policy Proposals*

We begin by considering whether governors are more likely to succeed at passing budgetary proposals. Remember that governors should be relatively advantaged when playing the budget as opposed to the policy game. When bargaining over the budget, lawmakers cannot ignore the governor – a new budget must be passed, and the failure to do so risks a government shutdown and serious political calamity. This brings lawmakers to the negotiating table. In the policy game, legislators are free to ignore or stonewall the governor. As a result, it may be difficult for the governor even to get lawmakers to the bargaining table, let alone to get them to enact her proposed policy changes.

Our data support this expectation, even without regression analysis. Of the budget proposals in our sample, 66 percent ended in either a full pass or a compromise, while the same can be said for only 54 percent of legislative proposals. Indeed, most governors (though not all) had a higher batting average for budgetary items than they did for policy proposals. If we dig a bit deeper, our data suggest that the difference

---

[10] In results not reported here, we estimate logit models that employ a dichotomous coding of the dependent variable – failures are assigned a value of 0, and any success (whether a full pass or a compromise) is assigned a value of 1. In these models, our findings remain largely unchanged, suggesting that the results we discuss here and display in the appendix are not driven by our approach to distinguishing between passes and compromises.

between these success rates is driven (at least in part) by governors' ability to secure compromises on budgetary items. There is only a very small and insignificant difference between the share of budgetary and policy proposals that end as full passes. The big difference is in the ability of the chief executive to secure compromises – 27 percent of budgetary items end in a compromise, compared to only 12 percent of policy proposals. This is consistent with our expectation that legislators will often ignore gubernatorial policy proposals but are forced to come to the table and negotiate over budgetary items.

To evaluate our hypothesis more fully, we turn to our regression results. These tell us whether a budgetary proposal is more likely to succeed, even after controlling for other potential determinants of bargaining outcomes. It may be, for instance, that we observe a higher success rate for budgetary items because they tend to represent smaller changes to status quo than do the policy proposals. After taking such factors into consideration, however, we still find that chief executives are more likely to win passage of budgetary proposals. This is indicated by the positive and statistically significant coefficient on *Budget Proposal* in both regression models.

To show the size of this difference, we turn to predicted probabilities. Assuming a typical governor and bargaining environment, the probability of securing either a full pass or a compromise on a budget item is between 5 and 11 points higher than securing the same on a policy proposal (depending on whether we use model 1 or model 2 from Table 4.3). If we assume a less favorable bargaining environment for policy proposals – an unpopular governor whose political party controls a relatively small share of the seats in the legislature – the difference grows to 15 points.[11] The governor only does better on policy proposals when she either enjoys numerous strategic advantages in the policy game or experiences large disadvantages in the budget game (i.e., is negotiating with a very patient legislature). On average, though, we find strong and robust evidence that governors do better on budget items.

Because this is such a strong effect and so central to our argument, it is worth considering alternative explanations of gubernatorial strength in budget bargaining. One possibility is that governors only *appear* to do better in budgeting because it is in this game, rather than in policy negotiations, that weak governors offer compromise agendas. If this were

[11] Assuming the governor's popularity and her party's legislative seat share are both one standard deviation below the mean.

true – if budgetary agendas reflected strategic bargaining situations, whereas policy agendas reflected governors' personal preferences – it would cast doubt on our finding. But in fact, as Chapter 3 demonstrates, we see exactly the opposite pattern. There is much more evidence that governors' policy agendas are shaped by their bargaining circumstances than are their fiscal agendas. Insiders also tell us that when it comes to the budget, governors have the freedom to shape their agendas as they see fit.

A second alternative explanation is that most budget proposals are, by their very nature, divisible, while many policy proposals may not be. A proposal such as the one made by Maryland's governor Parris Glendening in 2001 to "provide $45 million to expand Community Parks and Playgrounds over the next 3 years" could easily be cut into compromise of a $20 million expansion. While this outcome would be less than ideal for Gov. Glendening, it would still allow him to secure a partial legislative victory. If many executive policy proposals are not divisible (meaning that no possible compromise exists), similar deals cannot be struck. This might then translate into more failures in the policy negations.

Our very strong impression, though, after reading hundreds of executive policy proposals, is that potential compromise outcomes exist in nearly all cases. Still, this potential concern calls for a more systematic analysis. We hired two research assistants (who had not previously been involved in this project) to code the divisibility of policy proposals in our data set. In particular, they were told to code a proposal as indivisible if they could not anticipate a possible compromise.[12] Research assistants were not told in advance the actual outcomes of the proposals they were coding. Working independently, they found low rates of indivisibility, even among policy proposals that ultimately ended as failures. Additionally, and perhaps most surprisingly, governors and legislators were able to reach compromises on a large percentage of the proposals that appeared to our coders to be indivisible (indeed, among the policy agenda items that our assistants coded as indivisible, the share that ultimately ended as compromises was statistically indistinguishable from the share that ended as failures). For instance, in his 2001 address, Alaska governor Tony Knowles called for marketing North Slope natural gas and supplying it to Alaska communities, a proposal linked to the eventual construction of a natural gas pipeline. Our coders judged this an indivisible

---

[12] We focused exclusively on policy proposals because budget items are, in essence, always divisible. Research assistants coded the 284 policy proposals that ended as failures as well as the 71 that ended as compromises.

proposal, apparently judging that gas would either be marketed and sold through a pipeline or not. But when legislators responded with a bill to study the issue and prepare a report about the state's participation in the complicated public/private partnership that would be required, the end result was a clear compromise. This suggests to us that elected officials are quite skilled at unearthing compromises even when none seemingly exist. After undertaking this analysis, we are even more confident that differences in the nature of budget and policy proposals are not driving our results.

4.3.2. *Bargaining Patience*

While governors are more likely to emerge victorious when negotiating over budgetary proposals, our model of the budget game predicts that their success will still vary across states, largely as a function of the relative patience of the players. We expect governors to do well in the budget game during their legacy year, that is, their last year in office. During this year, governors have little to lose from a late budget, making them very patient bargainers. Similarly, we anticipate that governors will be most successful in budget negotiations when they bargain with a legislature that meets in short sessions (i.e., citizen legislatures). In these chambers, lawmakers typically maintain careers outside of legislative service and pay high opportunity costs if the governor vetoes their budget and calls them in to a special session. Such opportunity costs are not paid by lawmakers in more professionalized legislatures. Dan Schnur, former communications director to Gov. Pete Wilson, suggests that lawmakers in professionalized chambers actually prefer long stays in the capitol. When discussing California lawmakers, he notes, "They love being in Sacramento. The average assembly member is anonymous in his own district, but he is a celebrity in Sacramento. They have lobbyists paying attention to them, the press; everyone knows their name."[13]

To test for the effects of patience, we use two variables. The first is a measure of session length, operationalized as the number of legislative days that lawmakers met during the relevant year.[14] In our sample, the average number of legislative days is 83, ranging from a low of 19 (New Hampshire, 2001) to a high of 274 (New York, 2001 and 2006). The second is a dichotomous variable indicating whether a governor is in her legacy year. Our sample includes five such governors.

---

[13] Telephone interview of Dan Schnur conducted by Thad Kousser, July 7, 2009.
[14] These data were obtained from the *Book of the States*. Where necessary, calendar days have been converted to legislative days by multiplying by 0.75.

Each of our regression models shows that as session length increases, the probability that a governor will secure the passage of a budget proposal meaningfully declines. For the typical governor, with session length set to its mean, the probability of securing a full pass on a budgetary item is 32 percent. If we change nothing about the governor or the bargaining environment except decreasing the length of the legislative session to that of New Hampshire, the probability of a pass rises to 38 percent. If, conversely, we increase session length to that of New York, the chance that the governor will secure a full pass falls to 17 percent. Lengthy sessions (about one standard deviation above the mean) eliminate the normal advantages the chief executive enjoys in budgeting, pushing the probability that the governor will be able to secure a full pass for a budget item below that of achieving a full pass for a policy proposal.

While our results show that governors are less influential in the budget game as session length increases, it is possible that patience is not the driving force behind this relationship. Legislatures that meet in long sessions also tend to possess an increased intelligence capacity (Rosenthal 1990); that is, they usually have a large staff dedicated exclusively to fiscal policy and a revenue-estimating capability that is independent of the executive branch. These features may reduce the governor's traditional informational advantages and enhance legislative independence and assertiveness in budget negotiations (National Conference of State Legislatures 2005). To test for this possibility, we estimated regressions that also include a measure of legislative staff. While we do not present these results here, the inclusion of a measure of staff has no effect on our results – increases in legislative staff do not decrease the probability of gubernatorial success in the budget game, but increases in session length do.[15] Thus, we are comfortable concluding that legislative patience counteracts executive power in state budgeting.

[15] In models not reported here, we also examine the potential effect of legislative term limits, an electoral law that much prior research has shown to shift power from the legislative to the executive branch (Peery and Little 2003; Thompson and Moncrief 2003; Kousser 2005; Carey et al. 2006; Powell 2007). The research design that we employ in our analysis here, though, is not a strong one for testing the effects of term limits. Instead of observing states both before and after the implementation of term limits, as much prior work does, we look at them in 2001 and 2006, when most term limit laws had already been implemented. Our cross-sectional test, then, simply compares states with term limits to those without. When we included a term limits variable in our models, its estimated coefficient was substantively miniscule (−0.02) and statistically weak (yielding a test statistic of 0.13). None of our other results changed. We omitted the term limits variable from our final models because the weakness of our research design prevents them from shedding any new light on the impact of term limits.

We do not anticipate that legislative patience will shape outcomes in the policy game. Unexpectedly, however, there is some evidence of a statistically significant (though modest) positive correlation between session length and the probability of passing a policy proposal. This effect is not particularly robust because it is only present in model 2. Ferguson's (2003) analysis of State of the State success in 1993–4 also found a positive link between legislative professionalism and gubernatorial success in the policy realm. Why might session length lead to increased success for gubernatorial policy proposals? One possible reason is that there is simply more agenda space and more time for the consideration of gubernatorial policy proposals in a lengthy session. In short sessions, the legislature is in a frantic race to beat the clock, and the clock often wins. Short sessions in states like New Mexico (whose legislature in even numbered years only meets for 30 days) are frequently cited as a reason that many popular bills fail. When complaining that several proposals backed by the powerful business lobby died in the 2006 legislative session, John Carey, president of the Association of Commerce and Industry of New Mexico, said, "Some things just didn't make it through the whole process.... Thirty days is a short period of time," while Terri Cole, president and CEO of the Greater Albuquerque Chamber of Commerce, noted that many bills "died more from the clock running out of time rather than full debate."[16] It is likely that governors experience the same frustrations. Ultimately, however, we are cautious about drawing much of a conclusion from this result, given that the finding is not robust across the regression model and given that its substantive magnitude is fairly modest. Furthermore, in Chapter 8, we observe that California governors have become *less* successful in policy negotiations after the legislature there professionalized and increased its session length.

Regression results also provide modest support for our hypothesis concerning chief executives in their legacy year. They consistently show that governors do better in the budget game during their final year of service (though this falls short of statistical significance in the model that includes popularity). Surprisingly, however, we find that legacy-year governors also do better when negotiating over policy proposals and that this effect is statistically significant in all estimations. This is the opposite of what we had anticipated. We discuss this result more fully when we consider the effects of side payments on gubernatorial bargaining success.

[16] Mike Tumolillo, "Given More Time, the Legislature Could Have Done Even More for Business in New Mexico. As It Is, Leaders Call It a Successful Session," *Albuquerque Tribune*, February 27, 2006, p. B1.

4.3.3. *Ideological Agreement*

We next turn to our expectations about how the partisanship of the legislature should shape bargaining outcomes. While the legislature always faces incentives to negotiate and compromise with the governor in the budget game, no similar incentives exist in the policy game. As a result, a governor's ability to shepherd policy proposals through the legislature should depend greatly on ideological agreement between the branches. As we show in the policy game, if the governor proposes a bill that both branches prefer to the status quo, some form of this bill will pass and be signed into law. The final outcome may be at the governor's ideal, the legislature's ideal, or some other point, but we would not expect to see failure. This means that a governor negotiating with a legislature located closer to her on the ideological spectrum should have a greater chance of passing a policy proposal.

Empirically, we measure distance between the branches using the share of legislative seats held by members of the governor's party, averaged across the two legislative houses. (Elsewhere, we simply use the presence or absence of divided government; this choice has no meaningful effect on our results.) Larger values on this measure should indicate a smaller ideological distance between the governor and legislature. While the partisanship of lawmakers is an imperfect proxy for ideological proximity, this is the same sort of rough metric used by governors and their advisors. It is also a metric that is employed throughout the state politics literature.

The governors in our sample confronted a diverse set of partisan environments. On average, the governor's party controlled 52 percent of the legislative seats. In 10 state years, however, this number was 35 percent or less, making the governor's party a small and relatively powerless legislative minority. The chief executive facing the most dire circumstances was Mitt Romney, whose Republican party controlled fewer than 14 percent of the seats in the Massachusetts legislature. At the other end of the spectrum, the governor's copartisans controlled 65 percent or more of the seats in 11 states, making the governor's party the only game in town. Democrat Bob Wise of West Virginia faced the most enviable position – 79 percent of the lawmakers in his state were also Democrats.

As anticipated, our results show that chief executives who bargain with ideologically similar legislatures do better. The coefficient on our measure of seat share is positive and statistically significant, indicating that as the share of seats controlled by the governor's party increases, so does the probability that the governor will successfully shepherd a policy proposal through the legislative process. Besides being statistically significant, this effect is substantively quite large. Moving from the partisan bargaining environment faced by Mitt Romney to that of Bob Wise (holding all else constant) more than doubles the probability of a full pass, from 16 to 38 percent. Having a large partisan majority, while clearly useful, does not guarantee success. This is consistent with observations made by our interviewees, many of whom noted that a governor's agenda items are often blocked within the legislature by the more ideological members of the governor's own party. In talking about the struggles of recent California chief executives, Phil Trounstine, former communications director to Gov. Gray Davis, commented that "Gray Davis' biggest problem was not the conservatives, but John Burton [President Prop Tempore of the state senate] and the liberal Democrats. Arnold Schwarzenegger's biggest problem was not Democrats, but conservative Republicans."[17]

Since the winner of the budget game should largely be a function of the patience of the players, we do not expect the ideological distance between the governor and legislature to matter much (or at all) when it comes to shaping the likelihood of gubernatorial success on budget proposals. This means that we should observe a negative coefficient on the interaction between seat share and the budget dummy variable. Indeed, the regression results confirm our expectation. The interaction term is negative in both regression models, reaching statistical significance in model 2. The size of this interaction effect means that the probability of gubernatorial success in budget bargaining changes only marginally as the governor's party gains legislative seats. For budget items, moving from the partisan bargaining environment faced by Mitt Romney to that of Bob Wise (holding all else constant) has no significant effect on the probability of bargaining success.

4.3.4. *Side Payments*

Absent ideological agreement in the policy game, the governor needs to induce lawmakers to the bargaining table by offering side payments. In Chapter 2, we argue that the size of the side payments a governor can make are affected by three factors. The first is whether she can credibly threaten to veto lawmakers' pet bills. Remember, bills are the currency of the legislature – "most members have multiple pieces of legislation they wants to get signed [by the governor] at the end of the session."[18]

[17] Phil Trounstine, communications director to Gov. Gray Davis, interview by telephone by Thad Kousser, July 8, 2009.
[18] Tom Hayes, Director of Finance to California governor Pete Wilson, conducted by telephone by Thad Kousser, July 16, 2009.

A governor who can use veto threats as bargaining chips should have a greater chance of passing her own policy proposals. Of course, the credibility of such threats depends on the governor's party occupying enough seats in the legislature to sustain her veto. A governor's popularity with voters and the amount of time she has remaining in office should also affect the size of side payments she can offer. A popular governor can do more to help supportive lawmakers, while a governor who is near the beginning of her administration can make more and larger promises because she has a longer period of time in which to repay legislators. Again, we do not expect these variables to have much of an effect in the budget game.

To evaluate the effect of veto threats, we rely on our existing measure of the share of legislative seats controlled by the governor's party. Certainly, the more seats her party controls, the greater the probability that the governor will be able to sustain her vetoes. In results not reported here, we replace the measure of seat share with a dichotomous variable indicating whether the governor has a sufficient number of copartisans in both legislative chambers to uphold her vetoes.[19] This alternative measure produces only minor differences in our results. Because seat share and having a veto proof majority are correlated conceptually and empirically, we do not include both in the same regression model. In our data, the correlation between the governor's seat share and a veto proof majority is 0.72.

To evaluate the effect of popularity, we use the approval ratings of governors obtained from the U.S. Officials' Job Approval Ratings (JARs) database. JARs is a repository for job approval ratings obtained largely from state-specific public opinion polls. This variable is operationalized as the share of survey respondents who report "approving" of the job the governor is doing. For each governor, we use the last poll conducted before she delivered her State of the State address. We do this to minimize the possibility that the governor's approval rating will be shaped by the proposals included in her speech or by events and policy debates that occurred during the legislative session.

Unfortunately, JARs does not contain approval data for nine of our sampled governors from 2001.[20] Subsequent efforts to locate these missing data through Internet and newspaper searches came up empty – there

---

[19] In our sample of states, the share of votes needed to override a gubernatorial veto ranges from a bare majority to 67%.

[20] There are no missing data for 2006 largely because a single national polling firm, SurveyUSA, conducted a monthly survey in all 50 states asking respondents to evaluate, among other things, the performance of their governor.

were simply no (publicly reported) opinion polls conducted about voters' attitudes toward these chief executives. The governors for whom we are missing approval data tend to be from relatively small states with less professionalized legislatures and who are often in the first year of their first term. The nonrandom nature of these missing data is potentially problematic for our regression analysis because they result in a slightly biased sample. For this reason, we report model 1 (which excludes our approval measure). Even beyond issues of missing data, however, the effect of public opinion may be hard to estimate in the cross-sectional models used here. Approval ratings may be shaped by some of the same institutional factors that affect gubernatorial bargaining success. For this reason, in Chapter 6, we also conduct detailed case studies about the effects of public opinion, which allow us to further explore the potential causal relationship between popularity and gubernatorial success.

The regression models include two dichotomous variables that capture the amount of time a governor has to repay legislators who cast tough votes for her agenda. The first identifies chief executives who are serving in their first term and should be positively correlated with gubernatorial success in the policy game. The second identifies chief executives who are in their legacy year. These governors should perform poorly in the policy game because they have very little time left in office to keep their promises.[21]

Overall, the regression results are consistent with our expectation that governors who can make larger side payments will do better in the policy game. The share of legislative seats controlled by the governor's party, gubernatorial popularity, and whether the governor is in her first term are all positively and significantly related to bargaining success. These effects are substantively meaningful. Holding all else constant and moving from the lowest approval ratings in our data set (18% for Gov. Taft of Ohio) to the highest (75% for Gov. Leavitt of Utah) nearly quadruples the chance that the governor will be able to secure a full pass for a policy proposal. Similarly, the chance of a first-term governor securing a pass is 19 points higher than for a governor in her second or third term (as long as that governor is not in her legacy year).

Importantly, our results show that the ability to make large side payments does not enhance governors' bargaining power in the budget game. Large increases in either popularity or the share of legislative seats

---

[21] Because some of our sampled states place no limitations on the number of terms a governor may serve, it is impossible for us to create a single variable measuring the number of potential years that a governor could remain in office.

occupied by the governor's copartisans result in only marginal and statistically meaningless changes in success. The same is true for first-term governors. According to our regression results, when the governor can offer large side payments, she is likely to perform as well (or better) in the policy game as she does in the budget game (assuming she is negotiating with an average as opposed to a citizen legislature).

Our results for chief executives in their legacy year are puzzling. Surprisingly, we find that governors in their final year of service do better when negotiating over policy proposals, and this effect is statistically significant and fairly large. Why are final-year governors so successful in the policy game? We do not have a clear answer. One possibility is that these governors work particularly hard at securing the passage of their agendas to enhance their gubernatorial legacy. Despite this one puzzling finding, the empirical analysis generally demonstrates that the ability of governors to make large side payments is a key determinant of success when they are bargaining over policy proposals.

4.3.5. *Position-Taking Bonus*

We also anticipate that governors will be less successful in the policy game if the position-taking bonus is particularly large – that is, if the chief executive has a lot to gain by signaling her sincere policy positions. When this bonus is large, our model indicates that the governor will make more dead-on-arrival proposals. Lawmakers will not take these proposals seriously and cannot be induced to the bargaining table even with the promise of large side payments.

To test this expectation, we consider a set of governors for whom the position-taking bonus is likely to be large – those who are flirting with a presidential bid. Anecdotal evidence seems to confirm that these governors often populate their agendas with proposals aimed at a national audience, particularly those individuals and interest groups whose support is important for a presidential campaign. In 2006, for instance, Gov. Pataki of New York surprised many observers by laying out a fairly conservative agenda, centered around deep cuts in income, property, and estate taxes as well as a series of tough-on-crime proposals. In the coverage of his State of the State address, the *New York Times* noted that Pataki's speech "courts a much different audience these days: the bedrock Republicans to whom he must appeal should he pursue a presidential run in 2008."[22] The governor's address even proposed funding refineries in

---

[22] Danny Hakim, "Pataki Stresses Tax Cuts in Address Reprising Early Themes," *New York Times*, January 5, 2006, p. B1.

New York to make ethanol, an alternative fuel made from corn that is beloved in Iowa, the home of the first presidential caucus. As noted in Chapter 2, Gov. Romney also made a number of proposals in his 2006 State of the State address that were clearly targeted toward Republican voters outside of the liberal electorate in his home state. These included abstinence-only sex education and ending welfare work exemptions for pregnant women, mothers of young children, and the disabled – none of which had a chance of passing in the very liberal Massachusetts legislature.

Lawmakers are adept at recognizing proposals aimed at bolstering a potential presidential bid and are often unwilling to play along.[23] While governors Pataki and Romney were positioning themselves for runs at the 2006 Republican nomination, Gov. Richardson of New Mexico was getting ready to jump into the Democratic contest. In his State of the State address, he proposed a sweeping and large agenda (44 items), seemingly aimed at traditional Democratic interests. His agenda included a large increase in the minimum wage, a proposal to ensure that all children under the age of five have health insurance, and expanded investments in education. Despite Richardson's partisan advantages (his party controlled approximately 60% of the seats in both legislative chambers), most of his agenda items went down to defeat. Commenting on the governor's poor results, state Republican party chairman Allen Weh said, "The governor's real priorities are himself.... He's one of 10 to 12 guys running for President, and he wants things to add to his resume."[24]

All else equal, we expect governors with presidential ambitions to be less successful at winning the adoption of the policy items in their agendas. To test this hypothesis, we have identified governors who are reported (in either state or national media) to be seriously considering a presidential campaign.[25] Even without controlling for other determinants of success, these data support our expectations. Governors with

---

[23] A notable exception to this pattern occurred in 2006. During this legislative session, Gov. Romney proposed a historically significant health insurance reform plan, aimed at providing insurance to all state residents. Though this plan was viewed by many as an attempt by the governor to raise his national profile, Democratic leaders in the legislature were more than willing to go along (though they pushed for an even broader reform). Romney's proposal was successful because it appealed to the long-held policy objectives of state Democrats.

[24] Kate Nash, "Lawmakers Temper Year of Zeal," *Albuquerque Tribune*, February 17, 2006, p. A1.

[25] Our data set includes five governors with presidential ambitions. In 2001, these were Howard Dean (Vermont) and Gray Davis (California); in 2006, they were George Pataki (New York), Bill Richardson (New Mexico), and Mitt Romney (Massachusetts).

presidential ambitions were only able to secure full passes for 28 percent of their proposals. Governors who were not eying a national campaign, conversely, won full passes 42 percent of the time. Both sets of governors had very similar proportions of their agenda items end in compromises – 21 and 18 percent, respectively.

These results hold up in our regression analysis. When we include a measure of presidential ambition as an explanatory variable, it is indeed a significant predictor of gubernatorial success in the policy game. Our results show that, holding all else equal, governors who are reported to be considering a presidential campaign are over 2.5 times less likely to win the passage of a policy proposal. The substantive importance of this relationship exists under a variety of strategic contexts. It does not, however, exist in the budget game; that is, we uncover no meaningful difference in success between governors with and without national ambitions when it comes to bargaining over budgetary items.[26] It is important to note that though we confirm the prediction that governors with presidential ambitions often lose on their overly ambitious proposals, we note that this does not imply that they lack power; instead, it simply suggests that they exercised their power of the bully pulpit to take a stand with their proposal rather than attempting to use their power to pass it.

4.3.6. *Features of the Proposal and Agenda*
Our regression models also include variables that capture the overall size of the governor's agenda and features of each proposal. We anticipate that as the size of the agenda grows, the probability that the governor will succeed on any individual item will decline. In the policy game, a governor's ability to make side payments should be depleted if she asks for numerous bills. In the divide-the-dollar logic of the budget game, there are only so many cents that can be allocated among the players, meaning that a governor winning a figurative amount of concessions must determine how to allocate these across her budgetary agenda items. To test for the effects of agenda size, we include a count of the total number of proposals included in a governor's agenda.[27]

---

[26] In regressions not reported here, we consider whether governors are less likely to be successful in election years. It is possible that governors will place a high value on signaling their true beliefs to voters when they are running in an election. We do not find any meaningful evidence supporting this hypothesis.

[27] Our results remain unchanged if we replace this with a measure of agenda scale – the product of the number of agenda items in the governor's State of the State address and their average magnitude (using the 5-point scale discussed in Chapter 3).

We include also four variables that capture features of each proposal. The first identifies agenda items that represent a liberal change in status quo policy. These are proposals that move policy in a leftward direction (e.g., environmental regulations, expansion of social services, strengthening of abortion rights). Proposals that move policy rightward or that have no clear ideological orientation are coded as zero. The second variable identifies proposals that would move status quo policy in the same direction as preferred by the legislature. So, a conservative (liberal) proposal would be assigned a value of 1 if the legislature were controlled by Republicans (Democrats). We always code ideologically neutral proposals as a 1, regardless of the partisanship of the legislative majority (though this assumption does not affect our results).[28] Though our models make no prediction about whether liberal proposals should pass more frequently than conservative or ideologically neutral proposals, we would expect those that move policy in a direction preferred by lawmakers to enjoy greater success.

We also include a variable identifying agenda items that constitute a significant departure from status quo policy – that is, those proposals that are coded as either 4 or 5 on our measure of policy impact. We anticipate that governors will be less likely to secure passage for these agenda items. Finally, we utilize a variable indicating proposals that are political reforms. Political reforms should be difficult to pass because they often require a constitutional amendment (necessitating a supermajority vote in both legislative chambers) or ask lawmakers to agree to new restrictions on their own behavior (such as campaign finance laws or tax and expenditure limitations). Even within our sample, we observe governors who were very successful at moving most of their legislative agenda but utterly failed when it came to their ideas for political reform. Governor Riley of Alabama, for instance, proposed a set of popular reforms that included legislative term limits, new disclosure requirements for lobbyists, and an amendment to the state constitution prohibiting local governments from using eminent domain to seize private property and then turn it over to private individuals or corporations.[29] By the end

---

[28] In regression results not reported here, we consider several alternative operationalizations of ideological agreement, including one that makes ideological agreement into a series of steps (party control of one house, party control of both houses, and party control of both houses with a veto-proof override). None of these alternatives change our finding of a null effect.

[29] This proposal was in response to the U.S. Supreme Court's decision in *Kelo vs. City of New London*.

of the legislative session, Gov. Riley did not secure the passage of any of his proposals for political reform, but his batting average for all other agenda items was over 70 percent.

As we expected, our regression results show that governors who propose larger agendas are less likely to win the adoption of any given proposal. This relationship is statistically significant and substantively important. For the typical governor, switching from an agenda size one standard deviation below the mean (15 total proposals) to an agenda size one standard deviation above the mean (35 total proposals) decreases the probability that a policy proposal will be adopted by about 10 points. While we do not report an interaction between agenda size and whether a proposal is budgetary, when we include this term in our regression models, it has no meaningful relationship to gubernatorial success, meaning the affect of agenda size is similar in the budget and policy games. Of the proposal-specific variables, only the indicators for liberal policy change and for political reform are statistically significant. Liberal agenda items are significantly more likely to pass; apparently, governors have an easier time selling legislators on new programs and regulations than on proposals such as the rollback of regulations or teacher merit pay. Perhaps interest groups play a role in creating this asymmetry in the direction of policy. Governors are also less successful when proposing political reforms, which, because many of these reforms seek to impose strict ethics rules on lawmakers and increase the power of the governor, should not be surprising.

4.3.7. *State Fiscal Health*

In our regressions, we consider one final determinant of success – the fiscal health of the state. When asked about the advantages governors may enjoy during periods of fiscal prosperity, Bill Hauck, who served as Gov. Pete Wilson's deputy chief of staff, responded (perhaps a bit facetiously) that "when times are good, and when the state has money, it's much easier to do the job."[30] While this response may understate the challenges of governing in good times, the consensus among our interviewees is that state chief executives have a much easier job winning support for their proposals when the state is not confronting a budget deficit. Qualitative accounts of gubernatorial administrations are littered

---

[30] Interview with Bill Hauck, former chief of staff to assembly speakers Willie Brown and Bob Moretti and deputy chief of staff to Gov. Pete Wilson, conducted by telephone by Thad Kousser and Justin Phillips, June 25, 2009.

with stories of governors forced to scale back their legislative agendas to accommodate worsening fiscal circumstances (cf. Beyle 1992). Dan Schnur, who also served in Pete Wilson's administration, recounted for us the effects that the troubled California economy of the early 1990s had on Gov. Wilson's agenda. "If you look at the inaugural address and the first State of the State address, you'll see a very ambitions agenda.... He'd been getting budget warnings, but the bottom fell out in the spring of 1991. Everything that he proposed had to fall by the wayside."[31]

To evaluate systematically the effects of state fiscal health, we include a lagged measure of the state's budget surplus. These data were obtained from the Fiscal Survey of States, which is published biannually by the National Association of State Budget Officers. The measure we use is the prior year's fiscal budget surplus as a share of total state expenditures. Positive values of this measure indicate a budget surplus, whereas negative values indicate a deficit (in our sample, however, we have no states that ran deficits). In both our regression models, we observe a positive and significant relationship between surplus and gubernatorial success. This effect is not all that large – moving from a perfectly balanced budget to one that has a 12 percent surplus (the mean in our sample) only increases the probability of bargaining success by a few points. The significance and size of this effect does not differ across the budget and policy games.[32]

4.3.8. *The Empirical Importance of Two Bargaining Models*
The results of the regression analyses consistently support our argument that there are two largely distinct models of interbranch bargaining – one for budgeting and another for negotiations over policy bills. This is indicated by the statistically significant (and substantively meaningful) coefficients on the interactions between budgetary proposals and our measures of political capital, the strength of the governor's party in the legislature, and legislative session length. This is also illustrated by Table 4.1, which shows changes in the predicted probabilities of bargaining success, conditioned on changes in the bargaining environment. It is clear from the table that the variables that play a key role in shaping gubernatorial success in negotiations over policy items have almost no effect when it comes to budgeting, and vice versa.

---

[31] Telephone interview of Dan Schnur, conducted by Thad Kousser, July 7, 2009.
[32] Alternative measures of state fiscal well-being, such as the unemployment rate, do not have a statistically significant relationship to success, even if we remove our lagged measure of budget surplus from the model.

TABLE 4.1. *Predicted probabilities of gubernatorial success.*

	Policy bills	Budgetary proposals
Variable shifts from...		
A **popular** governor (68% approval) to an unpopular one (44% approval)	−15%	−2%
A **first-term** governor to a governor serving in a later term	−19%	−3%
A governor not in her **legacy year** to a governor serving in her legacy year	+16%	+17%
A governor whose party holds a large **legislative seat share** (67%) to a governor whose party has a small seat share (34%)	−11%	−2%
A governor who holds no **presidential ambitions** to a governor who does	−16%	−3%
Legislature shifts from short **legislative sessions** (20 days) to long sessions (270 days)	+6%	−21%

Note: The table reports the change in the predicted probability of a bargaining success, conditional on a change in the explanatory variable of interest. All predicted probabilities use model 1 from Table 4.2, except predictions for the effect of popularity, which are calculated using model 2.

Readers may wonder, however, whether and how our results would differ if the interactions were excluded, that is, if we estimated regression models that looked more like those in the existing literature. Remember, most investigations into the determinants of gubernatorial success do not distinguish between bargaining over budgets and bargaining over policy bills. In regression models that exclude the interaction terms, many of our key variables no longer appear to be significant determinants of gubernatorial bargaining success, including the partisanship of the legislature, the amount of time a governor has remaining in office, and the patience of legislators. Public approval remains statistically significant, but the magnitude of its effect falls by nearly half. This dramatic change in our results suggests that ignoring the fundamental difference in bargaining over budgets and policy bills may lead researchers to falsely conclude that key determinants of gubernatorial success (such as the partisanship of the legislature) are not meaningful predictors of outcomes or that they only have substantively minor effects. That prior studies of governors do not make this distinction may help account for some of the puzzling and inconsistent findings in the literature. Ultimately, by including these theoretically driven interaction terms in our regression models, we uncover determinants of gubernatorial success that might otherwise be hidden.

4.4. Summary

This chapter presents baseline data on gubernatorial success, telling us the share of agenda items that become law and the amount of variation in bargaining success across governors. These data indicate that state chief executives are powerful, if not omnipotent, actors in the lawmaking process. Of the agenda items we identified in State of the State addresses, 41 percent passed in a form that closely resembled the governor's original request, and another 18 percent were adopted as half-a-loaf compromises. The data also show that legislative achievement varies widely across chief executives – some governors in our sample secured the adoption of nearly 90 percent of their agenda items, whereas others failed to shepherd even 25 percent of their proposals through the legislative process. Importantly, these data show that even the most strategically advantaged chief executives were defeated on some proposals, while the weakest governors had enough power to secure the adoption of at least a small portion of their agenda.

Using regression analysis and our data on gubernatorial success, we systematically evaluate the bargaining models developed in Chapter 2. The main findings from these analyses are summarized in Table 4.2. The table reports the relationship between each of our substantive variables and gubernatorial success in both budget and policy negotiations. If it is significant, we report a positive or negative sign, indicating the direction of the relationship. If a variable had no meaningful correlation with success, we report the effect as "none," and if the direction or statistical significance of the relationship differed across regression estimations, we report the effect as "mixed."

As anticipated, we find that what governors bargain over – policy or budgetary proposals – largely determines what factors will and will not shape gubernatorial success. In the budget game, chief executives do better when they are negotiating with impatient legislatures, that is, legislatures that meet in relatively short sessions. In the policy game, governors do better when their party controls a larger share of seats in the legislature and when they have more political capital, that is, when they are in their first term or when they have higher levels of public approval. Our results also reveal that governors generally have a higher probability of success when negotiating over budgetary items and when they propose smaller agendas.

Just as important as identifying the factors that affect the probability of success, our results tell us which variables *do not* meaningfully shape

TABLE 4.2. *Determinants of gubernatorial bargaining success*

	Policy bills		Budget proposals	
	Expectation	Finding	Expectation	Finding
Legislative Session Length	none	mixed	−	−
Governor's Legacy Year	−	+	+	+
Legislative Seat Share (Governor's Party)	+	+	none	none
First-Term Governor	+	+	none	none
Public Approval	+	+	none	none
Presidential Ambitions	−	−	none	none
Total Number of Proposals	−	−	−	−
Proposal is a Budget Item			+	+

bargaining outcomes. When negotiating over budget items, for instance, the partisanship of the legislature is not significantly correlated to success, nor are measures of political capital. This means that governors do not need partisan allies in the legislature or popularity to do well in budget bargaining. These findings represent a noteworthy departure from the existing literature, which typically argues for a strong positive relationship between these variables and success and does not distinguish, either theoretically or empirically, between sets of factors that should affect budget bargaining and those that should affect bargaining over policy proposals. Our results strongly support the notion of two distinct bargaining games.

4.5. Appendix

TABLE 4.3. *Determinants of gubernatorial legislative success*

	(1)	(2)
Budgetary Proposal	1.45**	3.96**
	(.71)	(1.40)
Session Days	.001	.004*
	(.002)	(.002)
Session Days * Budgetary Proposal	−.006**	−.007**
	(.002)	(.003)
Legislative Seat Share (Governor's Party)	.018*	.019*
	(.009)	(.011)
Legislative Seat Share (Governor's Party) * Budgetary Proposal	−.015	−.025**
	(.010)	(.012)

(continued)

TABLE 4.3. *(continued)*

	(1)	(2)
First-Term Governor	.80**	.76*
	(.32)	(.42)
First-Term Governor * Budgetary Proposal	−.64*	−.99**
	(.36)	(.36)
Public Approval		.03**
		(.01)
Public Approval * Budgetary Proposal		−.03*
		(.02)
Presidential Ambitions	−1.13**	−1.48**
	(.50)	(.56)
Presidential Ambitions * Budgetary Proposal	.99**	1.54**
	(.49)	(.60)
Legacy Year	.68*	.99**
	(.40)	(.53)
Legacy Year * Budgetary Proposal	.02	−.66
	(.35)	(.40)
Significant Policy Change	−.28	−.24
	(.19)	(.20)
Liberal Policy Change	.54**	.67**
	(.13)	(.14)
Ideological Unity	.11	.06
	(.13)	(.14)
Political Reform	−.82**	−.62*
	(.36)	(.37)
Number of Proposals	−.02**	−.03**
	(.01)	(.01)
Budget Surplus (Lagged)	.006**	.017*
	(.002)	(.011)
2001 Dummy Variable	−.21	−.55
	(.28)	(.34)
cut1	.72	2.43
	(.60)	(1.18)
cut2	1.52	3.24
	(.61)	(1.19)
N	1,088	891
AIC	2,209	1,790

Note: The units of analysis are individual gubernatorial legislative proposals. Both models are ordered logistical regressions, with standard errors clustered by state year. Two-tailed tests are used: * < .10, ** < .05.

5

Do Governors Set the Size of Government?

How powerful are governors in negotiations over the size of the state budget? Can chief executives stand up to legislatures when it comes to deciding how much government will tax and spend? A lengthy literature in state politics suggests that the answer to this question is no. Most quantitative studies find that governors are reduced to little more than bystanders when it comes to determining the overall size of the state public sector.

Early empirical work found little to no relationship between the size of the budget and the partisanship of either the governor or the legislature, concluding that elected officials are neutral translators of economic and demographic conditions into policy (Dawson and Robinson 1963; Dye 1966; Hofferbert 1966; Winters 1976). Although more recent work has uncovered a link between party control and state budgeting, this link is conditioned by the types of issues over which the parties divide (Dye 1984; Brown 1995), the way that party control is measured (Smith 1997), and the set of state political institutions (Phillips 2008). Importantly, it only appears that it is the legislature's party that matters. State houses that are controlled by Democrats spend more, whereas Republican-run legislatures are more frugal and conservative. Yet, in all these studies, the party of the governor seems to be irrelevant to models predicting the size of state government.[1] Can a Gov. Mitt Romney be no different than a Gov. Howard Dean? Can capturing the biggest prize in state politics really be irrelevant when it comes to setting the size of state government?

[1] In the few models in which governors do appear to exert some control, the effect runs in a counterintuitive direction, with states led by Democrats spending less than those with a GOP governor (Clingermayer and Wood 1995; Rogers and Rogers 2000).

In this chapter, we draw on our model of budget bargaining to argue that governors play a key role in shaping the size of the public sector, contrasting our model with those that have been commonly used to account for the apparent weakness of chief executives. We also argue that existing efforts to empirically evaluate gubernatorial budget powers have relied on tests that are simply too blunt to fully flesh out executive influence. Prior studies rely exclusively on measures of party control as a proxy for gubernatorial and legislative preferences, gaining their causal traction from the assumption that Democrats always and everywhere want government to expand (Dye 1966; Hofferbert 1966; Winters 1976; Dye 1984; Garand 1988; Smith 1997; Alt and Lowry 2000; Kousser 2002). Instead of using party affiliations as a proxy, we measure executive preferences directly by looking at what governors ask for in their proposed budgets. Furthermore, rather than analyzing total levels of spending or revenue, we focus on the *changes* to fiscal policy that the governor is requesting. Doing so allows us to isolate the governor's particular budgetary objectives.

Our analysis relies on *The Fiscal Survey of States*, a biannual publication of the National Association of State Budget Officers (NASBO). Each year, NASBO conducts two surveys of state budget officials to identify trends and changes in state fiscal policy. The spring survey reports how much money a governor asked for in her proposed budget as well as any changes (tax increases or cuts) to revenue policy that she requested. The autumn survey reports on the budget that was ultimately passed by the legislature and signed into law. Comparing the spring and autumn surveys allows us to see how much of what a governor asked for ends up in the final deal. This empirical strategy is very similar to the techniques used by scholars, such as Kiewiet and McCubbins (1988) and Canes-Wrone (2001), to gauge presidential budgeting power.

We collect gubernatorial proposals and final budget outcomes from the NASBO reports for a total of 21 fiscal years – 1989–2009. To these we add data for a host of economic, political, and institutional factors that may account for variation in gubernatorial success. This new analysis allows us to test the most important implications of our theoretical model of budget bargaining – that governors should get much of what they want in budget negotiations and that they will do best when negotiating with relatively impatient legislatures. Importantly, the NASBO surveys enable us to undertake a much more comprehensive analysis of budget bargaining than we were able to conduct in Chapter 4. These data allow us to include many more states in our regression models and a much larger number of governors (nearly 200). In this new analysis, we also have more precise measures of gubernatorial success as well as the magnitude of proposed changes – we no longer need to rely on qualitative evaluations of proposals and outcomes.

As expected, our analysis again reveals striking evidence of gubernatorial strength in budgetary negotiations. Across all types of states and legislatures, we find that the chief executive's proposed budget has a positive and statistically significant effect on the budget that is ultimately passed and signed into law. Importantly, gubernatorial influence is indeed powerfully and inversely related to legislative professionalization, particularly session length. Our findings further confirm that a staring match is the appropriate analogy for understanding the dynamics of state budget negotiations.

5.1. Competing Models of Budget Bargaining

We begin by comparing two competing models of budget bargaining – the setter or spatial model and the staring match model that we present in Chapter 2. The main theoretical differences between these models are revealed in their answers to two connected questions: can the legislature convert its formal monopoly on the power to pass legislation into a practical advantage, and what is the relevant reversion point that casts a shadow over negotiations? As a result of their different answers to these questions, the models produce distinct predictions about whether and when governors will be able to influence the size of state government, predictions that we are able to evaluate here.

Nearly all efforts aimed at assessing the budgetary influence of state chief executives have relied on setter models – the type of model that we apply to negotiations over policy proposals. In most setter models, the outcome of interbranch bargaining is a function of the various players' preferences, the order of interactions, and the location of status quo policy (Romer and Rosenthal 1978). Typically, the legislature is treated as a monopoly proposer, submitting "take it or leave it" offers to an executive, who possesses an absolute veto. The executive is then forced to choose between the appropriations figures contained in the bill and the reversionary or status quo point. In applications to budget bargaining, this reversion is almost always assumed to be last year's spending plan maintained, in the absence of executive–legislative agreement on a new budget, through a continuing resolution.[2]

---

[2] Continuing resolutions typically fund government activities at or near the prior year's level until a new budget can be agreed on.

These models set out a causal mechanism that explains the apparent weakness of governors. In spatial models, the legislature's proposal power, combined with its ability to credibly threaten to keep expenditures at the status quo level, gives the legislature substantially greater influence over budgetary outcomes than the executive. Kiewiet and McCubbins (1988), for instance, demonstrate this to be the case at the national level in the United States. Using a spatial model of presidential–congressional bargaining, they show that when the president prefers smaller expenditures than Congress, the circumstance most favorable to the president, he exerts only a limited influence over budgetary outcomes. When the president prefers a higher level of expenditures, they establish that he has no influence at all. These insights are supported in Kiewiet and McCubbins's empirical analysis as well as by a subsequent investigation by McCarty and Poole (1995).

In the study of American states, applications of setter models also predict legislative dominance. In their influential analyses of state budgeting under divided government, Alt and Lowry (1994, 2000) amend the spatial model developed by Kiewiet and McCubbins to account for the balanced budget requirements that exist in nearly all states. In their model, the legislature and governor must reach agreement on fiscal balance (whether there is a surplus, deficit, or balanced budget) in addition to fiscal scale. They also add an assumption, backed by Lowry et al.'s (1998) empirical work, that fiscal imbalance results in significant electoral losses for the governor's copartisans in the legislature.[3]

Alt and Lowry's model, like that of Kiewiet and McCubbins, suggests executive weakness. In the face of interbranch disagreement over the size of the budget, the legislature can use its monopoly proposal power to threaten the governor with fiscal imbalance by passing a continuing resolution (CR) rather than a new budget. Because deficits or surpluses put the governor's copartisans in the legislature at risk, she will be forced to make significant concessions to the legislature on fiscal scale in return for a balanced budget. After reviewing the empirical predictions of their model under different fiscal contexts and configurations of party control, Alt and Lowry conclude that legislatures are even stronger than predicted by Kiewiet and McCubbins (1988). According to Alt and Lowry (2000, p. 1043), "in no case does the governor achieve a significant shift in the

---

[3] It is not clear to us why voters would punish legislators rather than the governor himself or herself, especially when they are in the powerless minority during times of divided government.

budget target in the direction of her ideal point." Indeed, Alt and Lowry's model suggests that governors often face something akin to a "hostage crisis" when negotiating with a legislature controlled by the other party: the opposition party can hold up the budget until it receives, as its ransom payment, a budget of the size it desires.

While spatial models and their progeny have unquestionably provided important insights into executive–legislative bargaining, we believe that these models are not the most appropriate simplification for budgeting negotiations in most American states (though they may be an appropriate simplification for budget bargaining at the national level). First, their portrayal of gubernatorial weakness contradicts much of the existing qualitative scholarship in the state politics literature. Case studies (Bernick and Wiggins 1991; Gross 1991), surveys of political insiders (Abney and Lauth 1987; Francis 1989; Carey et al. 2003), and other qualitative works (Rosenthal 1990, 1998, 2004; Beyle 2004) all point to the extraordinary power of governors when it comes to budgeting. According to these analyses, governors can, and often do, dominate the legislature when it comes to the eternal question of how much to tax and spend.

Additionally, the conclusion in setter models that chief executives are weak is driven largely by the assumption that the reversion point in the absence of a budget agreement is the status quo, preserved through some type of CR. As we noted in Chapter 2, CRs are not common or important considerations in state budget negotiations. In the few states where CRs are allowed, they are only temporary solutions at best. None can become permanent, and a new budget must still be adopted. This is different from the federal government, where Congress and the president can avoid adopting a new budget entirely and instead use CR to fund government operations for an entire fiscal year (Meyer 1997; Davidson et al. 2007). Among the states, the reversion point in the absence of an agreement on a new budget is usually a partial shutdown of the government, resulting in the closing of many state facilities and parks, the furlough of public employees, and the suspension of nonessential services (Pulsipher 2004).[4] Some states can avoid an immediate government shutdown by relying on a combination of reserve funds, government-issued IOUs, borrowing, and the deferral of expenditures. However, once these options are exhausted, a shutdown cannot be avoided.

[4] Essential services often (though not always) include prisons, highway patrol, welfare, and public health programs (Pulsipher 2004). Jennifer Grouters and Corina Eckl, "Table 6.4: Procedures when the Appropriates Act is Not passed by the Beginning of the Fiscal year," accessed at http://www.ncsi.org/programs/fiscal/ibptabls/ibpcbty.htm in June 2000.

The absence of agreement on a new budget imposes political costs on both branches of state government by cutting deeply into their public approval (especially if a government shutdown is triggered). For many lawmakers, fiscal impasse also imposes personal costs by forcing them to stay in the state capitol for a potentially lengthy special session. Many lawmakers have jobs to which they need to quickly return and literally cannot afford to remain in session haggling over the details of a new budget. The impact of the legislature's proposal power should erode when it cannot fall back on an acceptable status quo. This means that the playing field in state budget negotiations should be more level than is allowed for in spatial models.

In Chapter 2, we present an alternative to the setter model. Our simplification treats budget negotiations as a staring match in which the players bargain in the shadow of a late budget and the political and private penalties it can bring. As a result, both sides face incentives to compromise. As in any staring match model, what matters is a player's patience, not his proposal power or the ability to credibly threaten to keep expenditures at the status quo level. The player who can stay at the bargaining table the longest will be able to secure the most concessions from the other side. If both players are patient, the model predicts a fairly even division of the budgetary dollar.

These competing models – the spatial hostage crisis and the staring match – generate different predictions about the gubernatorial budget power and the features of state politics that will shape gubernatorial success. First, unlike the spatial model, the staring match model predicts that governors will be quite powerful in the budgetary arena. In all states, the governorship is a full-time and well-paid job, meaning that governors are patient bargainers – they can afford to engage in long and protracted negotiations over the budget. Since governors are patient, any benefits that the legislature enjoys from its first-mover advantage are quite small. Second, the spatial model expects that governors will do best during periods of unified governments, that is, when they have many allies in the legislature. In our simplification of budget bargaining, controlling a committee or access to the floor is less vital because the legislative majority cannot ignore the governor's budget. The necessity of passing a state spending plan brings them to the table whether they are the governor's partisan allies or not, and the key to gubernatorial success is patience. Likewise, a governor's political capital should have little effect on her ability to prevail in these sorts of negotiations.

Third, though the staring match model predicts that governors will generally do well in budget negotiations, it also predicts that governors should do best when they are more patient than the legislature. In Chapter 2, we identified two instances in which this is likely – when governors are in their legacy year and when they are bargaining with part-time citizen legislatures. Spatial approaches to executive–legislative bargaining, at both the national and state levels, rarely consider the potential effect of patience on outcomes (Kiewiet and McCubbins 1988; Alt and Lowry 1994, 2000; McCarty and Poole 1995; but see Banks and Duggan 2006). Even when the patience levels of the players are allowed to vary, spatial models predict no effect. Primo (2002), for instance, examines how some of these dynamics might affect Romer and Rosenthal's (1978) model. He shows that even when spatial models are extended to multiple stages of bargaining, discount rates do not factor into the equilibrium. Primo's results suggest that impatient citizen legislatures should not face a bargaining disadvantage because "impatience and time preferences may not be key features of political bargaining" (Primo 2002, p. 21).

In the sections that follow, we evaluate these competing predictions by estimating the power of state chief executives when it comes to shaping the size of government. This effort builds on the empirical analyses conducted in Chapter 4, which already provide some key insights into these questions. Our analysis of proposals in State of the State addresses indicates that governors do indeed exert a powerful influence over the budget, securing either a full pass or compromise on approximately two-thirds of their budgetary proposals. Our prior analysis also uncovers patterns of success on fiscal matters that are more consistent with the expectations of the staring match model than those of the spatial model – governors did better when bargaining with legislatures that met in short sessions, while the partisanship of the legislature and the governor's political capital had little to no effect on success. Here, we subject these findings to further scrutiny using new dependent variables and a much larger sample of states and governors.

5.2. Measuring Governors' Proposals and Legislative Enactments

To estimate the influence of governors on the size of the state budget, one needs first to know what governors want out of the budgeting process. Traditionally, scholars have relied upon a governor's partisanship as a proxy for her fiscal preferences, assuming that Democrats always want to increase the size of the public sector and that Republicans prefer to shrink it. Using this assumption, scholars then estimate gubernatorial power by looking to see if state budgets grow more during Democratic administrations than they do during Republican administrations. The problem with the approach (which almost always finds that governors have little influence) is that it ignores the unique opportunity that governors have to adapt to their states' political environments. Unlike presidents, they do not have to carry their party's national banner. Unlike senators, they do not have to go to Washington, D.C. to vote on their party's national agenda, under pressure to toe their party's line. Governors have the flexibility to set their own paths. Because of this, Republican governors can win office in liberal states and Democrats can survive in conservative ones, but only by positioning themselves toward the middle of the ideological spectrum or by taking positions that might not normally be associated with their partisan identification. Governors possess both the means and the motivation to be relative centrists, and this moderation will make their party affiliations less predictive of their budgetary goals, as we demonstrated in Chapter 3. This, in turn, can leave their powers hidden in models that assume that the fiscal preferences of Democrats and Republicans will sharply diverge. Here, we measure the fiscal preferences of governors directly rather than assuming that their party affiliations tell us what they want.

To do this, we use our NASBO surveys of state budget officials to create two measures of gubernatorial preferences. The first is the governor's desired change in the overall size of the public sector. We operationalize this as a governor's proposed change (over the prior fiscal year) in per capita expenditures.[5] One potential problem with this measure (and the reason we do not rely on it exclusively) is that it may not fully isolate proposed changes to status quo policy. During periods of economic growth, the size of state government increases even if no changes are made to tax policy, while the reverse happens during periods of economic decline. The relationship may sometimes create the appearance that the governor is proposing large changes to the status quo, when in reality, she is not calling on the legislature to make any modifications to existing revenue policies but is simply adjusting the size of her proposed budget to match year-to-year fluctuations in revenue collection. Indeed, a governor proposing to increase the size of the public sector by $25 per capita

---

[5] These are total expenditures in the general fund budget, typically reported in Table A-3 of the *Fiscal Survey of States*.

through tax increases may have a very different probability of success than a governor calling for a similar increase in spending but who can get there simply by relying on economic growth.

To protect against this concern, we also utilize a second, more narrowly tailored measure – the governor's proposed changes to tax policy.[6] The spring NASBO survey lists any tax proposal in the executive budget that was anticipated to have an impact (either positive or negative) on state revenue collections. Included are increases or decreases in tax rates as well as less headline-worthy changes such as the creation or elimination of deductions and credits, the closing of tax loopholes, changes in fees, and the creation of tax holidays. In addition to reporting the specific revenue measures recommended, NASBO provides an estimate of the net fiscal impact of each. We simply sum these estimates for each budget, creating a single measure of the total per capita tax changes proposed.

Finally, to determine what made it into the enacted budget – the budget that is passed by the legislature and signed into law by the governor – we rely on the fall publication of the *The Fiscal Survey of States*. The fall survey reports on the size of the enacted budget as well as any enacted changes to tax policy and their anticipated effect on revenue collections. To determine the governor's success in budget negotiations, we compare what the governor originally asked for to what she was able to get. Ultimately, we obtained data on proposed and enacted budgets over 21 fiscal years – 1989–2009 (data for prior years are unavailable). The analyses we report subsequently use data from 48 states. Nebraska is excluded because of its nonpartisan legislature, and Alaska is dropped because the state budget relies heavily on severance taxes on natural resources (particularly oil). The use of severance taxes results in fairly dramatic year-to-year variation in tax revenues and expenditures that are driven by the global commodities market as opposed to the budgetary choices of elected officials (Matsusaka 2004). Since NASBO reports data in current dollars, we convert the values for each year into 2000 dollars using the Consumer Price Index for all urban consumers (CPI-U).

5.3. What Do Governors Ask for, and Why?

Before evaluating gubernatorial success, we consider the characteristics of executive budgetary proposals. Do governors usually propose to shrink or increase the size of state government? Are there, as researchers usually

---

[6] These data are usually reported in Table 7 of *The Fiscal Survey of States*.

assume, large differences between the fiscal objectives of Republicans and Democrats? Do governors shape their proposals to fit their bargaining circumstances?

Our data show that governors usually propose to increase the size of state government but that there remains a great deal of variation across governors and over time. Of the executive budgets in our data set, over 60 percent called for an increase in spending when compared to the prior enacted budget. Indeed, the average proposed change was a $9 increase in total per capita expenditures (with a fairly large standard deviation of $99). We observe a similar pattern when it comes to tax changes. A plurality of the proposed budgets in our sample (40%) called for a net increases in taxes, while a smaller share requested a reduction in taxation (35%) or called for no changes in revenue policy at all (25%).

To consider the factors that shape the governor's proposed budget, we again turn to multivariate regression analysis. In particular, we estimate a series of models that control for the partisanship of the governor and legislature, the health of the state economy, the professionalization of the legislature, and the governor's political capital. We estimate separate models for the proposed change in total expenditures and the proposed change in tax policy. Appendix Table 5.2 reports our full regression results.

Our regression results indicate that the governor's partisanship is not a consistent proxy for her preferences over the size of state government. In our models of proposed changes in total expenditures, there is not a statistically significant difference between the budget proposals of Democratic and Republican governors. This is true even after accounting for the various economic indicators and the liberalness of the state electorate. Indeed, like their Democratic counterparts, a large majority of the budgets proposed by Republican governors call for growth in the size of the public sector. The absence of a strong party effect is consistent with our argument that governors are ideologically flexible and can set paths in statehouses that diverge from their party labels. It also suggests that it is wrong to conclude that governors are weak in budgeting just because fiscal outcomes do not strongly correlate to gubernatorial partisanship.

In regressions that consider proposed tax changes, we do, however, observe a meaningful partisan difference. On average, the proposed tax changes of Democrats are larger by $17 per capita than those of Republicans, a difference that is statistically significant at the 95 percent level. Yet, this finding masks crucial variation that might surprise some observers of contemporary American politics. The years that we are observing here came mostly after the Republican Revolution of 1994 and the continuing polarization of national politics (Poole et al. 2006) left the two parties as polar opposites on the ideological spectrum in Washington, D.C. While Republicans in Congress seemingly oppose all tax increases and routinely call for new tax cuts, this is not the case for Republican governors. Of the budgets offered by Republicans, only 34 percent called for changes in tax policy that would result in a net reduction in revenues, while 30 percent proposed changes that would bring about a net revenue increase. Republican tax increases were not limited to states with liberal electorates or legislatures controlled by Democrats. Similarly, Democratic governors often act against partisan type. In total, 21 percent of the Democratic budgets called for revenue-reducing tax cuts. Again, this indicates that using direct measures of gubernatorial budget requests is preferable to assuming that preferences can be captured by partisanship alone.

Additionally, our regression models do not uncover any evidence that governors shape their proposed budgets to fit their bargaining circumstances. Governors who should be most advantaged in budget negotiations – those bargaining with a citizen legislature and those in their legacy year – do not offer budgets that included larger increases in either spending or taxes than do weaker governors. In models in which the dependent variable is a measure of the absolute size of the governor's proposed change to the prior year's budget, we also find no differences between institutionally strong and weak governors. There is also little evidence that a governor's political capital influences her proposed budget. Chief executives who can sustain a veto, are popular, or are serving in their first term send budgets to the legislature that are very similar to governors without these attributes.[7] This set of results is as expected under our theoretical framework. Because governors do not need to entice lawmakers to the bargaining table in the budget game, they do not need to be strategic when crafting their proposals.

Ultimately, the variables that appear to have the largest effect on proposed budgets are not those that capture the governor's partisanship or her bargaining circumstances but rather those that measure the health of the state economy. More precisely, the variable with the largest substantive effect in our regression models is the state unemployment rate. When the unemployment rate is high, governors call for much smaller increases in total expenditures and larger increases in taxes. As we noted

---

[7] The coefficient on *First Term* is significant and negative in one of our models, indicating that first-term governors propose smaller increases in taxes than do other governors. This finding is not robust across model specifications.

previously, a bad economy lowers revenue collections, which, when combined with state balanced budget requirements, makes new expenditures difficult and creates pressure on governors to raise taxes to prevent deep cuts to government services. Governors often bend to these practical considerations rather than adhering to rigid ideological positions.

5.4. Evaluating Competing Models

We now turn to our analysis of bargaining outcomes. We being by examining the bivariate relationship between the governor's proposed spending change (our independent variable) and the change in spending that is included in the enacted budget (our dependent variable). This is the same empirical strategy that Kiewiet and McCubbins (1988) employed in their influential study of presidential–congressional bargaining. The coefficient of our independent variable answers this question: for every dollar that the governor proposes to shrink or increase total spending, how many cents does the legislature deliver? We conduct a similar analysis for proposed and enacted tax changes.

The results of this analysis are consistent with the expectations of the staring match model. First, we find clear evidence of gubernatorial strength in budget negotiations. There is a strong and statistically significant correlation (at the 99% level) between the spending change proposed by the governor and spending change included in the enacted budget. On average, for every dollar increase or decrease in total expenditures the governor proposes, the legislature gives her 69 cents. When bargaining over tax changes, the governor is somewhat less successful but still manages to secure 35 cents of every dollar requested. Despite this lower level of success, the correlation between proposed and enacted tax changes is also statistically significant at the 99 percent level.

Second, even during periods of divided government, state chief executives are powerful bargainers. The correlation between gubernatorial budget proposals and enactments remains positive and statistically significant. This is true regardless of whether one or both legislative chambers are controlled by the opposition party. Furthermore, the impact of divided government on gubernatorial success appears to be inconsistent. Divided government only reduces the strength of the correlation between proposals and outcomes in negotiations over tax changes but not in negotiations over total spending. The predictions of the spatial model – that state chief executives will be ineffective bargainers during periods of divided government – are not supported, at least in our preliminary analysis.

TABLE 5.1. *Legislative Professionalization and Gubernatorial Bargaining Success*

	Citizen legislatures	Semiprofessional legislatures	Professional legislatures	All legislatures
Total expenditure changes				
Governor's Proposal	0.85**	0.83**	0.53**	0.96**
	(0.04)	(0.03)	(0.06)	(0.04)
Session Months				1.80**
				(0.65)
Governor's Proposal × Session Months				−0.03**
				(.003)
Constant	17.73	16.60	23.43	7.89
	(2.99)	(3.01)	(8.56)	(4.32)
N	372	451	218	1041
Adjusted R^3	0.56	0.57	0.27	0.47
Total tax changes				
Governor's Proposal	0.37**	0.43**	0.29**	0.53**
	(0.02)	(0.02)	(0.04)	(0.03)
Session Months				0.08
				(0.32)
Governor's Proposal × Session Months				−0.02**
				(0.003)
Constant	6.77	1.91	2.86	3.20
	(1.73)	(1.47)	(2.09)	
N	357	441	218	1008
Adjusted R^3	0.40	0.56	0.18	0.42

Note: Two-tailed tests are employed: * $< .10$, ** $< .05$.

Third, governors do better when bargaining with less patient legislatures. This is shown in Table 5.1, which reports the correlation between gubernatorial budget proposals and outcomes by type of legislature – citizen, semiprofessional, and professional – using the trichotomous categorization developed by the National Conference of State Legislatures (NCSL). The final column of the table combines data from all types of legislatures with an interaction testing the relationship between session length and gubernatorial success. Recall that this is the feature of legislative professionalization that we believe to be the single best indicator of legislative patience. The top half of the table considers bargaining over the total changes in expenditures, whereas the bottom half looks at total tax changes.

Across all three categories of legislatures, the coefficient on the variable that measures the gubernatorial budget proposal is positive and statistically significant at the 99 percent level. This indicates that governors are consistently powerful, regardless of the type of legislature with which they are bargaining. The magnitude of the effect, though, is clearly weakest when governors are bargaining with professional legislatures. Negotiating with citizen bodies, governors get 85 cents of every dollar that they ask for in expenditure changes and 35 cents of every dollar they request in tax changes. These figures fall to 53 and 24 cents, respectively, when governors are bargaining with the most professional chambers. We observe only minor differences in the success of chief executives between citizen and semiprofessional legislatures. Furthermore, when bargaining over total expenditures, the governor's budgetary proposal alone explains well over half of the variation in outcomes (see the adjusted R^2) in states with citizen legislatures but accounts for just 27 percent of the variation across states with more professionalized legislative bodies. The parallel figures for bargaining over tax changes are 40 and 18 percent, respectively.[8]

The final column of Table 5.1 provides additional evidence that gubernatorial success decreases as patience grows. In this column, we interact a measure of session length (the number of months the legislature was in session) with the governor's proposed change in either total expenditures or taxes. This interaction effect is strongly significant in the expected direction. The results indicate that a proposed $1 increase in the size of government should translate into a 90 cent increase in spending when negotiating with a legislature like New Hampshire's, which routinely meets in very short sessions (about one standard deviation below the national mean). Conversely, the identical proposal will only translate into a 60 cent increase when the governor is bargaining with a legislature that meets as frequently as California's (about two standard deviations above the national mean).[9]

While chief executives do best when negotiating with impatient legislatures, we do not find any systematic evidence that they enjoy more

---

[8] The correlation between the proposed and enacted budget remains positive and statistically significant even in multivariate models that control for the state of the economy and the political and bargaining circumstances that the governor confronts.

[9] We also examine the potential effect of another legislative institution, term limits, in models not reported here. To estimate the effects of term limits, we employed a fixed-effects rather than a random-effect model. Governors negotiating over tax changes with term-limited legislatures were marginally more powerful, with a negative estimated coefficient indicating that they had to compromise less, though this finding falls short of statistical significance. Term limits appeared to exert no effect on bargaining over changes in total spending.

bargaining success during their legacy years. In Chapter 2, we argued that a governor who is serving in her last year in office will have little to lose in the short term from a delayed budget and can stubbornly dig in until legislators give her what she wants. In other words, legacy-year governors should be particularly patient. In Chapter 4, we found evidence that they pass more of their State of the State budget proposals. Yet, we see no such effect in the NASBO data. The correlation between governors' proposed budgets and the enacted budgets is equally as strong regardless of whether a governor is serving in her final year in office or earlier in her term.

Next, we consider the competing expectations of the spatial and staring match models using a multivariate regression analysis. Here, the dependent variable is not the size of the enacted changes to the budget but rather the absolute difference between what the governor asked for in her proposed budget and what she was ultimately able to secure at the bargaining table.[10] The advantage of using this particular dependent variable is that we can estimate how an independent variable will shape gubernatorial success without interacting that variable and the governor's proposal (as we did in the final column of Table 5.1). This makes it easier to simultaneously evaluate the relationship between numerous independent variables and gubernatorial success. This strategy is similar to that of Clarke (1998), who gathered data on gubernatorial recommendations for agency budgets in 20 states and then measured the extent to which each was changed by the legislature. Again, we estimate separate regressions for expenditures and tax changes.

To evaluate the competing predictions of the spatial and staring match models, our regressions include a variable that indicates the presence of divided government, a measure of session length, and a variable that indicates whether the governor is in her legacy year. Though we do not expect a governor's political capital to shape outcomes in budget negotiations, we do include a measure of the governor's popularity as well an indicator for whether she is serving in her first term. To allow for the possibility that governors will do worse when they are calling for larger changes to the status quo, we also include a variable that measures the size of the governor's proposed changes to the budget or to tax levels, as

[10] For example, the absolute difference between the proposed and enacted budget would be $10 if the governor had called for a $5 increase in per capita expenditures but ultimately signed into law a budget authorizing a $15 increase. The same would also be true if, instead of agreeing to the proposed increase, the legislature were to cut total expenditures by $5 per capita.

appropriate. Finally, the regression models include various measures of the state's economic health. The results of several models are reported in appendix Table 5.3.

Our results largely confirm the intuition of the staring match model as developed here and in Chapter 2. We continue to find that as the patience of the legislature increases, governors' bargaining success declines (though we still find no evidence that serving in one's legacy year matters). In all the models reported in the appendix, the coefficient on *Session Months* is positive and statistically significant at the 95 percent level (here, a positive coefficient indicates that as session length increases, so does the size of the gap between the governor's proposed budget and the budget she signs into law). When it comes to bargaining over total expenditures, each month the legislature meets increases the gap between the size of the proposed and enacted budget by approximately $4 per capita. In negotiations over tax changes, each session month translates into an additional $1 per capita difference between the governor's request and the enacted budget.

The relationship between gubernatorial success and divided government is still inconsistent. In models of total expenditures, governors surprisingly appear to do better when they are negotiating with a legislature in which at least one chamber is controlled by the opposition party. In models of tax changes, divided government increases the size of the gap between the proposed and enacted budget (by approximately $4 per capita), but it is not statistically significant in models that include the governor's popularity. However, even when divided government performs as expected (and is statistically significant), its substantive impact is only about half that of session length.[11] This further indicates that legislative patience is a more meaningful determinant of outcomes than divided government.

Additionally, we find that some variables that mattered in the policy game – whether or not the governor is serving in her first term as well as the governor's popularity with voters – have no meaningful correlation with success in budget negotiations. This is as anticipated. We also observe that governors are less successful when they propose larger changes to status quo fiscal policy – as the size of a governor's proposed increase (or decrease) in total expenditures grows, so does the gap between the proposed and enacted budget. This is true when it comes to

---

[11] Session length also explains more of the variation in success than the presence or absence of divided government.

tax changes. This result is consistent with our finding in Chapter 4 that governors with larger agendas with more proposals are less likely to be successful in bargaining. Indeed, in each of the regression models reported in appendix Table 5.3, the size of the governor's proposed change has the largest substantive impact on outcomes.

5.5. Disentangling Session Length from Salary and Staff

Though we are clearly not the first to argue that full-time legislatures exert a greater influence over budgetary matters than their part-time counterparts, our treatment of professionalization differs significantly from much of the existing literature. Traditionally, it is argued that professionalized legislatures are more powerful because they possess an increased intelligence capacity (Rosenthal 1990). These legislatures usually have a large staff dedicated exclusively to fiscal policy, revenue-estimating capability that is independent of the executive branch, and a sizeable contingent of experienced legislators. These features are believed to reduce the governor's traditional informational advantages and enhance legislative independence and assertiveness (National Conference of State Legislatures 2005). While professionalization may indeed have these effects, we argue that its real advantage is that long sessions make legislators willing to endure extended and conflictual interbranch negotiations over the size of the budget.

Thus far, we have employed in our analyses either session length or a measure of legislative professionalization that aggregates the various components of this concept – session length, compensation, and staff – into a single indicator (the NCSL classification used in Table 5.1). The staring match model makes a prediction that session length will be the primary factor affecting the legislature's patience and thus the governor's power. Increased staffing, which adds to the legislature's informational capacity, should not affect the balance of power between the branches if the staring match logic drives the effect of professionalism. High salaries, which can free legislators from other obligations, might also affect patience, but members of houses that regularly meet for full-time sessions should exhibit the highest levels of patience. To examine this claim, we estimate models of gubernatorial success (not reported here) that, in addition to session length, include measures of lawmaker salary and staff.[12] When

---

[12] Our measure of salary is total lawmaker compensation, including both base salary and per diem expenses. Our measure of staff is the ratio of staff per legislator.

these variables are included, neither is a significant predictor of gubernatorial success or failure. However, session length continues to remain both substantively and statistically meaningful, indicating that it is indeed patience as opposed to expertise that gives legislators the ability to stand up to governors on the budget.

5.6. Conclusion

Attempts to assess the power of governors in budget negotiations have traditionally relied on spatial models of policy making imported from studies of presidents negotiating with the U.S. Congress. In these models, legislators, through their monopoly on proposal power and their ability to credibly threaten to keep expenditures at the status quo level, reduce chief executives to very weak negotiators, particularly during periods of divided government. Executive weakness has seemingly been confirmed by existing empirical studies of the states that rely on the governor's partisanship as a proxy for her fiscal preferences. In this chapter, we challenge the appropriateness of the spatial model for state budget bargaining, arguing that the staring match model we detail in Chapter 2 is the most appropriate analogy for negotiations over the size of state government. In the staring match model, governors are quite potent, and the power of governors should increase when they are particularly patient (in their legacy year) or when they are bargaining with an impatient legislature (one that meets for relatively short sessions).

We have explored the predictions of both the spatial and staring match models using an original data set of gubernatorial budget proposals and legislatively enacted budgets. These data allow us to directly measure what the governor desires out of the budget process rather than relying on assumptions about the governor's goals based on her partisanship. We show that Republican and Democratic governors in similar situations offer nearly identical budgets, charting a centrist course rather than pushing states toward fiscal extremes. When we look at the fates of their proposals, our results largely confirm the expectations of the staring match model. Overall, we find striking evidence of gubernatorial influence. Our econometric estimations show that across all types of states and legislatures, the chief executive's proposed budget has a positive and statistically significant effect on the budget that is ultimately passed and signed into law.

Most important, however, the influence of governors is closely linked to levels of legislative professionalism. Though state chief executives generally do quite well in budget bargaining, they are most successful when dealing with legislatures that meet in short sessions. Lawmakers in these chambers are eager to leave the state capitol, and their impatience leads them to make significant concessions to the governor. We do not find that gubernatorial success is contingent on the partisanship of the legislature or various measures of the governor's political capital. These results indicate that budget negotiations between governors and legislature unfold much differently than negotiations over policy, in which factors like the partisanship of the legislature and the governor's political capital are crucial determinants of success.

Broadly, we believe that the analysis presented in this chapter yields three more general lessons for the study of bargaining between governmental branches. First, when researchers apply formal models of bargaining, one size does not fit all legislatures. Although setter models may capture the key dynamics of federal budget bargaining in the U.S. Congress, where a continuing resolution is a realistic reversionary outcome, these models do not appear to fit well with states that demand that a new budget be passed every year. Second, while variation in legislative professionalism clearly determines legislative power, it is session length – more than salary or staff – that appears to drive this trend. Finally, directly measuring governors' preferences, rather than inferring them from party affiliations, allows scholars to uncover the significant influence that these preferences exert over state policy.

5.7. Appendix

To evaluate the factors that shape governors' proposed budgets, we estimate several multivariate regression models, the results of which are reported in Table 5.2. Separate models are estimated for (1) the governor's proposed change in total expenditures (i.e., the difference between the size of the governor's proposed budget for the upcoming fiscal year and the size of last year's enacted budget, measured in per capita dollars) and (2) the governor's proposed change in tax policy (i.e., the sum of the tax increases and cuts included in the governor's proposed budget, again measured in per capita dollars). In the first two models, the dependent variable is measured as an absolute value, allowing us to consider the factors that may lead governors to propose a larger change to the budget (irrespective of the ideological direction of that change).

All models control for the partisanship of the governor and legislature, the health of the state economy and budget, the professionalization of the

TABLE 5.2. *Governors' Budgetary Proposals, Fiscal Years 1989–2009*

	Proposed change in total spending (absolute value)	Proposed tax changes (absolute value)	Proposed change in total spending	Proposed tax changes
Session Months	1.43	−0.86	0.07	0.32
	(1.12)	(0.88)	(1.21)	(0.87)
Divided Government	0.21	−4.10		
	(5.15)	(4.80)		
Share Democratic Seats			0.17	0.24
			(0.30)	(0.21)
First-Term Governor	5.47	−5.26	−5.97	−12.80**
	(4.95)	(4.74)	(6.73)	(5.07)
Legacy-Year Governor	−4.50	6.22	−23.04	5.99
	(13.14)	(12.72)	(17.74)	(13.49)
Democratic Governor	10.70**	3.37	9.90	17.30**
	(5.10)	(4.78)	(6.70)	(5.02)
Income Per Capita	1.63	0.53	1.81	1.73*
	(1.06)	(0.89)	(1.23)	(0.90)
Change in Per Capita Income	−4.47	8.46*	6.84	1.59
	(5.05)	(5.04)	(7.14)	(5.53)
Unemployment Rate	0.04	2.31	−11.09**	7.41**
	(2.80)	(2.52)	(3.55)	(2.79)
Change in the Unemployment Rate	0.25	0.68	15.47**	−2.37
	(4.01)	(3.97)	(5.61)	(4.39)
Lagged Budget Surplus	1.18**	−0.02	0.58	−1.51**
	(0.44)	(0.39)	(0.56)	(0.42)
Voter Liberalness	0.86	0.90	−0.91	−1.78**
	(0.89)	(0.60)	(0.89)	(0.89)
South	−6.64	−10.22	−3.27	−6.00
	(12.91)	(7.75)	(11.03)	(7.62)
Intercept	4.37	25.26	−10.77	−101.43
	(43.14)	(36.57)	(55.47)	(40.79)
Standard deviation of state effects	32.68	15.14	19.18	11.44
Standard deviation of year effects	11.42	15.46	21.73	21.31
N	1018	1028	997	1007
AIC	11,632	11,658	11,964	11,540

Note: All models include random effects for state and year. Two-tailed tests are employed: * < .10, ** < .05. AIC = Akaike Information Criterion.

TABLE 5.3. *Determinants of Gubernatorial Success, Fiscal Years 1989–2009*

	Total expenditures (difference between proposed and enacted)	Total expenditures (difference between proposed and enacted)	Tax changes (difference between proposed and enacted)	Tax changes (difference between proposed and enacted)
Session Months	4.44**	4.02**	0.99**	0.99**
	(0.96)	(1.10)	(0.38)	(0.41)
Divided Government	−12.26**	−13.69**	4.06*	3.51
	(4.41)	(2.89)	(2.15)	(−2.64)
Size of Proposed Changes	0.30**	0.61**	0.61**	0.65**
	(0.03)	(0.01)	(0.01)	(0.02)
First-Term Governor	0.04	−2.49	−2.41	03.77
	(4.29)	(2.17)	(2.17)	(2.69)
Legacy-Year Governor	8.16	2.12	2.14	1.42
	(11.28)	(5.76)	(5.76)	(7.82)
Public Approval		−0.28		−0.03
		(0.22)		(−0.11)
Income Per Capita	−1.86**	−0.84	0.36	0.51
	(0.78)	(1.07)	(0.33)	(−0.39)
Change in Income Per Capita	0.66	−4.86	−2.24	0.56
	(4.10)	(5.33)	(2.11)	(−2.64)
Unemployment Rate	−1.99	−0.86	1.23	1.72
	(2.24)	(3.04)	(1.03)	(−1.31)
Change in the Unemployment Rate	2.96	1.86	−2.77*	−1.93
	(3.19)	(−4.23)	(1.59)	(−2.00)
Lagged Budget Surplus	0.32	0.13	0.18	0.45**
	(0.37)	(0.51)	(0.17)	(−0.21)
Voter Liberalness	1.02	0.86	−0.34	−0.37
	(0.72)	(0.94)	(0.24)	(−0.30)
South	−1.26	−3.78	−1.07	−0.43
	(10.69)	(13.29)	(3.15)	(−3.50)
Intercept	78.62	75.03	−18.95	−28.32
	(32.78)	(−46.13)	(14.01)	(−18.52)
Standard deviation of state effects	26.76	32.72	5.18	4.10
Standard deviation of year effects	4.53	7.21	2.57	3.78
N	1016	646	1028	655
AIC	11,323	7,234	10,073	6,400

Note: All models include random effects for state and year. Two-tailed tests are employed: * < .10, ** < .05. AIC = Akaike Information Criterion.

TABLE 5.4. *Gubernatorial Budget Requests and Enactments,*
Fiscal Years 1989–2009

Variable	Mean	Standard deviation	Minimum	Maximum
Proposed change in total spending	$9.37	$99.32	−$628.08	$1,246.76
Proposed tax changes	$9.22	$78.65	−$399.44	$711.96
Difference between proposed and enacted spending (absolute value)	$43.63	$75.47	$0	$1,182.99
Difference between proposed and enacted tax changes (absolute value)	$28.04	$54.77	$0	$701.30

legislature, the governor's political capital, the liberalness of voters, and a dummy variable indicating southern states (defined as states of the former Confederacy). In models not reported here, we also include a measure of gubernatorial popularity. (Again, there is a great deal of missing data, even more than in the models we report in the appendix to Chapter 4.) The inclusion of popularity does not meaningfully alter our findings, and we do not observe any statistically significant correlation between public approval of a governor and the size or ideological direction of her proposed budget changes. Data on state personal income and unemployment rates come from the *Statistical Abstract of the United States*. Our measure of voter liberalness is the state ideology measure created by Erikson et al. (1993). While in Chapter 3, we measured voter liberalness using the Kerry vote, here, we needed an index that covers a longer period of time.

Table 5.3 reports regression models of gubernatorial success in negotiations over the size of government. Here, the dependent variable is the absolute difference between what the governor asked for in her proposed budget and what she was ultimately able to secure at the bargaining table. This difference is measured as dollars per capita. The second and fourth models include a measure of the public's approval of the governor. Again, the inclusion of this variable notably decreases our sample size. Finally, Table 5.4 presents summary statistics for the dependent variables used in our regressions.

6

The Power and Perils of Popularity

Gov. Kathleen Blanco, whose political standing nose-dived amid her administration's response to Hurricane Katrina, emerged Tuesday from a 17-day
special legislative session with a string of victories on the state budget, business tax breaks, a statewide building code, and a partial takeover of the
troubled New Orleans public schools.
— The Times-Picayune, *November 23, 2005*[1]

Despite an all time-low approval rating and a major scandal exploding
around him, Republican Gov. Bob Taft appears on the verge of scoring the
biggest public policy victory of his nearly 6 and 1/2 years in office.
— Dayton Daily News, *June 3, 2005*[2]

When Louisiana's governor Kathleen Blanco and Ohio's governor Bob
Taft won major legislative victories in the face of plummeting polls, it surprised the statehouse journalists who covered them. And, well, it should
have. The link between popularity and legislative success is an important
part of the lore of American politics, buttressed by systematic studies at
the national level and frequent observations in states. Essential to the
notion of political capital is the understanding that chief executives can
spend it by translating strong public approval into policy persuasion. The
converse should also be true: unpopular leaders should be hamstrung by
their poll numbers, unable to convince legislators to pass the agendas they
propose.

---

[1] Jan Moller and Robert Travis Scott, "No Solace for Blanco in Session's 'Success' – She
Still Has a Lot of Work to Do on Image," *The (New Orleans, LA) Times-Picayune*,
November 23, 2005, p. 1.
[2] William Hersey, "Taft Nears Budget Victory – Tax Overhaul Left Mostly Intact by Senate,
House," *Dayton Daily News*, June 3, 2005, p. A1.

This idea drives one of the empirical hypotheses emerging from our model of policy bargaining in Chapter 2, but, of course, we are not original in positing a link between popularity and success. The link is drawn not only in political journalism but also in academic writings on presidents, the literature on governors, and even in the words of key players in state government themselves. In the national context, works by Ostrom and Simon (1985), Rivers and Rose (1985), and Brace and Hinckley (1992) find that popular presidents exert more influence over legislation. In the states, Beyle's (2004) widely used measure of gubernatorial power includes the governor's job approval as a key component of "personal power." Writing before such polling data were available, Lipson (1939, p. 60) argued that a governor's "powers could be enhanced by his personal force of character and by his influence in the party or among the people at large."

In our theoretical analysis, we lay out concrete reasons why popularity should help a governor. During elections, governors with higher approval ratings should be better at delivering money and votes to legislative allies and better positioned to work for the defeat of lawmakers who have opposed the governor's agenda. Similarly, these governors can more credibly threaten to veto bills that legislators favor, even if in doing so, they take political heat. The impact of popularity may even operate at a more subtle, psychological level. A California legislator who served during the administrations of four different governors, Patrick Johnston, tells us that "popularity matters because people who pass laws are hardwired to pay attention to public opinion. They have an instinctive interest in supporting a popular governor, or at least not publicly opposing him. [Popularity] dampens the will to fight."[3]

Yet, while there is reason to believe that political capital can pay dividends, the academic study of chief executives and the testimony of insiders alike also provide many reasons to doubt that chief executives can effectively translate their popularity into legislative achievements. National studies by Collier and Sullivan (1995), Covington and Kinney (1999), and Cohen et al. (2000) find little support for the idea that presidential popularity helps to sway congressional votes, while Edwards (1980), Bond and Fleisher (1990), and Canes-Wrone and de Marchi (2002) show that popularity only helps presidents move their agendas in specific circumstances. In the states, Ferguson (2003) finds no evidence that popular

---

3 Interview with former California assembly member and senator Pat Johnston, conducted by Thad Kousser in Sacramento, June 22, 2009.

governors are better able to move their legislative proposals, and Rosenthal (1990, p. 33) observes that "even if a governor is fortunate or skillful enough to build and maintain personal popularity, there is no guarantee that it will be converted into power in the legislature." The success of governors Blanco and Taft, despite very low levels of public approval, further casts doubt on the importance of popularity.

Does popularity determine the fate of a governor's agenda or only her political future? In part because it may work through complex, circuitous routes, testing the empirical link between executive popularity and legislative success is not straightforward. In Chapter 4, we present regression models showing that governors who had higher approval ratings when they delivered their State of the State addresses passed more of their policy bills, controlling for other measures of their power and the ambition of their proposals. But as we admitted, these tests were imperfect attempts at gauging the causal impact of popularity. Approval ratings may be "endogenous," potentially shaped by state political conditions and the actions of governors themselves. Approval ratings tend to fall when unemployment rises, are often lower in states with more professional legislatures, and can plummet when a governor takes extreme policy positions. This web of relationships may produce an apparent link between popularity and success when none is there or obscure a link that does in fact exist.

In this chapter, we look less broadly but more deeply at the effects of political capital. We take seriously the challenges to causal inference in testing this concept and trace out the causal path that may link approval ratings to policy victories. We use two events – Hurricane Katrina in the Gulf States and the "coingate" scandal that plagued Gov. Taft in Ohio – to study gubernatorial performance. For both, we match governors with control cases and measure the success of chief executives over time. Each of these case studies is designed to investigate the value of political capital by looking at how much governors get from legislatures before and after wide swings in their personal popularity, when these swings have nothing to do with the policies that they propose. We begin, in the next section, by explaining how a hurricane and a scandal can provide this useful research design.

Our two carefully chosen cases turn out to present an intriguing pattern. Statehouse journalists in both Louisiana and Ohio observed the same puzzling trend. They saw unpopular governors securing much of what they wanted from the legislature, after they had struggled to do so when they were popular. Their observations, quoted earlier, about the surprising relationship between popularity and executive achievement are seemingly confirmed by an initial analysis of the legislative success of these governors over time. In the second section of this chapter, we compute each governor's batting average in the legislature, just as the journalists did. We find that governors Blanco and Taft struggled to move their agendas when they were popular but that their success rose as their approval ratings fell. "'They predicted a total disaster, and it was a total success,' Blanco said at her session-closing news conference, pointing to a $1500 pay raise for teachers and passage of controversial bills that consolidate tax assessors, clerks of court and other New Orleans offices."[4] This does not fit with the conventional wisdom and in fact reverses it. It also appears to be inconsistent with the findings of our empirical analysis in Chapter 4.

This first glance at governors presents a puzzle. Is it the case that political capital does not work as currency in the states? Or, does a governor's popularity in fact matter, though in subtle ways that are hidden from statehouse journalists or an analysis that simply looks at batting averages? By looking more deeply at our cases, we show that high approval ratings can indeed help a governor move a policy agenda. But to uncover this power, we need to recognize that popularity can shape the scale of the agenda that governors propose in the first place. We focus on how public approval changed what these governors asked for in their State of the State addresses and how they attempted to package their proposals. These observations point our attention toward the strategic nature of the game – either the budget or the legislative game – that they choose to play, the scale of their agendas, the ideological directions in which they attempt to move, and the magnitude of the policy shifts that they propose. In short, it pushes us again to view governors as strategic actors who recognize when they may be strong or weak and pitch their proposals accordingly. Understanding this helps to answer the puzzle posed by Gov. Blanco's and Gov. Taft's surprising success and reveals both the hidden power and the perils of popularity.

6.1. What Hurricanes and Scandals Teach Us about Political Capital

What is the best way to pick case studies that teach reliable lessons about the impact of political capital? To explore the effects of a governor's popularity on her policy-making success, we need to look at cases in

---

[4] Jan Moller and Robert Travis Scott, "Blanco Declares Session a Success – Most of Her Agenda Cleared Legislature," *The (New Orleans, LA) Times-Picayune*, June 20, 2006, p. 1.

which a governor's approval ratings vary while other factors important to her success remain the same. We must hold all else equal, in the language of scientific inquiry. This will help ensure that the patterns we see in a governor's lawmaking success are due to her popularity rather than to the myriad other systematic and idiosyncratic factors that might be at work.

Keeping this in mind rules out several potential approaches to gauging the impact of political capital. For instance, it would not be wise to look at two states, one with a popular governor and one with an unpopular chief executive, and directly compare their success rates. Differential success might be due to any and all of the other differences between the states in the governing institutions, political dynamics, and economic conditions. Without a large number of cases and statistical controls (as we employed in Chapter 4), such state-to-state comparisons would be fraught with inferential danger. So, too, would be a governor-to-governor comparison within a state. Because each governor brings a distinct style of leadership, and because political times change, this sort of analysis would not isolate the impact of popularity. It might also be endangered by the endogenous nature of popularity, with approval ratings shifting in response to a governor's policy proposals. The right case study would identify an exogenous event that changes a governor's popularity, then examines success both before and after the event.

Hurricane Katrina brought horrendous human costs. But for political scientists, it also provides a natural experiment ideally suited to studying the impact of political capital. In the two Gulf States that would soon suffer the storm's worst wrath in September 2005, the two governors began the year in very different places.[5] When Louisiana's governor Kathleen Blanco delivered her April 25, 2005, State of the State address in Baton Rouge, she was still enjoying a long honeymoon after her election more than a year before. "Everyone's got an opinion on her, and it's usually positive," reported Loyola University's Ed Renwick, who conducted a poll on the governor for the *Baton Rouge Advocate*. "Blanco scored well regardless of the political party, race or gender of the respondents."[6] The trend in her popularity that Figure 6.1 tracks shows that Blanco remained well liked throughout spring and summer 2005, as Louisiana's

---

[5] It is also helpful to our research design that while these two governors began 2005 under different political circumstances, they each operated in similar institutional settings. Both Louisiana and Mississippi have part-time legislatures, and neither state implemented legislative term limits until Louisiana did so in 2007, after our period of study.

[6] Michelle Millhollon, "La. Voters Back Blanco in Poll," *The (Baton Rouge, LA) Advocate*, January 9, 2005.

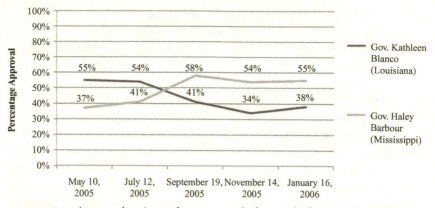

FIGURE 6.1. Approval ratings of governors, before and after Hurricane Katrina (September 1–5, 2005). *All polls conducted by Survey USA. Percentages report approval ratings among respondents with an opinion, with those voicing no opinion removed from the denominator.*

legislature considered her proposals while meeting in regular and special sessions.

Just to the west, in Mississippi, Gov. Haley Barbour's popularity had gone south. He had inherited a $709 million budget deficit after his 2003 election, trimmed it by cutting social services,[7] and seen his approval ratings plummet to below 40 percent. As the polls reported in Figure 6.1 clearly show, the struggling Barbour lagged far behind the soaring Blanco in the public's estimation.

Hurricane Katrina changed all that in a few short weeks. The storm devastated both states, wreaking destruction on Mississippi's low-lying coastal communities and on New Orleans's below-sea-level parishes. Each governor faced the same defining moment. In the eyes of their constituents, though, Barbour and Blanco performed differently. With his authoritative, direct manner during the hurricane and its immediate aftermath, Barbour earned comparisons to Mayor Rudolph Giuliani, whose response to the September 11 attacks is now the gold standard for political leadership in a time of crisis.[8] Blanco's name was not used in the same sentence as Giuliani's, except to highlight her shortcomings. She appeared shaken by the magnitude of catastrophe, missing the opportunity to be photographed wading into floodwaters or bringing immediate federal aid.

[7] Shaila Dewan, "In Mississippi, Soaring Costs Force Deep Medicaid Cuts," *New York Times,* July 2, 2005.
[8] Peggy Noonan, "After the Storm. Hurricane Katrina: The Good, The Bad, The Let's-Shoot-Them-Now," *Wall Street Journal,* September 1, 2005.

To be fair to Blanco, the challenges that Katrina posed for Louisiana's governor were more formidable than the tests confronting her Mississippi counterpart, and the political conditions less fortuitous. The loss of life in New Orleans was far greater. The city's anarchic drama that played out on national television for nearly a week highlighted the impotence of government in the face of cataclysmic disaster, while coverage of Mississippi depicted both devastation and response. Barbour also had a clearer path to the spotlight in which he performed so well. With no great metropolis, Mississippi provided no mayor to rival Gov. Barbour as the single leader in the state. He enjoyed a close relationship with President Bush, based on both their shared party affiliation and Barbour's role as the head of the Republican National Committee from 1993 to 1997. Blanco had none of Barbour's advantages in these areas; she was forced to sing an uneasy duet with New Orleans mayor Ray Nagin and often seemed out of tune with the Bush administration.

None of this was music to Louisiana voters' ears. Governor Blanco's approval ratings plummeted to 41 percent a few weeks after the storm, then to 34 percent by the middle of November. No longer popular with every type of voter, she lost support especially among blacks and residents of New Orleans.[9] Public opinion of Gov. Barbour moved in the opposite direction. His Giuliani-esque performance gained him 17 percentage points, as his approval rose to 58 percent by mid-September. It remained quite high even as his moment of poise in the face of destruction gave way to a messy winter of reconstruction. As Figure 6.1 clearly illustrates, after Hurricane Katrina, Barbour and Blanco traded places in the eyes of their respective publics.

This horrific disaster, then, provides an ideal opportunity for scholars to gauge the effects of popularity on a governor's ability to move a policy program. When they gave their 2005 State of the State addresses, Blanco had an overflowing account of capital on which to draw, while Barbour, with his 37 percent approval rating, was nearly bankrupt. By the time they gave their 2006 State of the States, Barbour was as rich in capital as Blanco was popularity poor. If a governor's public standing translates directly into legislative success, we should see their fortunes reverse in this arena as well. Governor Blanco's success in moving the policy proposals contained in her 2006 speech should have declined – compared with her record in 2005 – just as sharply as her popularity did, while Barbour's should rise along with his approval rating.

---

[9] Robert Travis, "Dive in Blanco's Popularity Reflected in Post-Storm Poll," *The (New Orleans, LA) Times-Picayune*, November 30, 2005.

The strength of this natural experiment lies in the clear link between Hurricane Katrina, an exogenous event sent quite literally by nature, and gubernatorial popularity. The direction of the causal arrow here is clear. Blanco did not become unpopular because of the ideologically extreme nature of her 2005 State of the State proposals. She was not being punished for failing to turn her 2005 proposals into enacted policy. Clearly and simply, she lost her capital because of her response to Katrina. Barbour won his with calm in the face of a terrible storm.

While each governor's performance during the Katrina might have revealed something about his or her mettle, the public perception of the governors' performaces was as much determined by the different circumstances that each governor faced during the hurricane as it was by his or her ability to govern. It is almost as if a medical researcher injected Barbour with a popularity booster shot, while extracting some of Blanco's popular appeal. We observe the same governors leading the same states, forced to deal with the same set of disaster-related issues. Only their popularity varies; *other features of the bargaining environment remain unchanged*. Because of this clean design, any resulting shift in their legislative success in 2006 can be attributed not to their past policy achievements or current ideological stances but to their approval ratings.

A second case study that allows us to test the effects of popularity took place in Ohio, where a series of scandals sent Gov. Bob Taft's approval ratings spiraling from a high of 68 percent in 2001 to some of the lowest levels in the history of gubernatorial polling by the close of the 2005 session. When he first came to office, Taft combined his family's venerable political tradition with a series of pragmatic, moderate policy stances to win wide popular acclaim. He rode high in the polls, won reelection in 2002, and then had to deal with the toll that the nation's economic slump took on Ohio. Taft's popularity began to fall in 2003 as he made unpopular choices, including backing what came to be known as the Taft tax, a decision that cost him support in his own party. "Perhaps the first sign of trouble for Ohio's governor was a 2003 Fourth of July rally with President Bush at Wright Patterson Air Force Base near Dayton. Mr. Taft was booed by an invitation-only, GOP-friendly crowd."[10] The initial slide in his popularity, because it was due to the nature of his policy proposals as well as the economic downtown, does not provide a clean natural experiment as does Hurricane Katrina.

[10] Jim Provance, "State Woes Reduce Taft to Political Punching Bag – Democrats, GOP Candidates Take Swings as Lame-Duck Steers Clear of Campaigning," *The (Toledo, OH) Blade*, November 5, 2006, p. B1.

The scandal that erupted in April 2005, however, is an event that was both independent of any of Taft's policy pronouncements and harshly damaging to his political capital. That month, the *Toledo Blade* broke a story that eventually led to the politically connected Tom Noe's conviction on 29 felony counts for stealing more than $2 million from the rare-coin funds he managed for the Ohio Bureau of Workers' Compensation. The muckracking investigations of Noe's links to prominent GOP office-holders soon embroiled Taft in the scandal and "derailed his legacy."[11] It became known that Taft had accepted 52 free golf outings and other gifts over the past four years that he had failed to disclose.[12] He played one of those rounds, in 2002, with Noe. In August 2005, Taft became the first governor to be convicted of a crime in Ohio when he pleaded no contest to failing to report the gifts and was fined $4,000. "He's always said that it was unintentional," Rickel, Taft's spokesperson, said. "He came forward, he fully disclosed, he admitted to his errors and accepted all the consequences."[13]

Voters punished Taft as well. Throughout spring and summer 2005, as the legislature considered the policy proposals that he had made that February, Taft's popularity plummeted, reaching an abysmal 19 percent in May. His popularity never recovered throughout the remainder of his tenure. These historically dismal levels left him very little political capital, setting up a clear expectation that his legislative productivity should follow the path of his popularity. To return to the medical analogy, if unpopularity is a pill, Taft took one dose (of his own making) in 2003 and was administered a double dose in 2005. To help gauge its effects, we need to find a similar governor who received the placebo.

Florida's governor Jeb Bush provides just such a comparison. A scion of another GOP dynasty, Bush was first elected the same year as Taft, 1998, to lead a populous, sprawling state. Like Taft, Bush worked with a legislature controlled by Republicans, and one with a similar level of legislative professionalism to Ohio's (Squire 2007). Both saw their states' economies expand, contract, and then expand again over the course of their tenures. The two governors shared much in common, except for Taft's roller-coaster popularity ride. As Figure 6.2 shows, Jeb Bush's

[11] Mike Wilkinson and Steve Eder, "Taft Urges Stiff Penalty in Noe Case – Governor Says He Won't Grant Coingate Pardons," *The (Toledo, OH) Blade*, November 15, 2006.
[12] Alan Johnson, "Taft's '05 Report Has No Free Golf on It," *The Columbus Dispatch*, April 18, 2006.
[13] Andrew Welsh-Huggins, "Ohio Supreme Court Reprimands Gov. Taft," *The Cincinnati Post*, December 28, 2006.

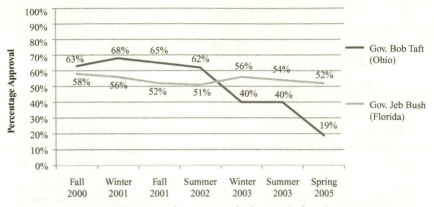

FIGURE 6.2. Approval ratings of governors, before and after the "coingate" scandal. *All polls taken from the U.S. Officials' Job Approval ratings website. Percentages report approval ratings among all respondents.*

approval remained remarkably steady from 2001 through 2005, consistently registering just above 50 percent. Because his level of popularity was constant, Gov. Bush's legislative record can serve as a baseline against which to judge Taft's. The Floridian's achievements may rise and fall because of economic circumstances, but their variation cannot be explained by Bush's popularity because it never varied. Bush took the placebo, and it is in comparison to his ability to move policy proposals through the legislature that the impact of Taft's popularity swings can best be gauged.

6.1.1. *A First Look at Gubernatorial Success: Batting Averages*

Using the Katrina natural experiment and the Ohio case study, we evaluate the effect of gubernatorial popularity on legislative achievement by first looking at the most basic metric of success: a governor's overall batting average. This measure takes all of the policy and budgetary proposals in a governor's State of the State address, traces their legislative histories, and records the percentage of items that eventually become law. Like the proposal-level database described in Chapter 4, this aggregate measure counts compromises as half a success. Unlike our regression analysis in Chapter 4, looking at batting averages does nothing to take into account the magnitude of these proposals, the ideological direction in which they seek to move the state, or even the total number of requests. A batting average does not tell the full story of gubernatorial achievement. Still, it provides an instructive first look at how a governor fared during a

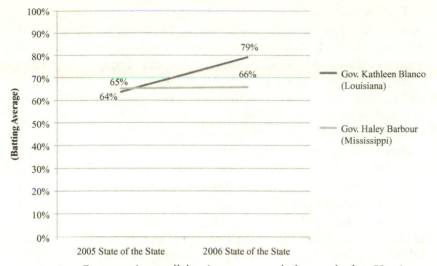

FIGURE 6.3. Governors' overall batting averages, before and after Hurricane Katrina.

legislative session, drawing on the same clear signs of success that state-house reporters often use when they evaluate governors. The batting averages displayed in Figures 6.3 and 6.4 tell the same story that journalists told about Kathleen Blanco's and Bob Taft's extraordinary accomplishments in the face of low approval ratings.

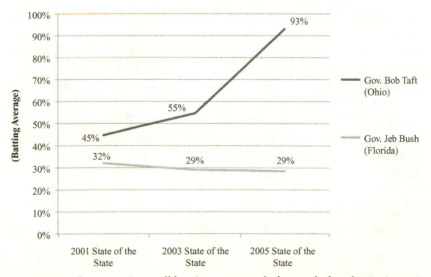

FIGURE 6.4. Governors' overall batting averages, before and after the "coingate" scandal.

First, consider the Gulf States before and after Hurricane Katrina. In spring 2005, when water levels were still low and Kathleen Blanco's popularity high, the Louisiana governor had only a partially successful legislative session. Measured by a simple batting average, she was able to secure 64 percent of the items that she proposed in her State of the State address. There were successes, to be sure, but also frustrating failures. She made a push for more education spending, but when the legislature sent her the final budget, her public reaction was; "Our teachers lost."[14] Governor Blanco had hoped to secure teachers raises averaging about $3,300, but the proposal, SCR 125, failed.[15] The *New Orleans Times-Picayune* summed up the session this way: "Gov. Kathleen Blanco came into the session pushing for a sizable teacher pay raise, a package of ethics reforms, a reduction in funding for nursing homes, several tax breaks for businesses and the elimination of fatty, sugary snacks on high school campuses. Legislators did pass an array of business tax breaks, but the ethics reforms died a quick death, nursing home owners managed to hold onto their oversized slice of the budget, and the snack food bill was weakened so much as to be meaningless."[16]

This mixed record, compounded with Blanco's popularity free fall in the wake of Katrina, seemed to set the stage for a difficult 2006 session. She gave that year's State of the State with her approval rating below 40 percent. The *Times-Picayune* opined that "for Blanco, the session was loaded with political significance. Ever since Katrina damaged her reputation on a national scale, and Time magazine last fall named her one of the three worst governors in the nation, she has been trying to rebuild her political fortunes."[17] Remarkably, she succeeded. Instead of declining along with her popularity, Blanco's batting average rose to 79 percent. Statehouse journalists noticed, reporting that "the Legislature ended a freewheeling three-month session Monday on a high note for Gov. Kathleen Blanco, who achieved nearly all her goals."[18] When Blanco's popularity fell, the simplest metric of her success rose.

By contrast, in Mississippi, Haley Barbour saw no significant post-Katrina bump in his legislative achievements. In early 2005, when Gov.

[14] Jan Moller, "Lawmakers Send Blanco $18.7 Billion Budget – 'Our Teachers Lost' Is Governor's Reaction," *The (New Orleans, LA) Times-Picayune*, June 24, 2005.
[15] "Lawmakers Clear Budget – $18.7 Billion Plan Heads to Blanco for Signing – What Passed – and Didn't," *The (Baton Rouge, LA) Advocate*, June 24, 2005.
[16] "Did Anything Happen?," *The (New Orleans, LA) Times-Picayune*, June 26, 2005.
[17] Jan Moller and Robert Travis, "Blanco Declares Session a Success – Most of Her Agenda Cleared Legislature," *The (New Orleans, LA) Times-Picayune*, June 20, 2006, p. 1.
[18] Ibid.

Barbour's popularity lagged far behind Gov. Blanco's, his batting average on State of the State proposals was actually a tick above hers. With his popularity at 37 percent, Barbour convinced the legislature to pass 65 percent of his proposals. This achievement did not come without its setbacks, exertions, and ultimate frustrations. Mississippi's three-month regular session went badly for the governor. The legislature did not settle on a budget, nor did it pass Momentum Mississippi, the governor's plan to attract service industries to the state and to invest in high-tech R&D efforts at universities.[19] It took four extraordinary sessions for the governor and legislature to complete their work. They agreed on a budget in the second extraordinary session, and passed Momentum Mississippi in the third, but the governor never convinced the legislature to back his six-part UpGrade Education Reform Act of 2005, the centerpiece of his agenda.[20]

By January 2006, when he began his first post-Katrina legislative session, Barbour's approval ratings had risen to 55 percent. This political capital appeared to lead to some clear successes. After the governor signed his appropriations bills, the *Jackson Clarion-Ledger* proclaimed that "there was reason to celebrate – $90.5 million added for universities, including 5-percent salary hikes; and two-year colleges getting a 12.2 percent boost – with Barbour the star of the show."[21] Yet, not everything went perfectly for the popular governor in the 2006 session. His proposals to free agencies from legislative restrictions and to give local governments the power to assess more fees on new development went nowhere, and his overall batting average was 66 percent. Governor Barbour had a successful session, to be sure, but his 2006 average was only one percentage point higher than the one he achieved when his popularity was in its pre-Katrina doldrums.

A first glance at Gov. Bob Taft's record in Ohio – in comparison to Jeb Bush's in Florida – again provides no evidence that governors can cash in their political capital for legislative success. For our analysis of Ohio, Florida serves as a control case. Governor Jeb Bush's popularity remained remarkably steady from 2001 to 2005, and, as Figure 6.4 shows, so did his record of legislative success. Bush recorded batting averages of 32 percent, 29 percent, and 29 percent as he clashed with fellow Republicans

[19] Andy Kanengiser, "Gov. Consults Lawmakers on Session," *The (Jackson, MS) Clarion-Ledger*, April 15, 2005.
[20] "Barbour Expands Session Agenda," *The (Biloxi, MS) Sun Herald*, April 15, 2005.
[21] Editorial, *The (Jackson, MS) Clarion-Ledger*, April 7, 2006.

in the legislature over contentious issues like class-size reduction, merit pay for teachers, and the adult prosecution of juvenile offenders.

In Ohio, Gov. Taft started out performing only slightly better than Gov. Bush, even though his popularity was sky-high. With an approval rating of 68 percent when he delivered his 2001 State of the State address, Taft seemed primed for success with the legislature. Yet he was only able to convince his fellow Republican lawmakers to move 45 percent of his agenda. To wrap up the legislative session, the *Toledo Blade* wrote an article titled "Clashes between Taft, Lawmakers Typify Turbulent Year in State Capital." The article quoted a legislative leader (Senate President Doug White), who characterized the record of mixed success in more colorful language: "We did some very excellent work under adverse conditions.... Moving 20 yards in a blizzard to go after a freezing calf can be better than a mile on a sunny day to do much less."[22]

By 2005, after the coingate scandal broke, Taft's 19 percent approval rating certainly portended gloomy days for his agenda. But somehow, Gov. Taft recorded one of the highest batting averages of any governor we analyzed. The legislature passed 93 percent of his proposals, including a major tax overhaul. This surprised, but did not shock, one Columbus insider. "'There's a certain irony to it," said former Dayton-area state representative J. Donald Mottley, a lobbyist and tax policy expert. It says a lot about him and about the current leadership in the General Assembly. He's very steady. He may not be the most colorful political official out there. He may not be the most articulate. He is very capable. He is focused."[23]

6.2. Why Popularity Shapes Both Agendas and Success

Can focus and steadiness really override charisma and popular sentiment in determining the success of a governor's legislative agenda? Put another way, does political capital have any currency inside a statehouse? The lesson from a first glance at batting averages would seem to be that personal popularity has little impact on gubernatorial success and that our regression results may have falsely concluded that popularity is a key determinant of executive success. Looking more deeply into our records of executive–legislative interactions – and considering the strategic nature

---

[22] Jim Provance, "Clashes between Taft, Lawmakers Typify Turbulent Year in State Capital," *The (Toledo, OH) Blade*, December 28, 2003.
[23] William Hershey, "Taft Nears Budget Victory – Tax Code Overhaul Left Mostly Intact by Senate, House," *Dayton Daily News*, Friday, June 3, 2005.

of these negotiations (particularly over policy items) – reveals a subtler story and a different conclusion. Approval ratings do not merely exert an effect on the success of a gubernatorial policy proposal; they cause governors to make different types of proposals.

This dynamic has important implications for analyzing executive success broadly. Looking at an overall batting average will not tell the whole story of a legislative session. First, we need to focus on the portion of the agenda that ought to be most affected by the governor's strategic situation – her policy proposals. Second, we must gauge how ambitious the policy agenda is: how many items are included, how fundamentally would they shift state policy, and in which ideological directions. Before revisiting these measurement issues, though, we review our argument that gubernatorial popularity shapes both what a governor asks for in the policy game and what she gets.

Why should a governor's popularity shape her policy agenda? Before governors deliver a State of the State address, they anticipate how receptive legislators might be to their policy proposals. In Rosenthal's (1990, p. 41) words, "the measures presented by governors may be tailored to fit whatever they think the legislature will accept." Governors craft agendas that stay true to their principles and personal priorities but also include nods to legislative sentiment. Realizing that politics is the art of the possible, savvy governors consider what legislators want as well and take stock of how strong their own bargaining position will be. When a governor is possessed of the full arsenal of executive powers – public popularity, a strong item veto, unified government – that governor can afford to aim high. Governors who lack these advantages must pitch their proposals more modestly, asking for bills that legislators are amenable to passing.

Popularity, in particular, should shape the breadth and ambition of a governor's policy agenda. A chief executive who can speak loudly from the bully pulpit knows that she can use public pressure to persuade legislators to work with her. She feels she can ask for what she wants, then rely on her public standing to coax reluctant legislators into passing her proposals. Indeed, she may even ask for too much. Though our model assumes that governors are rational actors who are perfectly informed about what a legislature will accept, they are, of course, human. Some will make mistakes, overestimating their own power and overshooting with their demands. Our model does not predict that strong, popular governors will fail to pass any of their policy proposals (unless they place huge value on taking sincere positions), but if they do fall off the equilibrium path, they may do so by asking for big policy shifts. Simply put, a popular governor is at risk of proposing an overly ambitious agenda.

By contrast, an unpopular governor foresees an uphill battle with the legislature and reacts accordingly. Instead of delivering a wish list, her policy agenda should include ideas vetted with legislators or designed to curry their favor. With low approval ratings, she knows that securing final passage will be a challenge and cannot take it for granted that the bills she desires will even be introduced or granted hearings. She will have to scale back her aspirations simply to bring the legislature to the bargaining table. This is different from budget negations where lawmakers must come to the bargaining table regardless of the type of proposals offered by the governor.

In our general theoretical model of policy negotiations, governors who can afford to make larger side payments (S) can propose bigger policy shifts. This pattern is not repeated always and everywhere, as we saw in Chapter 3, because the link between popularity and the spatial location of a governor's proposal depends on a number of factors, including the policy preferences of each player, the value that governors place on taking public positions, and their armory of other powers. These factors are hard to measure in large data sets. In our case studies, though, these factors are by and large held constant. As a result, the strategic dynamics that we have just described should produce a clear empirical pattern: the policy agendas of popular governors should be more ambitious than those of unpopular executives. This difference may take many forms.

First and most simply, popular governors should have the power to devote more of their State of the State to policy, rather than budgetary, items. Recall that the institutional arrangements of state government give chief executives, regardless of their political clout, significant influence over the state budget. In policy negotiations, where legislatures possess the institutional advantage, governors must earn their bargaining power though things like high approval ratings. Unpopular governors will retreat from playing the policy game, where they are at a natural disadvantage. They will shift their agendas toward items that let them play the budgetary staring match, which puts them on more equal footing. Popular governors, by contrast, can afford to ask for policy bills.

Second, popular governors should, all else being equal, propose more policy items in their State of the State addresses. With more political capital to spend, they can spread their efforts across many legislative items and still hope for success in each. In our formal policy model, every idea that they float requires them to ante up a chit of value S from their account of political capital, and popularity can boost the size of this account. Third, their proposals can be a closer match to their own ideologies rather than the ideologies of the most influential members of the legislature. Governors who lack personal popularity will have to ask for policies that are popular with the legislature. Those with high approval ratings can push proposals that more closely reflect their preferences. Fourth and finally, popular governors can be expected to float bigger ideas, anticipating that their approval ratings can provide the momentum to move policies of a greater scale. These predictions about our cases can be summarized as follows:

Hypothesis 6.1: As a governor's approval ratings increase, she will devote a larger share of the proposals in her State of the State address to policy rather than budgetary items.

Hypothesis 6.2: As a governor's approval ratings increase, she will make a larger number of policy proposals in her State of the State address.

Hypothesis 6.3: As a governor's approval ratings increase, she will propose policy items that more closely match her own, rather than the legislature's, preferences.

Hypothesis 6.4: As a governor's approval ratings increase, she will propose policy items that seek a greater magnitude of policy change.

Of course, not all chief executives will spend their political capital in the same way. Some might decide to pursue policy proposals that are larger in scale or that more closely reflect their ideology, while others might simply ask for more bills but keep the ideological tilt or the scale of their requests unchanged. Thus, we prefer to think of Hypotheses 6.1–6.4 as a menu from which popular governors can choose. Some will undoubtedly order everything off the menu, while others will be more cautious. Regardless of which menu items a governor chooses, the overall or aggregate ambitiousness of her policy agenda should grow as she becomes more popular (and, conversely, it should decline as her political capital wanes).

Thus, we assert that governors shape their public agendas to fit their strategic situations, and then use whatever leverage they have to move that agenda. With an enhanced power to reward cooperative lawmakers, popular governors should be more successful than their unpopular counterparts, holding constant the nature of their proposals. Applying our theoretical model to these case studies produces an explanation to the puzzle that began this chapter. Popular governors will propose larger, more ambitious agendas. Though their rate of success moving the more

174 The Power of American Governors

ambitious items on this agenda may be no higher, they will in sum achieve
more and owe their achievement to their popularity.

6.3. A Closer Look at Gubernatorial Success: Agendas and Weighted Success

On the basis of this view of the subtle link between a governor's public
popularity and her success – as a two-stage process that leads first to
agendas and then to accomplishments – we reevaluate the records of the
chief executives in our case study states. In doing so, we uncover the power
of popularity that was hidden in a first glance at overall batting averages.
In the following, we present a new set of quantifications designed to
test our hypotheses. We focus on governors' policy agendas, charting the
number of policy proposals included in the State of the State address,
the ideological direction of these items, and their magnitude or potential
impact. To hold constant the nature of proposals, we look for instances
of repeated agenda items and special sessions with similar topics.

6.3.1. Hurricane Katrina Natural Experiment

We begin by revisiting the Gulf States before and after Hurricane Katrina.
As our initial analysis showed, Gov. Kathleen Blanco seemed to get more
out of the legislature after her popularity plummeted, while the rise in
Gov. Haley Barbour's approval ratings led to no discernable boost in his
legislative success. A second look at their records amends this story. Katrina changed not only the governors' popularity but the ambition of their
agendas as well. First and most apparent is the fact that these governors
chose to play the policy game when they expected their popularity to
give them leverage but retreated to the safer ground of the budget when
they could no longer rely on their public images to sway reluctant lawmakers. After his response to Katrina had won him rave reviews, Gov.
Haley Barbour devoted 84 percent of his 2006 State of the State agenda
to policy proposals and only 16 percent to budget items. This was a significant shift from the composition of his agenda when he had been less
popular in 2005 and pitched only 56 percent of his ideas as policy bills
and 44 percent through the budget process. Correspondingly, when her
popularity declined, Gov. Kathleen Blanco dedicated a larger share of her
agenda to fiscal items. In 2005, when she was popular, 68 percent of the
proposals in her State of the State were for policy bills, but that share
declined to 58 percent as her approval ratings fell in 2006. This is consistent with Hypothesis 6.1's prediction that unpopular governors shift

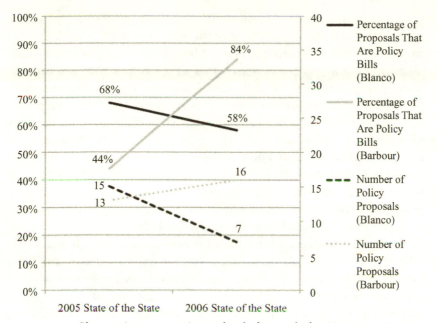

FIGURE 6.5. Changes in governors' agendas, before and after Hurricane Katrina.

their agendas toward the budget process, in which they hold a stronger bargaining position, when low approval ratings weaken them politically.

There is also support for our contention, made in Hypothesis 6.2, that higher popularity increases the number of proposals in each governor's policy agenda. When she was quite popular, in 2005, Gov. Blanco made 15 discrete policy proposals. After her approval sank by 2006, Blanco narrowed the focus of her State of the State to a mere seven policy items. With dwindling political capital, she could invest more of her energy and persuasive power in each proposal. One might argue that this winnowing was simply a reaction to the policy challenges posed by Hurricane Katrina – that mass devastation ruled out a wide-ranging agenda and necessitated focus. Governor Barbour's record in Mississippi shows that this was not the case. As he became more popular, Barbour expanded his policy agenda from 13 items in 2005 to 16 in 2006, scaling up his aspirations. Figure 6.5 summarizes these changes, illustrating the support that our Katrina case study provides for Hypotheses 6.1 and 6.4.

A close look at the potential policy impact and ideological direction of executive proposals reveals more evidence that popularity matters. So far in this chapter, every measure that we have used gives equal weight to each proposal that a governor puts forward. This makes some sense (in a limited way) because these are the agenda items deemed important enough to merit mention in a State of the State address. Yet, it is apparent to anyone who reads through these addresses and their journalistic coverage that not all proposals are created equal. A governor can propose major policy changes (such as the creation of new regional organizations to deliver public services like water) or big spending shifts (such as a 7.1% increase in the K–12 education budget), as Haley Barbour did after his popularity rose in 2006, or a governor may push for more modest changes, such as hiring an additional 50 state troopers or targeting meth use by making it more difficult to purchase pseudophedrine, as Barbour did in 2005, when he was less popular. Distinguishing between these qualitatively different types of proposals is critical to uncovering trends in gubernatorial agendas that are otherwise obscured.

To tell the difference between governors who aim high and those who play it safe, we rely on the same sorts of expert judgments that we introduced in Chapter 3. We gave each expert descriptions of a set of proposals, from a variety of State of the State addresses, with state names redacted and with dollar figures put into per capita terms. The experts were asked to code the potential policy impact of each proposal on a 5-point scale, with a 1 signifying that it would have a minor policy impact if it were enacted and a 5 identifying the sort of change that would be highly consequential.

Though our coders spotted few landmarks, they were able to make qualitative distinctions between the magnitudes of the proposals. They also gauged the ideological direction of each agenda item using a 3-point scale. They designated as liberal (−1) the proposals aimed at moving policy in a leftward direction ("for example, environmental regulations, expansion of social services, or strengthening abortion rights," according to the coding instructions we issued). Bills that moved policy to the right in these areas they dubbed as conservative (1), and they placed ideologically neutral (0) bills into a middle category. Our coders – Ethan Rarick, a former statehouse reporter from Oregon; Gary Hart, the former state senator from California who later served as the governor's education secretary; Paul Schuler, a former statehouse reporter from North Carolina; Prof. Alan Rosenthal of Rutgers; and former California director of finance Tim Gage – each coded approximately 36 proposals. We also judged these items ourselves, as a check on the reliability of these figures across independent coders, though in all of the analyses that we report here, we rely exclusively on the judgments made by our panel of experts.

The measures proved quite reliable,[24] allowing us to quantify the sorts of qualitative differences between proposals that would be obvious to the legislators who sit as the audience for State of the State addresses. The experts scored as a 4 two of the ambitious proposals that Haley Barbour made in his 2006 address: the proposal for new regional service delivery organizations (which eventually passed as a compromise in the form of SB 2943)[25] and the dramatic education spending increase (which passed in full as SB 2604).[26] They judged the service reorganization to be an ideologically neutral proposal and the increase in school expenditures as a liberal one. By contrast, the experts assigned only a 2 to the meth control proposal (an conservative law and order idea which passed as HB 607)[27] and a 1 to the state trooper increase (an ideologically neutral proposal which was included in the final budget), both of which were proposed by Gov. Barbour in 2005.

With these richer measures in hand, we can summarize the magnitude and ideological direction of all the legislative proposals in each State of the State address. Hypothesis 6.4 predicts that governors ask for bigger policy shifts when they are popular. This certainly appears to be the case in Louisiana. In 2005, when Kathleen Blanco's approval ratings were high, her State of the State called for significant policy changes. We have already seen that it contained a large number (15) of policy proposals. The expert codings reveal that six of these proposals scored a 3 or higher, including proposals to redesign all high schools to decrease

---

[24] The expert panel's judgments do in fact line up quite closely with the scores that we gave. On the 5-point policy impact scale, the score that the experts assigned to a proposal matched exactly with the score that we assigned for 70 of the 180 proposals. These scores were within one point of each other – for instance, an expert coded a proposal as a 3 when we scored it as a 2, or vice versa – for 166 of the 180 proposals. Rarely did we disagree much with the independent experts, increasing our confidence in this measure. On the 3-point ideology scale, our author scores matched exactly with the expert scores on 113 of the 180 proposals, and the correlation between the two sets of scores was 0.63, a correlation so strong that it would be observed by chance alone in fewer than 5 out of 100 cases.

[25] Barbour signed the compromise bill on this critical item in his agenda, according news reports. "Gov. Haley Barbour, who helped secure the funding in Washington, pushed for a regional wastewater authority, but county supervisors feared loss of control over development to a regional board. The bill passed Tuesday is a compromise representing weeks of haggling in Jackson. 'We need this badly,' said Rep. Roger Ishee, R-Gulfport. 'We need to get pipes in the ground.'" Geoff Pender, "Regional Water Board Passes, Bill Took Weeks of Haggling," *Sun Herald (Biloxi, MS)*, March 29, 2006, p. A3.

[26] Nancy Kaffer, "Bill Signing Relieves Local Educators," *Hattiesburg (MS) American*, March 28, 2006.

[27] "Lawmakers Have Passed Key Reforms," *Hattiesburg (MS) American*, April 2, 2005.

dropout rates, to pursue major industries to invest in the state, and to amend the constitution to funnel significant federal funds toward coastal erosion prevention projects. Overall, the impact scores for her policy proposals averaged 2.3. That average declined to 2.0 when Gov. Blanco's popularity plummeted by the next year, even as she cut to seven the number of proposals included in her agenda. These ideas – which included reducing the number of property assessors in New Orleans from seven to one – scored mostly 1s and 2s with our panel of experts. Quite sensibly, Gov. Blanco pushed for more modest agenda items after the ordeal of Katrina left her political capital greatly diminished. Indeed, the total scale of her policy agenda – calculated by multiplying the number of proposals by their average scale – dropped from 34 in 2005 to a quite modest 14 in 2006.

After her popularity fell, Gov. Blanco also asked for policy items more closely in line with the ideology of key legislators, providing support for Hypothesis 6.3. A relatively centrist governor working with a strongly Democratic legislature with many liberal representatives from New Orleans, Blanco shifted toward the Left when her popular approval shrank. According to our experts, the average ideological score of her proposals moved from −0.1 (almost neutral) in 2005 to −0.3 (leaning Left) the next year. Governor Blanco shifted from proposing an agenda with centrist goals, such as job creation and legislative ethics, when she was popular to one that contained more government service expansions. She appeared to be pitching ideas that would find an ideologically receptive audience in the legislature and that would appeal to her political base in New Orleans.

At the same time, in Mississippi, Haley Barbour's growing popularity was freeing him to move away from the ideological leanings of key lawmakers and pursue a more moderate agenda. The legislature, with a Republican upper house and a lower house controlled by Deep South Democrats, was dominated by conservative lawmakers. When Gov. Barbour was unpopular in 2005, his policy proposals averaged a conservative 0.5 on our scale. After his popularity skyrocketed in 2006, he shifted to the center by proposing legislation that averaged a nearly neutral 0.1. We find more modest evidence when it comes to the total scale of Barbour's policy agenda, which rose only slightly, from 34 to 39 points, after he became popular. This increase is due to a jump in the number of policy items included in his post-Katrina State of the State address, as opposed to a growth in the average of scale or impact of his proposals. Overall, the record from Louisiana and Mississippi provides support for our argument that governors make a strategic calculation about what they might get out of a legislature, and ask accordingly. As expected, popular governors forward more ambitious agendas.

The next crucial question, of course, is whether popularity helps them get what they ask for. We have learned that to answer this question, we must be cognizant of the strategic nature of governors' agendas and recognize that some legislative victories count for more than others.

One way to find out whether governors can turn political capital into policy influence is to ask whether a popular governor does better than an unpopular governor when asking for essentially the same things. Fortunately, we have the opportunity to make this comparison in Mississippi by looking at Haley Barbour's success when he made the same set of education proposals two years in a row. A major thrust of Barbour's 2005 State of the State was the UpGrade Education Reform Act of 2005, a six-point plan that, in the governor's words, "focuses on the classroom and puts teachers first."[28] Included in Barbour's reform were proposals to "link teacher pay raises to student performance, redesign high schools, and privatize non-education functions."[29] Yet, that spring, House negotiators rejected the governor's plan. The reform package, contained in Senate Bill 2504, died in conference committee at the end of the Regular Session, and the governor, though he criticized legislators for killing it,[30] declined to put it on the agenda of any of the four Extraordinary Sessions called that year before Katrina.

Perhaps the unpopular Barbour feared that he did not have the clout to convince the conference committee to release his bill. After his approval rose sharply in 2006, Gov. Barbour again made the package central to his State of the State address. This time, he succeeded in securing from the legislature two of its biggest items – performance pay for teachers (SB 2602) and a law that allowed high school seniors to take classes for both high school and college credit (HB 1130). It is possible that his success was simply because he had another year to try harder. But it is also likely that when Barbour convinced legislators to pass in 2006 two proposals that they had killed in 2005, he was flexing the newfound power of his popularity.

---

[28] 2005 Mississippi State of the State address delivered by Gov. Haley Barbour in Jackson, MS, on January 11, 2005.

[29] Laura Hipp, "House Panel Nixes Barbour's Upgrade School Reforms Plan," *The (Jackson, MS) Clarion-Ledger*, March 29, 2005.

[30] Goeff Pender, "Budget Haggling Deadline Extended – Lawmakers Add One Day," *The (Biloxi, MS) Sun Herald*, March 29, 2005, p. A1.

Another opportunity to evaluate the relative effectiveness of popular and unpopular governors in moving similar agendas comes from the Extraordinary Sessions that each Gulf State held in the immediate wake of Hurricane Katrina. Convened hastily after the storm, these sessions were aimed entirely at disaster relief and economic recovery. Because of this, the agendas laid out by the two governors had very similar content. Governor Barbour's "call" for Mississippi's 5th Extraordinary Session (convened on September 27, 2005) asked for items such as an emergency aid program for local governments, authorization for state agencies to purchase business property insurance for their buildings, and personal income tax exemptions for disaster relief payments. Governor Blanco's call for Louisiana's 1st Extraordinary Session (convened on November 6, 2005) asked for a statewide sales tax holiday, the creation of new local levee districts, and the establishment of an interest-bearing escrow account for homeowners' insurance settlements. Faced with similar challenges, the governors requested similar solutions.

Yet, they issued their calls under very different political circumstances, with Barbour's popularity already rising and Blanco's already falling. How did each governor fare, compared with his or her past performance working with his or her state's legislators? Using the same approach that we take to track State of the State success, we plumbed journalistic and legislative archives to find out how many of the items issued in each governor's call passed, or yielded a compromise, during the session. In a sign that popularity matters when agendas are held equal, Gov. Barbour received 81 percent of what he asked for, whereas Gov. Blanco won on 72 percent of her proposals. Both did better than they had in their 2005 State of the State addresses, perhaps because the crisis of Katrina made legislators more receptive. Still, the rise in Gov. Barbour's performance from that prehurricane speech to this postdisaster session was steeper, at 15 versus 9 percentage points. When they set out to meet the same policy challenges, the more popular governor did somewhat better.

Looking at the types of proposals on which popular governors did better in regular sessions also allows us to test one of the specific predictions derived from our policy and budget games in Chapter 2. According to these models, popularity should help governors convince legislators to pass their policy proposals but should be of little help in budget battles because the executive branch is already in a position of relative strength in these staring matches. Governor Barbour's record in Mississippi fits with this pattern. He was consistently powerful in budget negotiations, securing a full pass on 8 of his 10 budget proposals in 2005 (while reaching compromises on the other 2) and passing all three fiscal items in 2006. It was in his policy success that his rise in popularity paid clear dividends. He passed 6 of the 13 policy items in his 2005 State of the State, but his success rate rose to 9 full passes and 1 compromise out of 16 proposals when his popularity increased in 2006. The pattern in Louisiana is more complicated. Remember that Kathleen Blanco's raw batting averages rose even when her popularity fell in 2006. Perhaps this was a result of the need to pass proposals responding to Katrina, combined with the narrowing and shifting of her agenda that we just noted. In this case, if her batting average turned upward for other reasons, we would expect a slower growth, at least, in her policy average if it were hampered by her poor approval ratings in 2006. This is what we observe, with her policy batting average rising only from 73 to 78 percent, whereas her budget batting average rose from 43 to 80 percent.

To sum up all these complex dynamics, we use a single metric that captures a governor's performance more fully than a simple batting average. The impact score that we introduced in Chapter 4 counts the total number of gubernatorial proposals that the legislature passes, weighted by their policy impact and whether or not the governor was forced to compromise. To summarize its policy impact, if a proposal was coded as a 3 by our expert coders, full passage contributes 3 points to the governor's impact score. If the governor agrees to sign a compromise measure offered by the legislature, this counts for half of the proposal's magnitude (or 1.5 points in the case of a proposal with a magnitude of 3). Because there is no denominator that divides accomplishments by the number of proposals, governors are not penalized for pursuing lengthy agendas. This summary measure gives governors points for each of their accomplishments, with a higher score coming when they win bigger and more complete victories.

Looking at the policy impact scores of Gulf State governors before and after Katrina yields a very different picture than we saw by glancing at their batting averages. Importantly, the trends in Figure 6.6 – which give a more complete illustration of the impact of popularity – come much closer to following the patterns in each governor's approval ratings. Even though her batting average rose after Katrina, Blanco's impact score plummeted from a 26 before the storm to an 11.5 afterward, a decline of well over 50 percent. When Blanco was popular, she was able to secure the adoption of more and bigger policy items, and this score reflects it. Governor Barbour was also more successful when he had a greater store of political

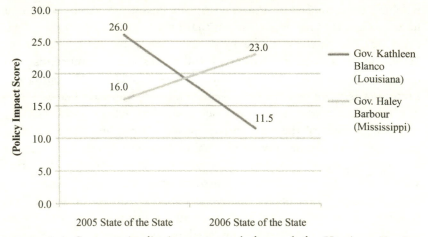

FIGURE 6.6. Governors' policy impact scores before and after Hurricane Katrina.

capital. Though his batting average was nearly identical in 2005 and 2006, his impact score grew by 7 points (over 40%) in the legislative session following Katrina. The importance of political capital is also underscored by the fact that Gov. Barbour was only able to successfully shepherd his UpGrade Education reforms through the legislature after his popularity grew.

6.3.2. Ohio's Coingate Scandal

Applying these new measures to the record of Republican governor Bob Taft of Ohio again demonstrates the power of popularity. How did Taft's overall batting average continue to increase as his approval sank lower and lower? Our first glance suggested that becoming one of the least popular governors in history helped Gov. Taft become one of the most successful at getting what he wanted out of the legislature. As Figure 6.4 showed, Taft's overall batting average rose dramatically from 2001 to 2003 to 2005, while Jeb Bush's in our control state of Florida remained steadily low as his popularity remained stable. It was in late 2005, after his public standing was hugely damaged by the coingate scandal, that Taft scored some of his most important successes. Political scientist John Green, assessing Taft's legacy in the press, said that "history will be kinder to Mr. Taft than immediate popularity polls." Green commented that "the governor's role in overhauling the state's tax system, the Ohio Reads tutoring program, the Third Frontier bond issue for high-tech research, and construction of new Ohio schools will get high marks when examined through a rear-view mirror."[31]

While these were indeed important accomplishments, looking more closely at what Taft was able to do when he was still quite popular in 2001 – and how he shifted strategies as his approval began to fall – shows that his popularity was not irrelevant to his legislative fortunes. In 2001, Taft had great success with his policy proposals, passing eight of his nine proposals in full and signing a compromise bill for the ninth. His overall batting average, which was a modest 45 percent, only suffered because this moderate Republican governor's budget called for many large, expensive, and arguably liberal items. Spending proposals made through his State of the State included things like expanding full-day kindergarten to cover 12,000 more children and spending more on schools, colleges, in-home services for the elderly, and residents with developmental disabilities. The state's Republican legislature – the seventh most professional according to Squire (2007) – had the patience to stand up to the governor on many of these fiscal items. Reflecting on the budget battles of 2001, Taft recalled that "Speaker Larry Householder brought in a more conservative caucus. I don't think they were too excited about the money that I proposed spending.... They said that after I gave the State of the State, the Republicans would look at each other and say 'Who's going to give the Republican response?'"[32] Though Taft was able to leverage his popularity into numerous successes in the policy game, his political capital meant little in budget negotiations, where patient lawmakers had the power to reject much of his center-left fiscal agenda.

As Gov. Taft's popularity eroded, his policy agenda become notably less ambitious. At the height of his popularity, the governor's State of the State address included nine policy proposals, with a total scale of 23 points. In 2003, faced with a weaker economy and eroding public support (his approval rating had fallen 25 points since 2001), Taft included only one policy item in his State of the State address, for a total scale of 2 points, the least ambitious policy agenda of any governor in our data. This lone proposal was a request that lawmakers place a $500 million bond measure on the state ballot to partially fund Taft's Third Frontier program, an initiative designed to draw high-tech industries and jobs to

---

[31] Jim Provance, "State Woes Reduce Taft to Political Punching Bag – Democrats, GOP Candidates Take Swings as Lame-Duck Steers Clear of Campaigning," *The (Toledo, OH) Blade*, November 5, 2006, p. B1.

[32] Interview with Governor Bob Taft, conducted by telephone by Thad Kousser and Justin Phillips, October 1, 2009.

Ohio. Using what remained of his political capital, the governor was able to successfully shepherd his proposal through the legislature, securing a 100 percent batting average for his very limited policy agenda. Unfortunately for the governor, his falling popularity proved to be an albatross around the neck of his bond measure, and voters narrowly rejected the proposal in the following election.

In 2005, after the coingate scandal and facing even lower levels of public approval, the governor again proposed a modest policy agenda. This time he included only five policy items in his State of the State address, for a total scale of 15 points. Though this was clearly a more ambitious agenda than Taft had proposed in 2003, it is still notably less than what he had requested at the height of his popularity. Again, focusing on a smaller number of items seemed to pay dividends. Taft was dealt only one failure and managed to secure a full pass on each of his remaining four proposals.

Although Gov. Taft scaled back his policy agenda in response to his declining popularity, we see little evidence that he did so in the budgetary arena. In 2003, for example, the governor's State of the State address included as many fiscal proposals – 20 – as were in his 2001 agenda. Though he cut back somewhat in 2005, he still offered twice as many budget items as policy proposals. The one change that we observe in Taft's fiscal agenda is that it became more conservative once his popularity began to decline. On our ideological scale, the governor's 2001 budget agenda averaged a relatively liberal −0.4, while his 2003 and 2005 agendas were more moderate, averaging −0.1 and 0.1, respectively. Though we did not anticipate this type of change (given our expectation that governors do not need to be strategic when it comes to budgeting), Taft was bargaining with a legislature that was unlikely to support liberal fiscal proposals and that could afford to be very patient in budget negotiations. This shift led to increased success in the budget negotiations, where his batting average rose from 25 percent in 2001 to 53 percent in 2003 and, finally, to 100 percent in 2005 (the year in which he had the most conservative fiscal agenda).

Taft's own judgment about the nature of his budget proposals – and the link between their ideological composition and his ultimate success – comports with what our coders found and suggests an intentional strategy. "There were three important factors behind our success in 2005," he told us in an interview. "We had a more experienced team, better relationships with legislative leaders, and did better groundwork. But it was also that the tax reform package was pretty appealing from the standpoint of the legislature. Big new spending initiatives probably would not have been well received."[33] Looking at the substance of his 2005 budget proposals, one can see why the Republican majority in the legislature liked them. Taft's proposals included four tax cuts, three Medicaid cuts, and a higher education tuition cap.

It is clear that Gov. Taft, despite his declining political capital, was able to keep his overall batting average up by reducing the number of policy proposals in his public agenda, focusing on the budget game, and shifting his fiscal agenda to the right. These patterns confirm two of our four hypotheses. What we do not observe, however, is evidence that Taft responded to his declining popularity by shifting the ideological direction of his policy agenda or by offering proposals that would, if adopted, have a more modest impact on the status quo. The average magnitude of Taft's policy proposals was 2.6 in 2001 and increased slightly to 3.0 by 2005. A similar pattern is evident when it comes to the average ideological direction of Taft's policy proposals, which moved from a fairly liberal −0.3 in 2001 to a slightly more liberal −0.4 in 2005. That we do not find the same patterns we observed in our analyses of governors Blanco and Barbour highlights the fact that there is no single path governors take when they need to reduce the ambitiousness of their agendas in response to dwindling political capital. Governor Taft scaled back his policy agenda by asking for fewer items but kept the overall ideological title of his policy proposals constant and continued to ask for items that represented significant departures from the status quo.

The governor's high batting average, however, masks a clear decline in his policy influence. At the height of his popularity, Taft's policy impact score was a relatively high 19.5. By 2003, that number fell to 2, though arguably, the governor's impact should be scored as 0 because voters ultimately rejected the bond measure that constituted the governor's lone policy accomplishment. For the 2005 legislative session, Taft's impact score improved to 13, an impressive performance given the governor's staggeringly low approval rating. Recall that by 2005, only 19 percent of survey respondents told pollsters that they approved of the job Taft was doing as governor. Although Taft's success in 2005 was certainly a testament to his political skills, his impact score still remained 33 percent below what he had achieved when he enjoyed a much greater store of political capital.

Can the patterns that we observed in Taft's agenda and policy accomplishments be explained by the demands of the time? The answer to this question appears to be no. None of these patterns are present in the

[33] Ibid.

State of the State addresses of Gov. Jeb Bush, whose popularity remained constant from 2001 through 2005, as did his overall batting average. If anything, Gov. Bush's policy agenda became more ambitious, particularly over the years when Taft cut his agenda the deepest. From 2001 to 2003, Bush tripled (from three to nine) the number of policy proposals in his State of the State and notably increased their average scale (from 1.7 to 2.6). The governor's policy agenda during the 2005 legislative session was equally as ambitious as in his 2003 agenda. Additionally, unlike Taft, Gov. Bush did not see a decline in his overall policy impact score. Indeed, Bush did better in both 2003 and 2005 than he did in 2001.

6.4. Lessons from a Hurricane and a Scandal

Looking in depth at just a few governors in carefully chosen states allows us to uncover patterns in their legislative records that we might otherwise miss. At first glance, these chief executives appear to be harmed by popularity, as they pass a smaller percentage of their State of the State proposals when their approval ratings are high. Moving beyond simple batting averages, however, reveals a more complex pattern. Quite clearly, governors act strategically by changing what they ask for when their popularity shifts. As anticipated by our bargaining models, this strategic behavior is most prevalent when it comes to a governor's policy agenda. When their public image is strong, ambition leads governors to issue more policy proposals, to ask for bigger changes to status quo policy, to push for bills that more closely reflect their own governing philosophies rather than those of key lawmakers, and to pitch more policy bills rather than simply retreating to the budget process. Popular governors take risks, banking on their political capital.

Sometimes these risks pay off, and sometimes they do not, revealing both the power and the perils of popularity. Before Katrina, when Gov. Kathleen Blanco's popularity soared, she aimed high and ultimately achieved more than she did through a narrower agenda after her popularity plummeted. On balance, Blanco's political capital yielded a payoff, though it did not prevent her ambitious agenda from suffering some stinging defeats along the way. Governor Taft's political capital also allowed him to achieve a great deal of success, at least in the policy game. When his popularity was high, he, like Gov. Blanco, proposed a very ambitious agenda. Taft did quite well in the policy game, securing a full pass on nearly every policy proposal included in his State of the State address, though he was less successful in budget bargaining, where Republican lawmakers found many of his proposals too liberal and had the patience to stand their ground. As his popularity plummeted, Taft compensated by narrowing the size of his policy agenda and shifting his fiscal proposals in a conservative direction. This strategy allowed Taft to improve on his overall batting average, though his policy impact declined. Taft's experience points out the flip side of the complex link between popularity and achievement. A savvy governor can, with a focused agenda and realistic expectations, adapt to plunging popularity and survive.

In sum, this chapter provides lessons both in how governors can respond to shifts in their popularity and how political scientists should study them. For scholars, it points to the paramount importance of holding constant the nature of a governor's agenda when assessing the impact of popularity on passage rates. Keep in mind that if we had estimated the models of gubernatorial success reported in Chapter 4 without holding constant the nature of the agenda, we would not have seen popularity exert a significant effect on the probability of passage.[34] In other words, by holding constant what governors asked for, our models revealed the otherwise hidden power of popular governors.

The substantive lesson of these case studies, though, is that although popularity can help a governor, it is no guarantee of success, just as low approval ratings are not an insuperable barrier. Popularity does pay off in political capital, but the legislature often has power to resist an overreaching agenda. Correspondingly, governors have a menu of strategies they can pursue when their popularity plummets. We find that chief executives often change their behavior to face the challenge of a lack of popularity rather than sitting idly by and dooming themselves to failure. Governor Bob Taft's summation of his dealings with the legislature provides a fitting coda: "I wasn't trying to be popular, I was just trying to get things done."[35]

[34] The model reported in the second column of Table 4.2 yields an estimated coefficient of 0.30 for approval ratings on the probability of passage for policy bills. When we reestimate this model and omit controls for the scale and ideological direction of a proposal, as well as the total number of proposals contained in a speech, the estimated coefficient for policy bills drops to 0.18 and falls short of statistical significance. (In neither model do popular governors appear to perform better on their budget proposals.)
[35] Telephone interview with Gov. Bob Taft, conducted by Thad Kousser and Justin Phillips, October 1, 2009.

7

The Item Veto

A Negative or a Positive Power?

Legislators would say I really need funding for a school in my district. I'd say I absolutely understand it, I know that is important and want to be helpful to you, and as soon as I see my smart growth bill pass, I will turn my full attention to the supplemental budget.

> – Maryland governor Parris Glendening, describing the dynamic
> that allowed him to leverage his power to line-item capital budget
> items into support for his policy program[1]

There are no quid pro quos. Governors just line out things that they want to line out.

> – Bill Hauck, deputy chief of staff to California governor Pete
> Wilson and chief of staff to assembly speakers Willie Brown and
> Bob Moretti, describing the item veto as simply a budget-trimming
> tool[2]

In 1994, Newt Gingrich and his Republican revolutionaries became strange bedfellows with President Bill Clinton, making the line-item veto the first pledged reform in the "Contract with America." Proponents viewed this reform, which conveys to chief executives the power to nullify

---

[1] Interview with Gov. Parris Glendening conducted by telephone by Thad Kousser and Justin Phillips, July 13, 2010. Maryland's "supplemental" budget is the capital construction budget that contains all of the district projects that legislators so desperately want to see built, and the governor has the authority to line out any item in it. For the rest of the budget, Maryland's governor has the extraordinary power of being able to propose any spending line that he or she favors, with legislators possessing only the power to decrease this spending but not to insert their own spending lines. This gives the governor a functional ex ante item veto power (National Conference of State Legislatures 2008).

[2] Interview with Bill Hauck conducted by telephone by Thad Kousser and Justin Phillips, June 25, 2009.

individual expenditures in appropriations bills without having to reject the entire bill, as a way to eliminate wasteful spending in the federal budget and "restore fiscal responsibility to an out of control Congress."[3] Indeed, after he had been granted and exercised this new executive power, President Clinton observed, "I think that having it has made it much easier to control spending."[4] Veteran legislative leaders, who felt a stake in defending congressional control over the nation's purse, objected. They argued that though the item veto might trim some fat, it fundamentally shifts important policy-making powers from the legislative to the executive branch. The U.S. Supreme Court agreed. Its 6–3 decision in *Clinton v. City of New York* held that the Line Item Veto Act altered the balance of power in a way that could only be permissibly accomplished through a constitutional amendment. Still, Justice Breyer's dissent again advanced the argument that the item veto was, at best, a constrained, negative power, arguing, "Nor can one say the Act's grant of power 'aggrandizes' the Presidential office. The grant is limited to the context of the budget."[5]

This controversy raised a question – with the highest constitutional stakes – about the essential nature of the item veto.[6] Exactly what powers does it confer on a chief executive? Is it simply a tool for exercising fiscal responsibility, a precise scalpel that allows the executive to line out spending favored only by legislators, trimming government without resorting to the blunt instrument of vetoing an entire spending bill? Or is it something more? The item veto might grant chief executives leverage that reverberates across many spheres of interbranch bargaining. Savvy negotiators might be able to turn this negative power into a positive one, making a promise to refrain from lining out legislators' pet projects in return for securing the legislature's support for executive priorities (even outside of budgeting). Through this sort of informal mechanism, chief executives may be able to transform the item veto from a fiscal scalpel

[3] See "Republican Contract with America," accessed at http://www.house.gov/house/Contract/CONTRACT.html in August 2011.

[4] Quoted in Wolf Blitzer, "Clinton Disappointed by Line-Item Ruling; Welcomes McDougal's Release," posted on CNN All Politics, June 26, 1988, accessed at http://articles.cnn.com/1998-06-26/politics/clinton.comments_1_lineitem-veto-veto-specific-items-clinton-said-by?_s=PM:ALLPOLITICS in August 2011.

[5] *Clinton v. City of New York* (97-1374) 95 F. Supp. 168, affirmed.

[6] We use the terms *line-item veto* and *item veto* interchangeably in this chapter, just as they are used synonymously in the public debate and the academic literature. One difference in usage that we do note, however, is that *line-item veto* is more prominently used in the national discussion.

into a broader source of influence that radically shifts power from one branch to the other.

Though the two sides in the national debate made each of these claims – that the line-item veto is a negative power that effectively controls the growth of government or that it bestows a positive power to move executive projects through the legislature – the academic literature provides little support for either of them. To predict the impact of federal reform, scholars have looked to the states. With most governors possessing the item veto but some lacking it, the states are a fertile testing ground to explore the item veto's effects. Existing studies, whether they employed sophisticated empirical analysis, surveys of state budget officers, or case studies, have found little or no evidence of a relationship between the existence or use of the gubernatorial line-item veto and fiscal restraint (Abney and Lauth 1985; Abrams and Dougan 1986; Gosling 1986; ACIR 1987; Nice 1988; Carter and Schap 1990). Abney and Lauth (1985, p. 375), for example, not only fail to uncover any evidence that the item veto trims spending but conclude that "on this basis of these data it could be argued that the presence of the veto discourages legislative discipline."[7] One exasperated review of the empirical literature is titled "Line-Item Veto: Where Is Thy Sting?" (Carter and Schap 1990). Research by Holtz-Eakin (1988), later confirmed and expanded on by Besley and Case (2003), finds some evidence of an item-veto effect. Researchers show that this power helps some governors cut spending, but only during periods of divided government.[8] As we note in our introductory chapter, the prevailing wisdom was encapsulated in the 1992 congressional testimony of CBO director Robert Reischauer, who reported that "evidence from studies of the states' use of the item veto indicates that it has not resulted in decreased spending."[9]

So, is the item veto a negative power, a positive power, or a nonexistent one? In this chapter, we explore the use of this institution and revisit the

[7] It is important to note that Abney and Lauth's (1997) follow-up survey identified a highly conditional impact of the item veto: it could be used to promote fiscal responsibility when governors could both reduce (rather than simply eliminate) budget items and delete the narrative portion of spending bills.

[8] The authors, unfortunately, are unclear as to why we should expect to observe this particular contingent effect. They also do not explore the possibility that the impact of the item veto may be, in part, a function of gubernatorial preferences over the size of the budget.

[9] See "Statement of Robert D. Reischauer, Director Congressional Budget Office before the Subcommittee on the Legislative Process, Committee on Rules, U.S. House of Representatives, September 25, 1992," accessed at http://www.cbo.gov/doc.cfm?index=4945& type=0/ on November 2, 2010.

academic literature about its effects. To probe the mechanisms by which the line-item veto may grant governors formal authority and informal leverage, we begin with the eyewitness testimony of those who have used the line-item veto as well as with legislators who have seen it used against them. We also draw on statehouse journalism. These insider statements and anecdotes yield support for both sides of the debate. Some portray the item veto as tool that can only be used to cut spending, whereas others depict it as a horse that can be traded to achieve other executive aims. We present these two views separately, tying them to our theoretical models of executive power and laying out the empirical expectations that each yields. Existing research may be equivocal about the item veto's ultimate effect, yet it traces out clear theoretical rationales for how the item veto can work. These rationales sharpen our sense of how to test for item veto effects.

If the item veto is indeed a negative power, it should be a powerful tool only for frugal chief executives, that is, those who want to keep government spending low. If the legislature passes a budget that includes more spending than the governor desires, she can, in theory, simply item veto expenditures until the size of the budget more closely matches her preferences. When governors want to increase spending or spend more than legislators do, a situation that may occur, for example, where a liberal Democrat heads a divided government, the item veto may go unused and appear ineffective. Recognizing this asymmetry allows a more precise test that asks whether the "blue pencil"[10] gives governors the power to cut, when they have an incentive to wield it.

If, by contrast, the item veto confers a positive power, then it should enable both frugal and spendthrift governors to get a budget that more closely matches the size they desire. Furthermore, the effects of the item veto should be seen not simply in the budget but in other areas of executive–legislative bargaining. In exchange for sparing expenditures favored by legislators, governors may be able to extract support for their policy as well as their budgetary proposals. Testing for this effect requires a broader investigation of how the line-item power might reverberate into other areas of interbranch bargaining.

Whether it is a positive or negative power, the item veto is not an absolute power. It can be overridden by legislators, making this constitutional authority contingent on political dynamics. Governors will look

[10] When governors exercise their item veto power, they are said to be using their "blue pencil" to line out spending (and some governors choose to use an actual blue pencil when marking up the budgets that legislators send them).

toward the endgame, feeling free to line out items when they have enough legislative allies to sustain their cuts but realizing that they lack the ability to trim budgets in states where they can easily be overridden, and they may refrain from using the blue pencil.

Finally, we note that because states were not randomly assigned to adopt the item veto, the systematic forces at play in the political process of adoption have left the states that lack the item veto not fully comparable to the states where governors possess it. This creates a research design challenge to answer the counterfactual question, How powerful would a similar governor in a similar state be, if she lacked the item veto? We address this challenge in two ways. First, we use econometric "matching" techniques (Rubin 1973, 1979; Ho et al. 2007) to create comparable sets of states, with and without the item veto, before employing traditional statistical models. Second, we conduct a detailed case study, observing how executive power shifted when the Iowa Supreme Court's 2004 *Rants v. Vilsack* decision dramatically restricted the line-item powers granted Iowa's governor.

7.1. Observations and Expectations about How Governors Use Item Vetoes

The first appearance of the line-item veto on American soil came in the constitution of the Confederacy. After the Civil War, this institution was included in most of the new constitutions written by its former members as they rejoined the union. Many western states embraced the item veto as they wrote and rewrote their constitutions in the late nineteenth century, and 16 additional states adopted it during the twentieth century (de Figueiredo 2003, pp. 2683–4). Most recently, Maine became the forty-fourth state to add the item veto to its constitution, doing so via a ballot measure that voters approved by an overwhelming majority in November 1995.[11] Today, the only states in which governors lack this power are Indiana, Nevada, New Hampshire, North Carolina, Rhode Island, and Vermont (Council of State Governments 2010).

For the governors who possess it, the item veto varies considerably in the details of how it can be used. This variation is recorded comprehensively by the Council of State Governments (2010) and described colorfully in Rosenthal (1990, pp. 160–2). We will harness that variation

---

[11] See Maine State Law and Legislative Reference Library, Enacted Constitutional Amendments, 1834–, accessed at http://www.maine.gov/legis/lawlib/const.htm in August 2011.

in our case study, but for our main empirical analysis, we focus on the qualitative difference between governors with and without the item veto.

7.1.1. *The Item Veto as Negative Power: A Fiscal Scalpel*

One way that the line-item veto can operate is simply according to the letter of its law: by granting governors the authority, at the end of the budget process, to cut lines of spending. This is potentially a very important strategic advantage. As we argue in Chapter 2, governors face great political peril if they veto an entire spending bill, especially if doing so means that the state will begin the fiscal year without a new budget. Recall that the absence of a late budget may force the state into temporary reductions in service provision, delay the payment of its bills, and (in many places) trigger a partial government shutdown. When governors use the item veto, they can avoid all of the costs associated with fiscal gridlock and yet still delete spending that they oppose, whether these spending lines are egregious examples of pork or simply spending choices that governors oppose on ideological grounds. Using the item veto this way makes it, in our terminology, a purely negative power. Governors can cut spending that legislators favor but are not able to advance budget projects or policy programs that they would like to see enacted. Of course, just because governors cannot leverage their power into support for their projects does not mean that they get no payoff from wielding their blue pencils. Total spending goes down, and governors can claim credit.

Recognizing this dynamic points to a key asymmetry in the power granted by the item veto – it should primarily help frugal governors, especially those in negotiations with spendthrift legislatures. If the chief executive favors a lower level of spending than lawmakers do, and expects to be rewarded for constraining the growth of pork-barrel spending, the item veto is a powerful weapon. It allows a governor to achieve a policy goal and, perhaps most importantly, to receive political plaudits. Yet, such a negative power confers fewer benefits on a governor who would like to see government grow but faces a low-spending legislature. Using the item veto to cut overall spending will not push policy in the direction that this type of governor favors. She will not be rewarded by her key constituencies because they likely favor more spending as well. If the blue pencil provides no leverage to advance her own policies or protect executive priorities in the budget, then she will have little incentive to use it. A negative power does nothing for spendthrift governors facing frugal legislatures.

Statehouses across the nation provide plenty of examples of governors using the item veto in a simply negative fashion when they favor less spending than legislators do. In his final year in office in 2006, Republican New York governor George Pataki vetoed 202 line items from the state's budget, totaling a massive $2.9 billion. "In wielding the veto pen," the *New York Times* observed, "Mr. Pataki is seeking to restore part of his image that has been somewhat tarnished in recent years: a reputation for fiscal conservatism."[12] The same year, Democratic governor Bill Richardson lined out $269 million from a New Mexico budget that he called a "feeding frenzy." Legislators countered that he was doing so only to aid his planned presidential campaign. "Some lawmakers accuse the governor of trying to burnish his national reputation," the *Albuquerque Journal* reported. "Richardson is widely thought to be setting up a presidential bid in 2008. An overflowing emergency savings account would strengthen the view that he is a responsible steward of the people's money." This interpretation downplays policy goals but serves to highlight the political payoffs than can be won through aggressive use of the item veto.[13]

Governors can and often do use this power, even against legislatures controlled by their own parties, if the legislature collectively wants to spend more than the governor does. In fact, the item veto gives governors the opportunity to show off their stinginess. California governor Gray Davis, a moderate Democrat, used it for these purposes when he negotiated with more liberal leaders in the legislature. "The governor gets credit from the public for wielding a heavy veto pen," explained his communications director, Phil Trounstine. "It shows that he's fiscally responsible."[14] After Florida governor Jeb Bush lined out $219 million in local projects from Florida's budget in 2001, he said that he did so based on the criteria of "whether projects provided a statewide benefit and had been openly and fairly debated by elected officials."[15] When he did not see those benefits, Gov. Bush blue-penciled millions of dollars of projects sponsored by fellow Republicans.

Even if it is primarily a negative power, the item veto is a scalpel that can be used discriminately. According to Gary Hart, who served both

[12] Michael Cooper, "Pataki's Supervetoes," *New York Times*, April 13, 2006, p. 7.
[13] Trip Jennings, "Lawmakers: Gov. Playing Politics – Legislators Dispute Richardson's Claims of Overspending," *Albuquerque Journal*, March 11, 2006, p. A1.
[14] Interview with Phil Trounstine, communications director to Gov. Gray Davis, conducted by telephone by Thad Kousser, July 8, 2009.
[15] S. V. Date, "Million in State Projects Vetoed," *Palm Beach Post*, June 16, 2001, p. 1A.

in the California state senate and in the executive branch as education secretary, "as a legislator I knew the power of the pen; if you pissed off a governor, you really ran the risk if you had a program that you cared about or a bill that you wanted, he would veto it. I recall shortly after Pete Wilson was elected, Delaine Eastin ripped him in a speech and I thought at the time that was not a smart move. And I believe it cost Delaine any chance of getting any meaningful legislation enacted into law while Wilson was governor."[16] On a wider scale, New Mexico governor Bill Richardson meted out his item vetoes in a partisan fashion. According to an *Albuquerque Journal* report, the Democratic governor used his line-item veto to strike nearly 33 percent of the projects sponsored by Republicans. Democratic sponsors lost only about 15 percent of their projects. The analysis found that lawmakers who either have been outspoken critics of the governor or who opposed key legislation in the recent session were more likely than Richardson allies to see their projects vetoed.[17]

Governors who use the item veto with such vigor come from different parties, harbor different ambitions, and look to settle different scores. One thing that they do have in common is that they want to spend less than the legislature does and see political advantage in trimming the budget. Pataki wanted to finish his term with a reputation as a fiscal conservative, Richardson planned to begin his presidential campaign with the same image, and Davis and Jeb Bush wanted to show that they were stingier than their copartisans. None of these governors expected anything in return from legislators, who often reacted with outrage when the budget axe fell on their pet projects.

But what about governors positioned to the left of the legislature on the ideological scale? For governors who want to spend more than lawmakers do, a purely negative line-item veto is of little use. Indeed, this power is little used in many states where chief executives want to spend but legislators are relatively frugal. This dynamic often occurs where Democratic governors negotiate with legislatures controlled by Republicans or conservative Democrats. In Florida, after Jeb Bush lined out so much spending in 2001, some Republican lawmakers observed that they brought home more projects to their districts under Democratic governor

---

[16] Interview with Gary Hart, former California state senator and education secretary, interview by telephone conducted by Thad Kousser, July 16, 2009.

[17] Trip Jennings and Gabriela C. Guzman. "More Republican Projects Were Vetoed – Gov.'s Critics Also Faced More Cuts," *Albuquerque Journal*, March 17, 2006, p. A1.

Lawton Chiles because he was less apt to use his blue pencil.[18] This was a repeat of the pattern that had been set in the 1980s, when Democratic governor Bob Graham used the item veto sparingly, working with key staff to scrutinize hundreds of district projects in 1986 but ultimately lining out only a handful. His successor, Republican Bob Martinez, cast 136 item vetoes in 1988 and 250 in 1989 (Rosenthal 1990, pp. 161–2). In Florida, the item veto had a huge impact when Republican governors wanted to trim government but hardly any effect when it gave Democratic governors an authority of which they were loathe to make use.

Noting that the impact of this institutional power may be contingent on political dynamics provides a clear empirical prediction: its presence should lead to reduction in spending only when governors are frugal. Surprisingly, we have not seen this prediction made or tested in the existing literature. Both Holtz-Eakin (1988) and Besley and Case (2003) show that the effect of the item veto is present only under divided government. This is an important advance, revealing the first clear evidence that the item veto has any fiscal impact, but it is a somewhat puzzling approach. It lumps states with a Democratic governor and a Republican legislature together with states that have a Republican executive and Democratic legislature, possibly leading scholars to underestimate the impact of the veto in the latter case. In our analysis, we will allow the effect of the item veto to vary with the frugality of the governor, relative to the legislature, in what we see as the most direct test of its budget-trimming potential.

We also test for another contingency that is suggested both by stories from the states and by the strategic logic of bargaining but has not yet been fully explored in the existing literature. The item veto should only reduce spending when governors have the votes to make it stick, sustaining vetoes against legislative override. Item vetoes may come toward the end of the budgeting process, but they do not mark the endgame of legislative–executive bargaining. In all states that grant governors the item veto, legislators may attempt to override these cuts, with the vote threshold necessary varying by state. Overriding an item veto takes a 60 percent vote in most legislatures, while states such as Massachusetts, Minnesota, and Louisiana make it more difficult with a two-thirds threshold. Only a simple majority is needed to override in Alabama, Maine, Oklahoma, and Tennessee, leaving item vetoes especially vulnerable (Council of State Governments 2010). For governors, the relevant calculus is whether they

---

[18] S. V. Date, "Million in State Projects Vetoed," *Palm Beach Post*, June 16, 2001, p. 1A.

have enough partisan allies in the legislature to keep the other party from reaching the state's prescribed threshold. If so, they can expect that their copartisans will side with them on policy grounds or hope for support on the principle of political allegiance. If not, governors will know that any item veto is unlikely to stand, making their constitutional authority essentially a dead letter.

In our analysis, we identify the legislative sessions in which the governor's party holds enough legislative seats to stop an override, predicting that the item veto will only trim spending in such circumstances. In our conversations with insiders, we found many examples of this dynamic at work. When governors had enough allies to defend it – even when they lacked a legislative majority – the item veto gave them great power. Because Republican governors George Deukmejian and Pete Wilson had sufficient support to defend their vetoes, they could stand up to Democratic legislative majorities, according to Deukmejian advisor Larry Thomas. Asked whether he could remember either being overridden, Thomas replied, "I don't think Duke was, and I have no memory of it for Wilson. If you can assure that your caucus will hang with you on any veto, it hugely enhances your power."[19]

In Alabama, by contrast, the blue pencil did little to help a Republican governor constrain spending by the Democratic legislature because he could be overridden by a simple majority. After the legislature passed a record $6 billion educational spending budget in 2006, Republican governor Bob Riley attempted to reduce school spending by $60 million to broaden his proposed tax cut. He did so using his "amendment" power,[20] functionally equivalent to an item veto in this case. "But the House of Representatives by 63–38 rejected Riley's proposed amendment, or veto. Most Democrats voted to reject it. Most Republicans supported it. Then the House voted 89–10 to pass the education budget over Riley's veto."[21] Without enough allies in the House to sustain his amendment, Gov. Riley

---

[19] Interview with Larry Thomas, press secretary and campaign manager to California governor George Deukmejian, conducted by telephone by Thad Kousser and Justin Phillips, June 30, 2009.

[20] Alabama's governor possesses a variety of item-veto authority to allow greater flexibility but is more at risk of override: "The governor may veto the bill entirely or offer executive amendments. The legislature may accept the amendments or may pass the original bill again with a majority vote, causing it to go into effect without the governor's signature," according to National Conference of State Legislators, Gubernatorial Veto Authority with Respect to Major Budget Bill(s).

[21] David White, "Education Budget OK'd over Riley's Objections," *Birmingham News*, March 30, 2006, p. 1-B.

was forced to accept the spending plan and had less money to give back to taxpayers during an election year.

When governors lack votes to sustain an override, the item veto shifts from a budget-trimming power to nothing more than an act of political theater in a play that is repeated year after year. During the run-up to Massachusetts governor Mitt Romney's first presidential run, overrides of his item vetoes by the Democrat-dominated legislature became a matter of course. In 2005, legislators overrode all but 0.8 percent of the spending that he had lined out from the budget. After Romney vetoed $573 million in spending in 2006 – "putting his final stamp on the state budget as he looks to a possible presidential run in 2008" – legislative leaders were nonplussed. House Ways and Means Chair Robert A. DeLeo, after glancing over Romney's item vetoes, predicted, "I will tell you, if the items he vetoed are the ones I just quickly see, I don't think we're going to have any problem at all overriding any of those vetoes."[22]

When governors look ahead toward the endgame and realize that an item veto will eventually be overridden, will they use their blue pencil in the first place? They have some strong incentives not to use it. Being overridden can be embarrassing to governors, making a very public demonstration of their political weakness. An override battle is typically a high-profile event that can take governors off their agendas and damage their relationships in the capitol. But for governors concerned about their image on the statewide or even national stage, an override battle can allow them to cement their reputation as fiscal conservatives as voters see them fighting, albeit futilely, against spendthrift legislators. In Mitt Romney's 2006 Massachusetts budget battle, a key national political player urged him to use his item veto, even though it would not be sustained. Grover Norquist, an antitax advocate and president of Americans for Tax Reform, called on Romney to resist an assessment on businesses that the legislature had included in its budget. "It's not his responsibility that the Republicans are in the minority in the Legislature," Norquist said. "If he gets overridden, that is not his fault. It could be a centerpiece of how he governs in a state with a strong opposition party."[23]

Yet, while governors may score rhetorical points by casting a doomed item veto, this action does nothing to reduce state spending. The item veto should only be effective if it cannot be overridden. While other scholars

---

[22] Michael Levenson, "Romney Vetoes $573M from State Budget – Lawmakers Vow Overrides," *Boston Globe*, July 9, 2006, p. A1.

[23] Frank Phillips, "Romney Is Urged to Veto Health Fee," *Boston Globe*, March 17, 2006.

TABLE 7.1. *Predicted Effects of the Item Veto, by Political Condition*

	Governor has votes to sustain veto	Governor lacks votes, leaving item vetoes vulnerable to override
Frugal governor	Effective	Ineffective
Spendthrift governor	Ineffective	Ineffective

have noted the frequency and importance of overrides, statistical models assessing the importance of the item veto do not include variables that measure whether or not a governor has the votes to sustain it against an override. We do so, predicting that the power of the blue pencil will be contingent on this legislative support. As we have noted earlier, we also expect that the presence of legislative support will cut spending when governors are more frugal than legislators but that it will have no effect where the chief executive favors higher government spending. Together, these contingent predictions of where and how the item veto should be effective, if it is indeed a negative power, are summarized in Table 7.1.

7.1.2. *The Item Veto as Positive Power: A Horse to Be Traded*

While the letter of item-veto laws grant governors a power that is merely negative, it is also possible that strategic executives can turn it into the positive power to advance their own agendas. The logic underlying this sort of bargain is straightforward, working just the way Maryland governor Parris Glendening explained in the epigraph that began this chapter. When a governor with item-veto powers negotiates with a legislator who would like to see a district project or a pet program funded in the budget, the governor can promise to refrain from blue-penciling this money in exchange for the legislator's support for executive priorities. The power of the item veto – or rather the governor's commitment to forsake this power – is yet another horse to be traded in a wider bargaining game. It can win the governor support for a budget item or a bill such as Glendening's smart growth legislation. It can help a governor move her own budget items, and its power can reach from the budget realm into the policy game. In this way, the item veto's effect can be modeled just like the other powers that increase executive leverage in the policy-bargaining game. Like governors who are popular, those who are early in their terms, and those with a sustainable bill veto, governors who possess item-veto powers can pay legislators larger side payments and thus are more likely to win support for their own proposals when playing the policy game.

Many key players in statehouse bargaining point out this dynamic when they discuss sources of gubernatorial strength. "California's governor is pretty powerful," observes longtime Golden State senator Pat Johnston, "with the veto and especially the item veto. They can use that to get the legislature to give them a lot of what they want in a budget."[24] "California's governor is particularly powerful because he has that blue pencil," argued Larry Thomas, Gov. George Deukmejian's advisor. "A lot of legislators, once they get something in the budget, they get on their hands and knees and plead not to get it blue-penciled. . . . Sometimes, a governor might cut a deal."[25]

Dan Schnur, communications director to Gov. Pete Wilson, spelled out the logic of how the item veto can work as a positive power. "When the budget is sent to the governor, he can eliminate a particular budget item with his blue pencil," Schnur explained. "It might be a $1,000 expenditure in a $100 million budget, but it is something that is important for a particular legislator. A staff member lets the legislator know that if they want that playground or that off-ramp that they put in the budget to survive the blue pencil, then maybe they should think twice about voting no for what the governor proposed."[26]

These stories from California sound much like Gov. Glendening's use of the item veto in Maryland. Even in Ohio, where Republican governor Bob Taft worked with Republican legislative leaders, he still used (or refrained from using) the item veto to help his allies in the leadership corral their rank and file to support shared policy aims. "If a legislator had leverage – let's say the speaker or president needed their vote on something – if he was smart he'd get a commitment up front from us that he was on solid ground with the item veto," remarked Taft. "We tried to be credible. If we gave our word, we would honor it."[27] Governor Glendening noted that legislators lived up to their end of the bargain as well. "I've found, and especially when you are dealing with the leadership, they stand by their word," Glendening remembered. "If they said, 'Help

[24] Interview with former California state senator Pat Johnson, conducted by Thad Kousser in Sacramento, June 22, 2009.
[25] Interview with Larry Thomas, press secretary and campaign manager to California governor George Deukmejian, conducted by telephone by Thad Kousser and Justin Phillips, June 30, 2009.
[26] Interview with Dan Schnur, communications director to Gov. Pete Wilson, conducted by telephone by Thad Kousser, July 7, 2009.
[27] Interview with Gov. Bob Taft of Ohio, conducted by telephone by Thad Kousser and Justin Phillips, October 1, 2009.

me with this budget item, and I'll make sure your bill gets out of the committee,' then I can't remember ever being spun on that."[28]

The testimony of governors and legislators alike clearly shows that horse trading over the item veto sometimes occurs. It is difficult to find examples from the press of this exchange, however, because it is like the proverbial dog that does not bark. When the trade works, no item veto is issued. Because the exchange might appear unseemly to voters, these are exactly the sorts of political negotiations that occur most often in private. We can glimpse them only when they collapse, as they did in Mississippi during negotiations over the state's fiscal year 2002 budget. When Gov. Ronnie Musgrove attempted to extract legislative cooperation by threatening to use his item veto, house speaker and fellow Democrat Tim Ford refused to meet the governor's demand. In the end, Gov. Musgrove lined out $150 million in spending, and legislators set the state record for item-veto overrides.

When, by contrast, interbranch relations turn peaceful, the resulting cheer and goodwill provide circumstantial evidence that horses can indeed be traded. "Checks will be written, beer will flow and golf balls will fly, but not much else will happen this week as lawmakers return for the annual veto session," reported the *Kansas City Star*. "As required by the Missouri Constitution, lawmakers will convene at noon today for the veto session, which gives them the opportunity to override any bills rejected by the governor. Gov. Matt Blunt did not veto any bills this year and used his line item veto on only four budget items that are not expected to provoke overrides."[29] Perhaps Gov. Blunt was in such a generous mood because legislators had passed 11 of his 17 budget proposals and also delivered one compromise deal. The governor may have kept his blue pencil in his pocket in exchange for the positive progress that legislators made on his agenda.

We are far from the first scholars to suggest that governors can turn the item veto into a positive power to move budget and policy proposals. Alan Rosenthal observed that some governors are cognizant of the leverage that the blue pencil gives them: "A governor may invoke the item veto and excoriate the legislature on its Christmas tree of an appropriations bill

---

[28] Interview with Gov. Parris Glendening of Maryland, conducted by telephone by Thad Kousser and Justin Phillips, July 13, 2010.

[29] Tim Hoover, "Lawmakers to Gather for Tee – Golf and Glad-handing Are the Main Agenda Items in Jefferson City This Week," *Kansas City Star*, September 13, 2006, p. B7.

with presents for everyone. But a number of governors . . . also recognize pork to be a necessary staple of the legislative diet and important to the executive, as well as to leadership, for trading purposes" (Rosenthal 1990, p. 160). Yet, our original data set of State of the State proposals, both in the budget and in the policy realm, gives us the first chance to test whether governors can systematically turn the item veto into support for their own proposals.

If it is a positive power, the potency of the item veto should be contingent on a governor's ability to sustain a veto against override (just as it should be for negative power). A certain legislative override takes away the item veto's leverage. Yet, if the item veto confers positive powers, a wider range of governors should be able to use them. Both frugal and spendthrift governors would benefit because regardless of their spending preferences, all governors have items on their personal agendas that they would like to move. Even when a relatively free-spending governor faces a fiscally disciplined legislature, there are likely some items of spending in the budget that are of crucial importance to legislators but are inconsequential to the governor. A spendthrift but savvy governor may be able to threaten to line out that spending if legislators fail to pass her key proposals, reaping just as much positive reward as a frugal governor would in that situation.[30] This eliminates one of the contingencies that we expect to exist if the item veto is only a negative power, as illustrated in Table 7.1. Overall, if the item veto confers positive power, then we should see governors who possess it and who can sustain it against an override pass more of their budget and policy proposals, ceteris paribus, than other chief executives.

7.2. A Negative Power? Analyzing State Spending Patterns

Using our new data sets, we can begin by evaluating our hypothesis that the item veto confers a negative power on governors. When governors are frugal, and when they have enough legislative allies to sustain their item veto, this allows governors to use their blue pencil to reduce state spending more effectively compared with governors who lack the item veto. We

---

[30] This gives spendthrift governors a horse to trade. In an analogous way, even relatively frugal governors have some things that they would like to see included in the state budget (as evidenced by the extensive budget agendas that they present in State of the State addresses) and thus have something for which to trade.

conduct this test using the data set, described in Chapter 5, that charts per capita state spending patterns from the 1989 to 2009 fiscal years.[31]

However, unlike the existing literature, we take advantage of matching techniques to identify the effect of the item veto. With observational data (such as we use here), estimating the impact of the item veto on budget bargaining can be difficult if the existence (or absence) of the line item veto is correlated with other institutions that shape the balance of power between the executive and legislature. In this case, we are concerned about legislative professionalization, which has a critical influence on executive power. As we have already demonstrated, governors are significantly less likely to get their way in budget negotiations when dealing with professional lawmakers.

These sorts of problems are not new in the study of state institutions, and the usual approach is to gather data on other features of states to hold them constant in a multivariate analysis. Here we could simply include a measure of professionalization (such a session length) as a control variable, like we do in Chapters 4 and 6. Such an approach may not be advisable in this case because not only is the existence of the item veto strongly correlated with legislative professionalization but *all* states with legislatures that are classified as professional delegate item-veto authority to their governors. Correspondingly, five of the six states that deny the governor the item veto have citizen legislatures (the sixth state, North Carolina, is classified by the National Conference of State Legislatures as having a "hybrid" legislature).

This pattern poses a special challenge to causal inference and means that we need to be particularly careful when comparing outcomes in states that do and do not have the item veto. One solution, laid out in Ho et al. (2007a), is to "preprocess" our data set, essentially removing observations from the most professional states to make our "treatment" and "control" cases – the states with and without the item veto – comparable. We do so, employing matching techniques (Rubin 1973, 1979) that allow us to identify a set of states that are roughly similar, except for the fact that some grant governors the line-item veto and some do not.

---

[31] As in Chapter 5's analysis, observations from Nebraska are dropped from these analyses because the state's formally nonpartisan structure makes it impossible to measure the governor's party support in the legislature. Observations from negotiations with an independent or otherwise nonpartisan governor are dropped for the same reason. We also drop observations from Alaska, where state revenues received from natural resource extraction can lead to radical year-to-year spending shifts.

Figure 7.1 shows how matching helps us move closer to the experimental ideal in which the treatment and control groups look quite similar, except that one group is treated (in this case, the treatment is the item veto). Our data set begins with 1,029 observations, 134 of which feature governors who lack the item veto. Relying on the MatchIt program (Ho et al. 2007b), we conduct a 4–1 nearest-neighbor match that retains all 134 of these cases and matches them to the 536 most similar cases featuring a governor who possesses the item veto. We match on legislative professionalization using the same salary, session length, and staffing variables that we introduced in Chapter 5. We also rely on a summary measure of professionalization developed by Squire (1992).[32]

Comparing the bars in the top of Figure 7.1 shows, prior to matching, just how substantial the differences in legislative structure are between states with and without the item veto. After matching, the two sets of states look much more comparable.[33] We can now move on to conducting the same sort of multivariate analysis that state scholars typically do, holding constant not only legislative structure but a host of economic and political variables to isolate the effects of the item veto. As a robustness check, we also estimate regression models using our full data set (though we do not report these here).

We begin our empirical analysis by asking, In each year's budget battle, are governors who possess the item veto able to keep spending lower than governors who lack the blue pencil? To answer this question, we estimate regression models that explain variation in year-to-year changes in spending, measured in per capita constant dollars.[34] This model compares spending changes (fiscal differences) in item-veto states to spending changes states without the item veto (institutional differences).[35] We estimate multilevel models that include both year and state random effects. As in Chapter 5, we hold constant a range of economic indicators, measures of party control, citizen ideology, and whether the state is located in

---

[32] We rely on Squire's continuous measure of legislative professionalization rather than the three NCSL categories used elsewhere in the book. The Squire measures allow us to make the most precise matches.

[33] After matching, we obtain balance improvements of 64.5% for legislative salary, 74.3% for session days, 78.2% for legislative staff, and 69.8% for Squire's full index of legislative professionalism.

[34] We convert these figures, which are reported in current dollars in the NASBO reports from which we gather them, into constant 2000 dollars using the CPI-U.

[35] Though these institutional differences are primarily across states in our models estimating the effects of the item veto itself, our models that estimate the effect of a sustainable veto do feature significant variation across time within individual states as governors lose and then retake enough legislative seats to defend their item vetoes against overrides.

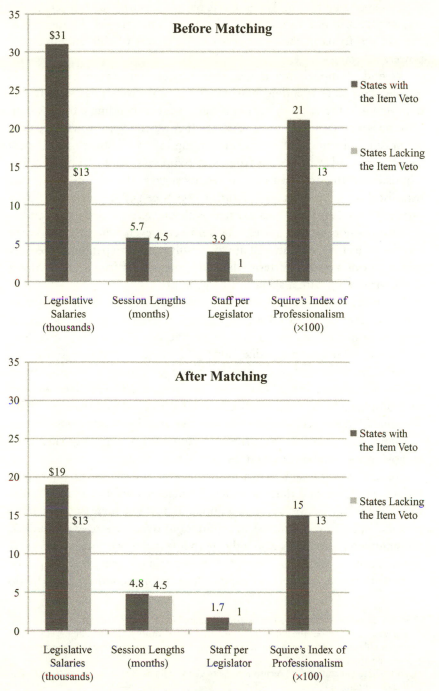

FIGURE 7.1. How matching makes cases more comparable.

the low-spending South. Appendix Table 7.2 reports our full regression results. Because our focus in this chapter is squarely on the item veto, though, we focus in the main text on the effects of this gubernatorial power.

We find, in model after model, that the item veto exerts only a weak influence on state spending patterns. Governors who possess both the item veto and the votes to sustain it sign budgets spending a bit less than governors who lack this power. Yet, whether we analyze the matched data set or our full sample of cases, this finding falls well short of statistical significance and ranges only from approximately $1 to $5 per capita. Consistent with past research, our results suggest that the item veto has little fiscal sting (cf. Abney and Lauth 1985; Nice 1988; Carter and Schap 1990). This result is not inconsistent with our expectations. Remember that we do not anticipate that the item veto, even when the governor has the votes to sustain it, will always result in lower spending. We only expect to observe this pattern when the governor is frugal, especially if she is bargaining with a spendthrift legislature.

However, when we investigate whether the effects of an item veto are contingent on the governor's spending preferences, as our theoretical analysis predicted, we again find suggestive but not conclusive results. In the last column of appendix Table 7.2, we interact the presence of a sustainable item veto[36] with a measure of a governor's fiscal objectives. This new variable, *Frugal Governor*, identifies chief executives who, in their proposed budget, called for either a freeze or a decrease in per capita spending.[37] We expect to observe a negative and significant coefficient on this interaction, showing that the item veto has greater sting when used by governors who wish to trim the size of state budgets.

The results of this new estimation are largely consistent with our expectations. First, we find that the enacted budget grows at a much smaller rate when the governor is frugal, a finding that is not surprising given the power of state chief executives in negotiations over the size of the budget. Substantively, our results also indicate that frugal governors who possess a sustainable item veto are better able to restrain the growth of the public sector (by an additional $6 per capita) than are their counterparts who do

---

[36] In our matched sample, the item veto is sustainable in 452 of the 536 cases in which a governor possesses the item veto, while in 84 of those cases the item veto is not sustainable (the governor does not have enough copartisans in either house to stop an override attempt).

[37] Forty-three percent of the executive budgets in our data set are classified as frugal using this definition.

not possess this power. Interestingly, for all other governors, the size of government grows by nearly the identical amount regardless of whether they have access to a sustainable veto. None of these differences, though, reach statistical significance.

In model estimations not reported here, we further refine our empirical analysis by comparing the effect of a sustainable item veto among frugal governors who are bargaining with a "spendthrift" legislature to those who are not. To do this, we must make assumptions about legislative preferences because we do not have a direct measure of what key lawmakers want from the budget (in our data, we only observe the size of the budget the governor proposed and the size of the enacted budget). We classify as spendthrift legislatures in which both chambers are controlled by Democrats, relying on the assumption, which is supported by our empirical analysis in Chapter 5 and the results reported in Table 7.2, that Democratic legislatures generally lead to larger year-to-year increases in the size of the state budget than Republicans legislatures. These results, which again are only suggestive, indicate that the item veto has its largest impact when frugal governors are bargaining with Democratic legislatures.

Finally, it is worth noting that our results are not sensitive to the type of regression models we estimate. Arguably, using a fixed-effects approach is preferable to the multilevel models we report here. In any state that allows for the item veto, the governor will in some years have enough partisan allies to sustain her blue pencil and in other years may not. Fixed-effects models measure the impact of a sustainable item veto by comparing, within each state, outcomes in those years in which the governor has access to this power to outcomes in years in which the governor does not, and then averages the item veto effect across all states. The limitation of a fixed-effects approach in our case, however, is that there simply is very little within-state variation (only 16 instances) in the availability of a sustainable item veto. This makes it very unlikely that the fixed-effects model will unearth evidence of an item veto effect, even if one exists.

When we do estimate fixed-effects models, our findings are very similar to those we discussed earlier. The only noteworthy difference is that the coefficient on *Sustainable Item Veto* is largest in fixed-effects models and, in one instance, reaches statistical significance at the 90 percent level. When we use our unmatched data set, the fixed-effects model shows that spending grows by $13 less per capita when the governor has an item veto and enough partisan allies in the legislature to back her up. We caution against placing too much weight on this result, given the limited amount of within-state variation in the availability of a sustainable item veto. Ultimately, though we observe patterns that are consistent with our expectations, we do not find robust evidence that the item veto gives governors the negative power to significantly and meaningfully cut state spending.

7.3. A Positive Power? Analyzing the Size of Government and State of the State Proposals

After finding no clear evidence that the item veto bestows a negative, budget-cutting power on chief executives (even those who are frugal), we test for its potential positive powers. This sort of power should manifest itself in the following pattern: governors who possess the item veto should enjoy greater levels of success in shepherding their budgetary and policy proposals through the legislature. Instead of simply cutting funding that lawmakers prefer, governors will turn their threats to use the blue pencil into legislative support for their policy agendas and increased concessions in budget negotiations. Because these threats must be credible, this power should (again) be contingent on the governor's ability to sustain an item veto.

We begin testing for positive powers by exploring the NASBO data set from 1989 to 2009 but consider a different dependent variable. Here, we parallel Chapter 5's analysis more directly by explaining variation in a measure that summarizes how well governors do when negotiating over the size of government. We look at the absolute value of the difference between changes in the size of the budget proposed by the governor and the changes ultimately enacted at the end of the session. The smaller the value of this measure, the less the governor budged and thus the more successful she has been – regardless of whether she wanted to grow or shrink the size of the budget. If the item veto provides governors with a meaningful positive power, it should yield a negative coefficient.

Using our matched data set, we find that there is no statistically significant or substantively strong correlation between the sustainable item veto and bargaining success (see appendix Table 7.3), though the coefficient does have the anticipated negative sign. The magnitude of the coefficient indicates that chief executives with the item veto and partisan allies to back it up sign into law budgets that are closer (by approximately $4 per capita) to their original proposal. We also estimate a regression model that includes an interaction between the presence of a sustainable item veto and our measure of frugal governors. If the item veto is a negative and not a positive power, it may be that only frugal governors are able to use the item veto to secure a budget closer in size to their original proposal. They could do this by simply using their blue pencil to line out spending they found to be wasteful or that they disagreed with for ideological or political reasons. In this case, we would expect a negative and significant coefficient on the interaction term and a coefficient of zero on our stand-alone measure of the item veto. As Table 7.3 shows, however, we observe a negative coefficient on both variables, neither of which achieves statistical significance. Substantively, the regression indicates that a frugal governor with a sustainable item veto secures a budget that is approximately $6.50 per capita closer to her original proposal. Among nonfrugal governors, access to this power helps secure a budget that is closer to their original proposal by an average $2 per capita. It is worth noting that the most meaningful driver of gubernatorial success when it comes to bargaining over the size of the budget remains the patience of the legislature. Even if the coefficients of sustainable item veto were statistically significant, the substantive impact of the item veto pales in comparison to that of session length.

Finally, in results not reported here, we look even more broadly for evidence of positive power, testing whether the item veto helps governors pass the proposals made in their State of the State addresses. To do so, we estimate regression models that predict the outcome of individual proposals, using the same data set, models, and variables as in Chapter 4. Recall that these models treat the probability of bargaining success as a function of the patience of players, the ideological distance between the branches, the ability of the governor to make side payments, the size of her agenda, features of each proposal, and the health of both the economy and state budget. The two differences between the ordered logit models estimated in Chapter 4 and those that we estimate here is that we now include a dichotomous variable that captures the presence of a sustainable item veto and preprocess our data using the same techniques described earlier, this time applying them to the states included in our sample of State of the State addresses.[38] We again find no strong evidence of an impact. Governors appear to do a bit better when they possess a

---

[38] Note that in Chapter 4, we do not need to use matching techniques because we are not testing the effects of the item veto in this chapter. On the key treatment variables in the models in Chapter 4, there is generally good balance between the treatment and control cases.

sustainable veto,[39] but the effect is not statistically significant. Overall, we uncover little support for the hypothesis that the item veto can be used as a positive power to move the governor's agenda. Simply put, in a systematic analysis that includes hundreds of governors, this much-debated executive power appears to have little potency. As a last effort to uncover strong item-veto effects, we turn to Iowa, where a decision by the state's supreme court resulted in a substantial shift in the type of item-veto powers granted to the state's governor.

7.4. Evidence from an Iowa Case Study

Although it is useful to examine the impact of the item veto across many states and governors, valuable lessons can also be learned from a single case study. For this we turn to Iowa, where the state's supreme court, in the case of *Rants v. Vilsack* (June 2004), suddenly reduced the item-veto powers granted to the governor. We study the decision's impact by measuring State of the State success in both 2003 and 2005 – the year before the supreme court's decision and the year after it went into effect. Focusing on a single state (over a brief period of time) as we do here allows us to hold constant the governor as well as other institutional arrangements, thereby isolating the impact of a sharp reduction in item-veto powers. This gives us a pretest–posttest research design. We also add a control case – the record of Virginia's governor – to help ensure that any changes we might observe in Iowa from 2003 to 2005 are not a function of national economic or political trends operating everywhere. Like Iowa's legislature, Virginia's statehouse is a hybrid between a citizen and a professional legislature. Like Gov. Vilsack, Democratic governor Mark Warner negotiated with a Republican-held legislature before and after the *Rants v. Vilsack* decision.[40] During the two legislative sessions we study, both states confronted similar fiscal and economic circumstances.

How did *Rants v. Vilsack* change the nature of the item veto in Iowa? Governors in the Hawkeye state can item veto not only spending lines

---

[39] Additional analysis interacting the presence of an item veto with whether a given proposal was a budget or a policy item shows that the item veto helps governors most on their budget proposals, but again, this interaction coefficient fell short of statistical significance.

[40] The only exception to these parallel patterns in party control is that Democrats tied (at 25–25) the Republican Party for control of the Iowa Senate after the 2004 elections, giving Gov. Vilsack more allies in the legislature in the session immediately after his veto powers declined. This trend should bias against finding any effect of the shift in item-veto powers.

but also statutory language in any legislation deemed an "appropriations" bill. In 2003, Democratic governor Tom Vilsack attempted to use his item veto power to advance a key element of his legislative agenda through the Republican-controlled legislature. At the beginning of the session, he proposed the Iowa Values Fund, an economic development program backed by a $500 million appropriation. Republicans in the legislature wanted to spend much less on the fund, while reducing income taxes and worker's compensation payouts and restricting tort liability. After a long standoff, the legislature, in a special session, eventually passed two bills: one providing $45 million for the fund and the other establishing the preferred structure for the governor. In the second bill, Republican lawmakers included the tax cuts and tort reforms that they wanted, making it a compromise package that gave each branch some of what it desired (Iowa General Assembly 2003).

When he signed the two bills, Gov. Vilsack used his item veto to separate the components of the package, keeping the funding and the structure of the fund, while lining out the tax and tort changes that the legislature wanted. Republican lawmakers quickly hired independent legal council to challenge the item vetoes, arguing that the items crossed out were in a policy bill, not an appropriations, bill and that therefore the governor's actions violated the state constitution. House speaker Christopher Rants argued that allowing governors to veto this type of language made interbranch compromise difficult. Though they initially lost in district court, Republicans prevailed in the state supreme court, which established a new precedent with its decision, striking down the item vetoes and narrowing the scope of what constitutes an appropriations bill. "This case is huge for us," remarked Rants shortly after the supreme court's decision. "It will forever change the relationship between the legislature and the executive."[41] An article in the *Iowa Law Review* agreed, concluding that "*Rants* indicates that with respect to the item-veto authority in Iowa, the separation of powers pendulum has once again reversed course and swung in favor of the Iowa legislature" (Scuddler 2005, p. 400).

Did the *Rants* decision weaken the power of the governor when it comes to interbranch bargaining? We do not anticipate that this decision affected whatever negative powers are conveyed by a sustainable item veto because the decision in no way altered the ability of the governor to line

---

[41] Quoted on p. 51 of Rich Jones and Brenda Erickson, "See You in Court: The Balance of Power between Governors and Legislatures Sometimes Gets Out of Whack," *State Legislatures*, July/August 2004.

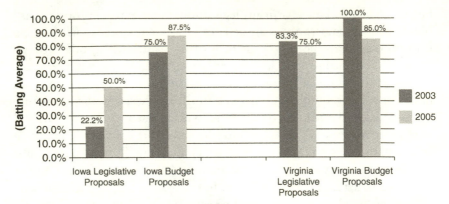

FIGURE 7.2. Case study: Success of State of the State proposals, before and after Iowa's court decision.

out expenditures in appropriations bills. However, since *Rants v. Vilsack* eliminated some of the leverage that Iowa governors formerly possessed to promise to let legislative policy language stand in return for support of executive priorities, the decision may have weakened the governor's ability to use the item veto as a positive power. If so, we expect the Iowa governor to be less successful at moving his fiscal and policy proposals after the supreme court's action. Importantly, throughout his terms in office, Gov. Vilsack always had enough copartisans in the legislature to sustain his vetoes. This means that if the item veto conveyed any positive power, he was well positioned to take advantage of it.

We begin by considering Gov. Vilsack's success at shepherding his State of the State proposals through the legislature before and after the *Rants* decision (see Figure 7.2). In 2003, Vilsack managed to convince the Republican-controlled legislature to pass only 22.5 percent of the legislative proposals in the 2003 State of the State, achieving success only on his proposals to establish the Iowa Values Fund and to streamline the state's property tax system. His proposals to raise the minimum wage, provide new mental health and substance abuse benefits, invest in housing for the disabled, and support nonprofits all stalled in committees. Governor Vilsack's legislative agenda (surprisingly) met with more success in 2005, with three of his six policy proposals passing. This increase cannot be explained by a change in the overall ambitiousness of his agenda.

We also observe a similar pattern in budget negotiations. In 2003, Gov. Vilsack did quite well, passing 75 percent of the fiscal proposals included in his State of the State address. In 2005, though, he did even better, securing money for early childhood development funding and teacher pay

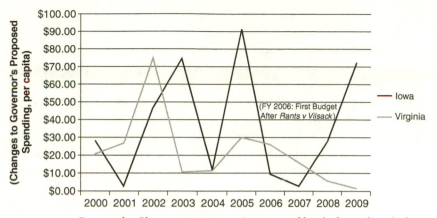

FIGURE 7.3. Case study: Changes to governor's proposed level of spending, before and after Iowa's court decision.

increases, along with $500 million of the $800 million that he had sought for the Values Fund. Like the increase in his policy batting average, the governor's growing success in budget bargaining cannot be accounted for by a change in the nature of his agenda. Nor can the governor's success in either game be explained away as an artifact of some nationwide shift toward executive power. At the same period of time, Virginia governor Mark Warner (from our control state) saw a slight decline in his effectiveness, which was impressively high in both 2003 and 2005. The decline in executive influence in Iowa appears to be real and damaging to the theory that the item veto confers positive leverage. Instead of facing a decline in his power, Gov. Vilsack actually won on more of his policy and budget proposals after he lost the *Rants v. Vilsack* decision.

We also look for evidence of a shift in positive powers using our measure of gubernatorial success in negotiations over the size of government. Figure 7.3 displays the absolute value of the difference between the proposed and enacted budget, with larger values indicating that the governor had to make more concessions to lawmakers. Here, we show the outcomes of budget negotiations for all the years in which Vilsack served as governor of Iowa – fiscal year 2000 through fiscal year 2009. As one can see, the absolute distance between the proposed and enacted budget fluctuates quite a bit from year to year, and no clear pattern emerges. Prior to the supreme court's decision, the average per capita distance between the proposed and enacted budget averaged $42.57, while it fell to $28.03 afterward. This works against our hypothesis, indicating that Gov. Vilsack was forced to budge from his initial proposal by larger amounts when his item-veto powers were at their strongest. Of course, one confounding factor is that in 2006 midterm elections, Democrats gained control of the state legislature. This means that beginning in fiscal year 2007, Gov. Vilsack was bargaining with his copartisans. Of course, the increase in gubernatorial success in Iowa could have been due to economic patterns as well. In Virginia, the average distance between the proposed and enacted budget also declined from \$28.97 to \$12.31 over the same period. Taking Virginia's pattern into account, it appears as if *Rants v. Vilsack* had no effect overall on this measure of gubernatorial strength, doing nothing to take Iowa off the path that Virginia followed.

7.5. Conclusion

We began this chapter by laying out two routes through which the item veto might empower governors: it could give them the negative power to exert fiscal discipline by cutting spending that legislators alone desire, or it might bestow a positive power to move a governor's own agenda. Both arguments have been made in prior scholarship and advanced in debates about the consequences of giving item-veto power to presidents. Through interviews with political insiders and our reading of statehouse journalism, we uncovered anecdotal evidence of each process at work. To determine whether the item veto systematically brings negative and potentially positive powers to governors, we probed our fiscal and State of the State databases and conducted a case study of gubernatorial success in Iowa following the *Rants v. Vilsack* decision.

The consistent lesson of our empirical investigations is clear: the item veto does not significantly increase gubernatorial power, either negative or positive. When governors have the authority to line out budget items, backed by enough legislative allies to sustain their vetoes, they appear to spend a bit less, particularly if they are frugal. Governors possessed of this power also appear to do marginally better in budget bargaining, signing into law a budget that is closer in size to their original proposal. These item-veto effects, however, almost always fall well short of reaching statistical significance. Though our empirical findings move in the expected direction, they do not provide convincing evidence that the item veto empowers governors.

In one sense, this should come as no surprise. The literature on item vetoes is full of null findings, which we once again replicate. Yet, all scholars who have studied it share a clear intuition that it should at least enable governors to shrink the size of government. Our archival research turns up many cases in which governors use their power this way, and interviews with governors and their advisors demonstrate just how much they cherish the authority. What can explain this disjuncture between, on one hand, intuition and the testimony of insiders and, on the other, the patterns revealed in a large-scale statistical analysis? We propose four possible explanations.

First, as we argue in the first half of this chapter, we should expect the item veto to exert an effect only under certain circumstances. Interviews and statehouse journalists remind us that since legislators often can override item vetoes of their favorite expenditures, this institutional power should only be effective when governors have the votes to block an override. Thinking through the logic of veto bargaining makes it clear that whereas the item veto may help a governor who is more frugal than the legislature, it may be useless in the hands of an executive who wants to increase, rather than cut, the budget put on her desk by lawmakers. Recognizing that it should not lead to lower spending everywhere and always perhaps provides a better explanation of the null finding that is typical in the literature. When we attempt to amend that literature by identifying cases where item-veto powers are sustainable and where governors are frugal, we find suggestive results. The line item appears to have more bite when both circumstances are present, though this finding is far from conclusive.

A second explanation of our weak findings is related: we may simply not have enough data to draw firm conclusions. Null findings can come when underpowered tests have too few observations. At first glance, this sounds preposterous, when our data set features nearly every state and ranges from 1989 to 2009. But note that the number of cases in which the item veto should matter – when governors can fight off overrides *and* when they are frugal – is relatively rare. It is possible that by analyzing more years (as time passes or as more data become available), these suggestive findings could become conclusive.

Third, it is possible that the item veto works, but only in the way it is explicitly intended: by giving governors a way to line out truly gratuitous legislative pork. In modern state governments, the dollars that go to small district projects are dwarfed by massive expenditures on education, Medicaid, and welfare programs. If governors use the item veto as a scalpel to cut out district projects rather than as a cleaver against major program areas, its impact will be difficult to detect in statistical models. Item vetoes may infuriate a handful of legislators when their pork is cut, but the savings will only amount to decimal dust compared to the grand scale of a state budget. The blue pencil may still be effective in this way, but its impact will be drowned out in models of total expenditures.

Fourth, we cannot rule out the explanation that the item veto is ineffective, even though it is in fact often used. In a state where the governor possesses the item veto, legislators may feel free to lard up a state budget with their pet projects, claim credit with their constituents for doing so, and perhaps not be too devastated to see these items eventually lined out. In states without the item veto, legislative leaders and governors themselves may work harder to instill fiscal discipline, keeping these objectionable lines out of the budget to preserve the collective reputation of their parties (Cox and McCubbins 1993) or to avoid a full-scale veto of the budget. If this explanation is correct, the item veto is used, but often only for show. Legislators take strategic positions for political advantage rather than for policy gain, much like ambitious governors often do in their State of the State addresses. If this explanation is correct, the null finding that we and so many other prior scholars have found should be believed: the presence of item veto may change the way that the budget bargaining game is played but will not alter its final outcome.

7.6. Appendix

In Table 7.2, we report the results of several regression models that estimate the effect of the item veto on the size of state government. The dependent variable in each model is the year-to-year change in state government spending, measured in per capita constant dollars. The first two models are estimated using our unmatched data set, while the final three use our matched data (the matching techniques we use are detailed in Section 7.2). Models report the effect of either an item veto or a sustainable item veto. The final model tests for the possibility that the impact of a sustainable item veto is greatest in the hands of a frugal governor, that is, a governor whose proposed budget calls for either no increase or a reduction in per capita government expenditures. A negative coefficient on *Item Veto* indicates that governors who possess this power are able to reduce the growth of the state budget. The negative coefficient on *Item Veto × Frugal Governor* suggests that the item veto has a greater impact on the growth of spending in the hands of a frugal governor.

Table 7.3 reports regression models of gubernatorial success in negotiations over the size of government. Here, the dependent variable is the absolute difference between what the governor asked for in her proposed budget and what she was ultimately able to secure at the bargaining table. This difference is measured as dollars per capita. Both models are estimated using our matched data set. Model 2 is identical to model 1, except that we add an interaction between *Sustainable Veto* and

Frugal Governor. A negative coefficient on *Sustainable Veto* indicates that governors who have the item veto and the partisan allies to back them up typically sign into a law a budget that is closer to what they proposed than governors without this power. The negative coefficient on *Sustainable Item Veto × Frugal Governor* indicates that the item veto is most useful in the hands of frugal governors.

TABLE 7.2. *The Item Veto and State Per Capita Spending Changes, Fiscal Years 1989–2009*

	Before matching		After matching		
	Any item veto	Sustainable item veto	Any item veto	Sustainable item veto	Sustainable item veto
Item Veto	7.78	−4.95	14.51	−0.80	0.40
	(10.10)	(8.59)	(12.26)	(11.08)	(11.91)
Income Per Capita	2.52**	2.50**	3.09**	3.08**	2.26**
	(1.11)	(1.12)	(1.39)	(1.41)	(1.21)
Change Income Per Capita	13.17*	13.26*	4.27	4.87	2.49
	(7.63)	(7.63)	(9.98)	(10.05)	(8.41)
Unemployment	−7.05**	−6.66**	−3.71	−3.20	−0.85
	(3.40)	(3.37)	(4.53)	(4.55)	(3.90)
Change Unemployment	6.71	7.08	3.10	2.51	−6.13
	(5.97)	(5.94)	(7.43)	(7.47)	(6.25)
Lagged Surplus	1.48**	1.50**	1.16**	1.69**	2.31**
	(0.55)	(0.55)	(0.69)	(0.69)	(0.58)
Voter Liberalness	−0.67	−0.63	−0.16	−0.38	−0.52
	(0.72)	(0.73)	(0.99)	(0.98)	(0.86)
Republican Governor	−2.98	−3.58	−4.31	−4.31	
	(6.68)	(6.82)	(9.21)	(9.50)	
Frugal Governor					−85.77**
					(15.76)
Item Veto × Frugal Governor					−5.99
					(17.87)
Share Democratic Seats	0.69**	0.63**	0.57	0.58	0.61*
	(0.26)	(0.27)	(0.36)	(0.38)	(0.32)
South	−7.38	−6.64	−8.98	−7.89	−5.63
	(9.16)	(9.15)	(12.04)	(12.12)	(10.61)
Constant	−72.12	−59.28	−88.99	−83.70	−47.83
	(50.84)	(53.28)	(62.51)	(66.57)	(57.09)
AIC	12,106	12,107	8,129	8,108	7,823
N	1,001	1,001	662	655	655

Note: The dependent variable in all models is the year-to-year changes in state government spending, measured in per capita constant dollars. All models include random effects for state and year. Two-tailed tests are employed: * < .10, ** < .05. AIC = Akaike Information Criterion.

TABLE 7.3. *The Item Veto and Gubernatorial Bargaining Success, Fiscal Years 1989–2009*

	Model 1	Model 2
Sustainable Item Veto	−3.68	−2.03
	(7.18)	(8.42)
Divided Government	−7.59	−7.58
	(6.13)	(6.13)
Frugal Governor		9.45
		(9.79)
Sustainable Item Veto × Frugal Governor		−4.41
		(10.95)
Session Months	5.46**	5.34**
	(1.87)	(1.86)
First-Term Governor	9.47*	9.22*
	(5.12)	(5.14)
Legacy-Year Governor	20.00	18.72
	(12.79)	(12.85)
Income Per Capita	−1.15	−1.05
	(1.01)	(1.02)
Change in Income Per Capita	5.77	5.59
	(4.93)	(4.96)
Unemployment Rate	−1.89	−2.27
	(2.73)	(2.75)
Change in the Unemployment Rate	0.53	0.83
	(3.84)	(3.86)
Lagged Budget Surplus	0.73*	0.73*
	(0.41)	(0.41)
Size of Proposed Changes	0.08**	0.08**
	(0.03)	(0.03)
Voter Liberalness	1.30	1.30
	(1.01)	(0.99)
South	4.96	5.32
	(13.97)	(13.78)
Intercept	60.95	57.11
	(42.32)	(42.67)
Standard deviation of state effects	33.03	32.48
Standard deviation of year effects	8.21	8.53
		56.86
AIC	7,203	7,194
N	655	655

Note: The dependent variable in all models is the absolute difference between what the governor asked for in her proposed budget and what she was ultimately able to secure at the bargaining table (measured in constant per capita dollars). All models include random effects for state and year. Two-tailed tests are employed: * < .10, ** < .05. AIC = Akaike Information Criterion.

8

Legislative Professionalism and Gubernatorial Power

> If states are to survive and prosper in our system, they need the tools
> of effective government. Proposition 1-a is a giant step toward that goal.
> California can lead the way.
> – Ballot argument in favor of California's Proposition 1-a

In 1966, California voters handily ratified a ballot measure that not only
transformed their state's legislature from a citizen house into a professional body but also precipitated a decade of legislative modernization
across the country. For California lawmakers, the passage of Proposition 1-a brought about a dramatic lengthening of legislative sessions,
an increase in their salary, and the expansion of the legislature's expert
staff. These reforms, part of a package proposed by the state's blue-
ribbon Constitutional Revision Commission, were not intended merely
to make life better for lawmakers. The proponents of the reform saw that
it could transform state government more fundamentally. They under-
stood that Proposition 1-a, by enhancing the effectiveness of the legislature, could alter the balance of power between the branches of government. Jesse Unruh, the speaker of the California Assembly and leader of
the reform effort, argued that professionalization was needed because it
would strengthen the hand of the legislature when it comes to dealing
with the governor (Squire 1992).

On the eve of professionalization, however, not everyone was in agreement with Speaker Unruh. The information guide mailed to California
voters prior to the 1966 election contained some surprising predictions at
odds with our intuition about the effects of professionalization. State senator Schmitz (Republican of Orange County), for example, urged voters

to oppose Proposition 1-a and hailed the citizen legislature as the one true check against executive power, calling it a "people's check" against governors and their professional staffs. The contestants in that year's gubernatorial race, incumbent Pat Brown and his charismatic challenger Ronald Reagan, both signed the ballot argument in favor of the proposition, suggesting that neither thought it would seriously undermine executive power. Indeed, this bipartisan support may have helped push Proposition 1-a toward its eventual electoral landslide.

Were Pat Brown and Ronald Reagan signing away some of the powers of the office they both sought? In this chapter, we use the passage of Proposition 1-a to further explore the effects of legislative professionalization on the power of governors. We have argued that gubernatorial influence cannot be measured solely by the powers possessed by the executive branch. Because legislatures house every governor's primary bargaining partners, the institutional resources of the lawmakers are crucially relevant. Our focus on California allows us to study the link between legislative professionalism and executive power by tracking how Golden State governors perform, first, in negotiations with a citizen body and, later, when they face off with the nation's most professionalized state legislature.

Through this analysis, we gain additional leverage on the hypotheses developed in Chapter 2. Our budget-bargaining model predicts that the ability of governors to move their fiscal agendas should decline when they face more professional legislators because full-time lawmakers can be more patient than their citizen counterparts when budget negotiations drag on into staring matches. We have already found strong evidence consistent with this prediction. In Chapter 4, we show that governors, when bargaining with a professional legislature, are more likely to lose on the budgetary proposals contained in their State of the State addresses, while in Chapter 5, we demonstrate that these governors are also less successful in battles over the size of government. By contrast, our policy bargaining model does not make any predictions about the role of professionalism. Indeed, our analysis of the policy proposals contained in State of the State addresses found either no relationship between professionalization and gubernatorial success or a small positive one (depending on the sample used).[1]

[1] The positive relationship was found when we considered the subsample of data from states with gubernatorial approval ratings. This sample excludes many states with citizen legislatures (see Chapter 4).

Tracking gubernatorial success over the course of California's legislative evolution brings time-series evidence to bear on a question that our other analyses examine only with cross-sectional data. Looking at one state over time allows us to hold constant many factors that we were unable to address in our prior empirical analyses. This approach controls for the presence of the nation's most muscular version of direct democracy (Bowler and Donovan 2008), a *plural executive* system that forces governors to share power with many other statewide elected officials, the particular constellation of powers with which Golden State governors are endowed (including the item veto and strong appointive authority), and all of the other unique attributes of California politics. For governors operating under a consistent political system, we can examine whether and how the adoption of Proposition 1-a shifted the balance of power between the branches.

Admittedly, this test is far from a perfect natural experiment. We cannot isolate the legislature's professionalization from the other changes that took place over the same time period in California. The state has faced many economic booms and busts, transitioned from a red to a purple to a predominantly blue state (Fiorina and Abrams 2006), become increasingly polarized along party lines (Masket 2007), witnessed a notable increase in the frequency of divided government, and seen its geopolitical divide shift from a north–south to an east–west axis (Douzet and Miller 2006). Legislative term limits, which were enacted by voters in 1990 and widely implemented in 1996, forced from office many career lawmakers, ushering in a new era of "amateur politics" in the legislature (Clucas 2003). Most importantly, for the purposes of our test, the state has been led by notably distinct governors. The same 1966 election that ushered in Proposition 1-a's era of professionalism also marked the defeat of two-term incumbent Pat Brown and the ascension of Ronald Reagan. When we look before and after professionalization, we will be comparing the records of very different governors.

We take steps to reduce the chances that our observations are driven by the idiosyncrasies of individual governors and their times. We look at all governors in the same point of their career arcs, tracking the success of their proposals in the State of the State delivered in the third year of each governorship. We also gather information on numerous governors, looking at three who served prior to the passage of Proposition 1-a (Earl Warren, 1945; Goodwin Knight, 1955; Edmund "Pat" Brown, 1961) and four who served after professionalization (George Deukmejian, 1985; Pete Wilson, 1993; Gray Davis, 2001; and Arnold Schwarzenegger,

2006). With a larger number of governors, individual quirks are more likely to average out.

We begin this chapter by showing just how fundamentally Proposition 1-a, and the changes that followed, transformed California's legislature. We then conduct a brief and indirect test of how professionalization shifted the budgeting dynamic, looking for evidence that legislators grew more patient when lawmaking became their full-time job. The bulk of our analysis looks at the records of seven governors in moving their State of the State agendas, drawing on the same sorts of journalistic sources that we have repeatedly used to track gubernatorial success. We examine success on both policy and budget proposals. The results of this analysis largely confirm our expectation that professionalization of the legislature has hurt the ability of the governor to successfully move her budgetary agenda. It also provides some unexpected evidence that professionalization has a similar effect when it comes to a governor's policy proposals.

8.1. The Professionalization of California's Legislature

Like nearly all of the houses described as "Those Dinosaurs – Our State Legislatures,"[2] the California Assembly and Senate were part-time bodies composed of citizen lawmakers in 1966. In their operations and resources, these chambers resembled the U.S. Congress of the nineteenth-century much more than the contemporary Congress (Polsby 1968; Squire 1992). Of course, California was not alone. Although a few states, such as New York, Massachusetts, Kansas, and Michigan, possessed surprising attributes of legislative professionalism, nearly every other statehouse met for only a few months every year or biennially, paid lawmakers either a meager salary or none at all, and provided small staffs that had little policy expertise. A series of reports by national organizations urged the modernization of state legislatures (Council of State Governments 1946; American Political Science Association 1954; National Legislative Conference 1961). Still, because many of the obstacles to professionalization – including specified session lengths and limits on salaries – were locked in by state constitutions, reform was difficult.

Transforming statehouses into something that resembled the twentieth-century Congress required energetic leadership and sustained

---

[2] This is the title of a *New York Times* magazine article authored by Thomas C. Desmond, quoted in Wahlke (1966).

effort. In California, that came from Jesse Unruh, the speaker of the assembly, who, when he was not dominating Sacramento politics and policy (Boyarsky 2008), supplemented his legislative salary by counting boxcars for a Los Angeles railroad (Squire 1992). When Unruh came to power after the 1960 elections, he ruled a citizen body. California's constitution restricted the length of time that lawmakers could meet to 120 days in odd-numbered years and only 30 days in even-numbered years. Legislators were paid between $7,200 and $8,000 per year for their service, which provided for "a modest standard of living while the legislature was in session, but most members still needed another job to make ends meet" (Squire 1992, p. 1029). Lawmakers had little staff support, relying on the executive branch and interest groups for their information (Jacobs 1997).

Wishing to boost his institution's power and his own influence, Unruh worked slowly but deliberately to create the constitutional revision commission that eventually placed Proposition 1-a on the ballot.[3] When it passed, he and his legislative allies used their newfound control over salaries and session lengths to turn the legislature into a full-time body that paid a high salary and employed the lawyers and policy analysts who ended the legislature's reliance on agency officials and interest groups for information. These reforms gave California the most professionalized state legislature in the nation, according to several early 1970s rankings (Citizens Conference on State Legislatures 1971; Squire 1992). Observers noted that lawmakers in the modernized statehouse treated legislative service as a profession, and many even opted to live year-round in Sacramento with their families (Dodd and Kelley 1989).

California was not alone in this movement. Other states pursued a parallel path, and Unruh (along with several of his staff members) worked closely with legislative leaders in these states to support the diffusion of professionalization (Kennedy 1970; Citizens Conference on State Legislatures 1971; Herzberg and Rosenthal 1971; Rosenthal 1974; Sittig 1977). Although these efforts were not always successful, they did help to bring about the most dramatic surge in legislative modernization seen in the history of American statehouses. In 1960, for example, only 19 states held annual legislative sessions, but by 1990, this number had risen to 43. Whereas a majority of states paid only per diem to their legislators in

[3] Proposition 1-a removed existing constitutional restrictions on session length, opening the door for the legislature to meet in sessions of unlimited duration. It also allowed legislators to set their own salaries via statute, eliminating the constitutional requirement that any increase must be approved by voters.

the 1943, by 2000, all but seven paid a regular (if modest) salary (Kousser 2005). The total legislative staff in all states rose to 16,930 by 1979 and continued to climb to 24,555 by 1988 and 26,900 by 1996.[4] This burst of professionalization manifestly transformed state legislatures. The relevant question for this chapter and book is whether the rising status of many legislatures brought about a decline in the policy making and budgetary powers of governors.

8.2. Professionalization and Delays in Budget Bargaining

We begin by considering whether increased professionalism led California's legislature to become more patient in budget negotiations. One way to do this is to look at changes in the length and frequency of late budgets. The argument we lay out in Chapter 2, based on a staring match model of budget bargaining, holds that governors can afford to be more patient than citizen lawmakers when budget deadlines loom. Though leaders of both branches know that they will pay a political cost if the budget is late, part-time legislators will pay the additional private costs of missing valuable time from their "day jobs" if they are called back into a special session to resolve a late budget. (In citizen chambers, the regular session usually ends well before the deadline for a new budget.) Their desire to avoid paying these private costs leads lawmakers to cave in to gubernatorial budgetary proposals. Professionalism, particularly lengthy sessions, should bring about increased legislative patience and a greater willingness to stand up to the governor on fiscal matters.

Without any personal hurry to pass a compromise budget and head home, California's legislators can now be as patient as their governor. This should lead to long delays as lawmakers stand their ground in budget negotiations, forcing negotiations past the state's deadlines to extract executive concessions.[5] The opportunity to observe this sort of evidence

---

[4] National Conference of State Legislators, "Six of State Legislative Staff: 1979, 1988 and 1996;" accessed at http://www.ncsl.org/programs/legman/about/stf1.htm in June 2001.

[5] In our formal model, these and any delays are technically "off the equilibrium" path; governors should have recognized the legislature's newfound patience after professionalization, anticipated that lawmakers would hold out, and offered concessions early. But politics rarely plays out quite as cleanly as this rational model, and under the new system, legislators likely had to enter protracted negotiations to prove their patience. We see in Figure 8.1 a wave of delays just after the passage of Proposition 1-a, then a return to many on-time budgets, and then a steep rise in delays again, especially in years of divided government. Perhaps the latter divergence from our formal prediction occurs because, under divided government, both parties were willing to venture far past deadlines because of uncertainty about which party would take the blame.

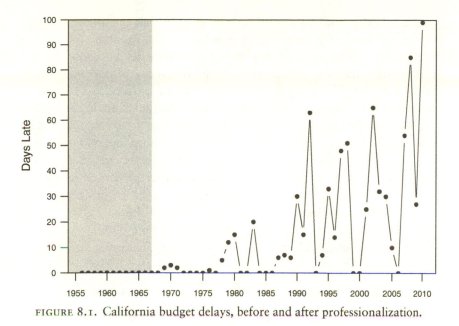

FIGURE 8.1. California budget delays, before and after professionalization.

along the causal path between legislative professionalism and executive power is a key strength of case study analysis (Brady and Collier 2004; Collier et al. 2010). In the next sections, we will probe for direct evidence of legislative power through the defeat of gubernatorial budget proposals. Here, we look for a preview of this power shift in the form of longer budget delays, showing that professionalization made legislators more patient in their staring matches with governors.

To do this, we draw on a data set of the timing of state budget adoption. These data were compiled by Klarner et al. (2010), using legislative journals and communications with state reference librarians. For each fiscal year (beginning in 1956), they identify late state budgets as well as the number of days each was adopted after the start of the new fiscal year. Figure 8.1 reports budget delays in California, before and after the passage of Proposition 1-a. As predicted, we see a dramatic increase in delay – indicating a rise in legislative patience – immediately after the proposition's implementation. In the 11 years prior to Proposition 1-a (the shaded portion of the graph), California did not experience a single late budget. Since Proposition 1-a went into effect, however, 64 percent of all California budgets have been late by an average of 27 days. By the 1990s, budget delays became as predictable as 100 degree heat in a Sacramento summer.

Although it is impossible to definitively say that professionalization of the California legislature is responsible for the dramatic increase in fiscal delay shown in Figure 8.1, two pieces of evidence support such a conclusion. First, a similar increase in the frequency of late budgets did not occur everywhere. Among states that kept a citizen legislature, late budgets were as rare in the 1990s and 2000s as they were in the 1960s. Second, our data show that states with full-time, well-paid chambers (like post-1966 California) are *much more likely* to adopt late budgets. Over the past five decades, a whopping 42 percent of the budgets adopted by professionalized chambers have been late, compared to only 3 percent in citizen legislatures. For these reasons, it appears that California's trend of increasingly late budgets is closely linked to Proposition 1-a. Once California's legislature transformed itself into a full-time body, its members became more patient when it came to budget negotiations.

8.3. Governors Bargaining with Citizen Lawmakers

To determine whether this increased legislative patience shaped the ability of governors to move their budgetary and policy proposals, we gauge gubernatorial success before and after legislative professionalization. Just as we did in our case study chapters on popularity and the item veto, we track the victories and failures of State of the State proposals. The added challenge of this chapter is that studying professionalization requires a long historical reach, tracking gubernatorial success over a time period not covered by today's journalistic search engines. While the News-Bank database that we use for our modern analysis allows us to search major California newspapers to determine the records of our postprofessionalization governors,[6] we turned to other sources to track pre-1966 governors.

As we have done for all of our State of the State analyses, we began by reading through the text of a governor's address and identifying the discrete policy and budgetary proposals it contained. Next, we worked with a team of research assistants to search for information on the legislative histories of each proposal. To do so, we relied on Proquest Historical Newspapers, which allows for keyword searches that retrieve PDF

---

[6] For instance, NewsBank covers the *Sacramento Bee*, California's legislative newspaper of record, from January 1984 onward. Because it only covers the *Los Angeles Times* from 2006 to 2009, we supplemented our NewsBank searches with searches of the *Los Angeles Times* in Proquest Historical Newspapers and Lexis-Nexis Academic Universe for our postprofessionalization governors.

images of articles in the *Los Angeles Times*. Our assistants also gathered relevant articles from the *Sacramento Bee*, reading microfilm copies of the newspaper from January 1 (in each year included in our analysis) through two weeks after the end of the legislative session. These searches typically retrieved a combined 50–70 articles about the items on each governor's agenda. We read through the articles to assess the final fate of each gubernatorial proposal, coding passages, compromises, and failures. With fewer journalistic sources for governors who served in the preprofessionalization era, we were unable to determine the fate of a larger share of their agenda items (21%). So that our analyses are not biased by the use of a different search process, all of the summary statistics that we report in this chapter exclude proposals for which we could find no news coverage. Because a reanalysis of our models in Chapter 4 that also excluded proposals with no definitive outcomes did not change any of the substantive results, we view this as the safest way to address one of the inherent challenges of archival research.

In the following, we present overviews of each of the seven California governors included in our analysis. We take care to highlight the bargaining circumstances each confronted, features of their agenda, and their records of failure or success. Doing so allows us to revisit many of the book's broader themes and, most importantly, to compare the ability of California chief executives to move their policy and budgetary agendas before and after legislative professionalization.

8.3.1. Earl Warren (1945)

Before he became chief justice of the U.S. Supreme Court, Earl Warren was three times elected governor of California. A moderate, he first won on the Republican ticket in 1942 but took advantage of the state's "cross-filing" system to win the nominations of the Republican, Democratic, and Progressive parties in 1945.[7] The State of the State address that he delivered to begin his third year in office leaned to the political Left. Speaking to the legislature on the afternoon of January 8, 1945, Warren argued that the people of California "expect us to start now cutting away the handicaps to social and economic progress."[8] The governor proposed the expansion of unemployment insurance, increasing government expenditures for the disabled, and even a universal health

---

[7] See Earl Warren College, University of California San Diego, "Earl Warren (1891–1974)," accessed at http://warren.ucsd.edu/about/biography.html in September 2011.
[8] From "Message of Governor Earl Warren to the 1945 Legislature," printed on pp. 13–17 of the *Assembly Journal*, January 8, 1945, Sacramento: California State Assembly, p. 14.

insurance program. In addition, Warren focused much of his speech on California's bureaucracy. He called for increased planning, the restructuring of several departments, and the elimination of some of the organizations created to help the state during World War II, including the California State War Council and the Farm Production Council.

The Republican-led legislature responded positively to Gov. Warren's agenda. Of the 12 policy proposals for which we were able to determine the outcome, Warren was successful on nine, for a batting average of 75 percent. Governor Warren's failures came on three proposals that sought to move the state sharply to the left. He urged the creation of a Commission on Economic and Political Equality "for the purpose of studying minority problems.... Under such a commission we could start to build a foundation for real political and economic equality for every citizen in the State."[9] The legislature, more conservative than Warren, rejected this call, forcing the governor to wait until he ascended to the Supreme Court to make his most significant contributions to civil rights. The governor's most stinging defeat, however, came on his proposal for universal health insurance, provided through private doctors and paid for by payroll deductions charged to both employers and employees. As future presidents would learn, moving this sort of program through a legislature brings tremendous challenges. The governor's proposal became the main focus of the legislative session, with 23 newspaper articles in the *Los Angeles Times* and *Sacramento Bee* charting the governor's deep engagement in moving his insurance package through the legislature. Warren came closer to victory than all the presidents who would take up this quest throughout the next half-century, with his full legislation losing on a 39–38 assembly vote in April and a compromise bill finally dying in that house on June 5.[10]

Though he suffered setbacks on his boldest and most controversial policy proposals, Gov. Warren was tremendously successful when it came to the budget. We were able to track down the final results of five of his six budgetary proposals, and he was successful on all five. Legislators backed Warren's proposals to maintain the tax reductions that he had won in prior sessions, to protect old age pension funding, and to increase expenditures on disabled children. Warren's call to earmark "sufficient funds" for the purchase of additional park and beach lands was met with an

[9] Ibid., p. 23.
[10] Herbert L. Phillips, "Legislature Sets Adjournment for June 16th; Kills Health Bill," *Sacramento Bee*, June 5, 1945, p. 1.

appropriation of $15 million for further beach purchases and the passage of AB 1620, authorizing the acquisition of beach land for recreation. He even succeeded in securing his most controversial budgetary proposal – a $90 million freeze on expenditures from the state's Postwar Reconstruction and Reemployment program. The governor was able to secure this freeze over the initial objections of lawmakers and without having any of the savings earmarked for other programs, despite the legislature's very strong preference to do so. The thorough nature of his victory was indicative of Warren's near-complete control of the budgeting process.[11]

8.3.2. *Goodwin Knight (1955)*

When Earl Warren's third term was interrupted by his appointment as chief justice in 1953, his longtime lieutenant governor, Goodwin Knight, ascended to the state's top position. The former Los Angeles Superior Court judge fit the same moderate Republican mold of his predecessor, and was elected in his own right as governor in 1954.[12] While the speech that he gave to begin his third year in office, 1955, was technically an inaugural address, it read like a typical State of the State. After hearing it, a reporter from *Sacramento Bee*'s capitol bureau observed that "the governor's inaugural speech was not one of oratorical generalities but rather a plain spoken and extensive recitation of policy, state government needs and administration recommendations."[13]

Governor Knight's agenda was not as ambitious as that of Warren, centering more on budgetary as opposed to policy proposals. That said, the governor did call for reform to worker's compensation and unemployment insurance as well as a bold proposal to reform the practices of the state's political campaigns. The newly elected speaker of the assembly, Republican Luther H. "Abe" Lincoln of Alameda County, quickly signaled his support of Gov. Knight's program. The day after the speech, news coverage reported that Lincoln called the address "a clear appraisal of the problems confronting our ever growing state" and predicted that both legislative chambers would follow Knight's leadership.[14] With citizen legislators inclined to work with their party's leader, Knight was able

---

[11] Herbert L. Phillips, "Warren Reveals New Plan to Break Deadlock," *Sacramento Bee*, May 3, 1945, p. 1.

[12] California State Library, "Goodwin Knight 1953–59," accessed at http://governors.library.ca.gov/31-knight.html in September 2011.

[13] Herbert L. Phillips, "Legislature Convenes, Knight Takes Oath as 31st Governor," *Sacramento Bee*, January 3, 1955, p. 1.

[14] "Frustration, Achievement Mark Session," *Sacramento Bee*, June 9, 1955, p. 1.

to secure a number of policy successes: he recorded five clear victories against the two defeats.

Again, the governor's defeats came on the two most controversial proposals. The failure of the first – a new Fair Campaign Practices Act – was predictable given our prior finding (Chapter 4) that political reforms are rarely successful. This act would have made the lives of legislators more difficult by dramatically increasing political contribution reporting requirements. Indeed, Gov. Knight's proposal encountered steep Republican opposition along its "fatal journey through the legislature."[15] Californians would have to wait until the passage of a 1974 proposition backed by Gov. Jerry Brown for serious political reform. Equally as contentious was Gov. Knight's proposal to create a Water Resources Department, which passed the assembly but failed in a senate dominated by rural lawmakers who were skeptical of consolidating executive control of water policy.[16]

The governor's fiscal agenda included proposals for significant new investments in educational facilities, infrastructure, water projects, and parks. The early reception to many of the governor's budget proposals was not entirely favorable, but his performance in this sphere was quite strong. After Knight's State of the State address, the senate's fiscal committee chair, Republican Ben Hulse of rural Imperial County, voiced his disagreements: "He [the governor] indicated that he plans to expand state services. I don't agree with any expansion that cannot be financed out of present revenues and reserves."[17] Yet, despite Senator Hulse's warnings against indebtedness, lawmakers put before voters the massive borrowing plans that Gov. Knight had called for: a $200 million bond to fund the construction of colleges, prisons, mental hospitals, and other parts of the governor's five-year institutional building program and a $100 million state bond issue for the construction of schools in needy areas.[18] Lawmakers quickly and favorably responded to the rest of Knight's fiscal program. With the state's gas tax due to drop from six cents to five and a half, the governor called for an urgency measure to keep the tax at its current level and accelerate highway construction. Legislators obliged,

---

[15] Richard Rodda, "Committee Kills Bill on Election Fund Accounting," *Sacramento Bee*, June 2, 1955, p. 1.
[16] See Chester G. Hanson, "Hopes Doused for OK on Water Department Bill," *Los Angeles Times*, June 1, 1955, p. 21, for coverage of the water bill, and Persily et al. (2002) for a treatment of malapportionment in California.
[17] Herbert L. Phillips, "Knight Message Draws Praise, Hints of Hassles," *Sacramento Bee*, January 4, 1955, p. 1.
[18] "Action Taken on Top Bills in Legislature," *Los Angeles Times*, June 9, 1955, p. 21.

sending him the bill by the end of a January session in which they introduced a record 5,405 bills.[19]

When legislators passed the annual budget, they left the governor's
proposed spending plan almost perfectly intact. "The Legislature trimmed
only $500,000 from Gov. Knight's budget, approving a record-breaking
bill for $1,529,000,000 to operate the State for the next fiscal year," the
Los Angeles Times reported. Future governors might have been surprised
at the small scale of the budget, but they would have been shocked at
how little of it (only 3%) the legislature changed. In the postprofessionalization, pre-term limits era, legislators routinely altered between 15 and
20 percent of governors' spending proposals (Kousser 2005). Overall,
legislators passed nine of Knight's budget proposals, delivering one compromise and failing to pass only one fiscal item. Like Earl Warren before
him, Gov. Knight saw decent success on his policy agenda but found
citizen legislators to be strongly supportive of his budget agenda.

8.3.3. *Edmund "Pat" Brown (1961)*

In 1958, Pat Brown became the first Democrat to win a California governor's race in 20 years and only the second to do so in the twentieth
century. Brown used his time as chief executive to push relentlessly for
the creation of programs that built the state's roads, waterworks, and universities, all of which won him wide praise. Of course, with an expanding
economy and a legislature taken over by his fellow Democrats, conditions were primed for Gov. Brown to move his program. The start of
his first term in office was so successful that he magnified rather than
narrowed his goals by his third year in office. In his 1961 State of the
State address, the governor declared, "In the past two years, more pio-
neering legislation has been enacted than in any comparable period since
the first term of Hiram Johnson," but warned, "There is no room for self-
satisfaction about our accomplishments. . . . Good government requires a
never-ending search for the best means of serving the people."[20]

This search led Brown to issue a stunning 38 legislative proposals,
accompanied by 20 budget items. The items on this massive agenda were
wide ranging, and the governor met with a great deal of success. Brown's
speech began with a call for education reform, including tighter teacher
training standards, an increased emphasis on basic subjects, a statewide

[19] Richard Rodda, "Gasoline Tax Bill Goes to Governor," *Sacramento Bee*, January 21,
1955, p. 1.
[20] From "Address by the Governor," *Assembly Journal*, January 3, 1961, Sacramento:
California State Assembly, pp. 68–9.

testing program, and a move toward greater equalization of funding across school districts. Each one of these ambitious proposals passed. Brown deemed the teaching training standards contained in Senate Bill 7, which required that all teachers hold a college degree in an academic subject, the "major bill of the legislative session."[21]

However, some of the governor's most far-reaching policy proposals were defeated, echoing our observation in Chapter 6 that governors' ambitions can trip them up. As Brown noted, "Outside of the MTA bill, we lost everything in our attempt to lay the foundation for regional planning."[22] The senate also stifled his call for unchecked authority to reorganize the administration, killed his proposal to prohibit racial discrimination in private housing, and was unmoved by his controversial attempt to repeal or moderate the death penalty.[23] Overall, though, Pat Brown's record of success playing the policy game was remarkable. We tracked down records on all but two of his policy proposals, and these revealed 27 passes, 2 compromises, and 7 failures.

The governor's ability to move his budget proposals was even closer to perfection. He passed 17 of them, accepted 1 compromise, and saw only 1 failure (we were unable to determine the immediate fate of his proposal to build a UC medical school in San Diego but are assured of his eventual success). His fiscal program included increasing benefits for the disabled, for worker's compensation, and for unemployment insurance, while raising revenues to shore up all three funds.[24] When the gavel had fallen on the 1961 session, Gov. Brown declared, "We can take pride in one of the most productive, most progressive sessions in the modern history of California."[25] Republican legislators were less complimentary, with one headline reading "Brown Praises 1961 Legislature, GOP Dissents."[26] Regardless of ideological perspective, the governor clearly succeeded in moving an astonishingly large agenda. Indeed, by nearly any objective standard, Gov. Brown had the most successful legislative session of any state chief executive included in this book. Brown was not

[21] Robert Blanchard, "Brown Praises Action on Water and Transit," *Los Angeles Times*, June 21, 1961, p. 2.

[22] Robert Blanchard, "Brown Praises Action on Water and Transit," *Los Angeles Times*, June 21, 1961, p. 2.

[23] Robert Blanchard, "California Lawmakers Head Home," *Los Angeles Times*, June 18, 1961, p. FA.

[24] Tom Arden, "Insurance Liberalizing Bills Pass," *Sacramento Bee*, June 5, 1961, p. A1.

[25] Robert Blanchard, "Brown Opens His 1962 Re-election Campaign," *Los Angeles Times*, June 20, 1961, p. 1.

[26] "Brown Praises 61 Legislature, GOP Dissents," *Sacramento Bee*, June 16, 1961.

shy about trumpeting his wins. To kick off his 1962 campaign, Brown toured the state and reported on his own batting average, counting both bills proposed in his State of the State address and in other communications, noting that 56 of his 68 major bills passed. "That adds up to a team batting average of .830 . . . which might just win the Democrats another pennant next year."[27]

8.4. Governors Bargaining with Professional Lawmakers

This burst of liberal legislation gave Brown a record to run on and helped the governor defeat national political power Richard Nixon in the 1962 gubernatorial election. However, the governor's momentum eventually slowed. The fair housing act he secured from the legislature in 1963 was overturned the following year in a referendum, and Gov. Brown took blame for both the causes of and the crackdowns on Berkeley protesters in 1964 and Watts rioters in 1965 (Rarick 2005). As the state turned rightward, Brown lost his 1966 reelection fight against political newcomer Ronald Reagan (Dallek 2004). This election also brought Proposition 1-a's decisive victory, setting the legislature on the path toward professionalism. In the coming years, Speaker Unruh and the legislature would assemble the greatest professional apparatus state legislatures had yet seen (Citizens Conference on State Legislatures 1971) by lengthening sessions, increasing salaries, and soon bolstering the staff for committees, personal offices, and expert units such as the Legislative Analyst's Office, the Office of Legislative Counsel, and the Assembly and Senate Offices of Research. Because the transformation of the legislature did not occur overnight, we pick up our case studies of governors after the houses fully transitioned into their modern forms. By studying governors from George Deukmejian onward, we are also able to buttress our archival accounts with the testimony of those who served in these administrations.

8.4.1. *George Deukmejian (1985)*

Republican governor George Deukmejian, the first of our governors to bargain with a professionalized legislature, was the antithesis of Pat Brown in his governing philosophy yet similar in his political career and personal style. Deukmejian ascended to the governorship from the

---

[27] Robert Blanchard, "Brown Opens His 1962 Re-election Campaign," *Los Angeles Times*, June 20, 1961, p. 1.

Attorney General's Office, just as Pat Brown had, and was also a skilled insider who was deeply engaged in Sacramento's politics and policy. Unlike Pat, though, he was a "real fiscal conservative,"[28] and instead of initiating some of the state's most expansive legislative agendas, he proposed very few new laws and programs. "He had little interest in using the bully pulpit for anything other than his pet causes: building prisons and cutting taxes," according to two statehouse journalists (Jacobs and Block 2006, p. 79).

When Gov. Deukmejian took office after his 1982 victory over the Democratic mayor of Los Angeles, Tom Bradley, he faced much stronger opposition in the legislature than did governors Warren, Knight, or Brown. Not only had the legislature professionalized but it was controlled by the Democrats, who were often hostile to the governor's legislative agenda. In his first year in office, Deukmejian saw how long a professional legislature could hold out in a budget conflict. The 1983 budget was nearly a month late as legislators, no longer inclined to rubber stamp the governor's fiscal plan, fought him bitterly. At the time, this was the longest budgetary stalemate in California history (a record that has long since been surpassed).

That year, according to Deukmeijian aide Larry Thomas, bargaining over the budget "got so nasty that the Democratic majority denied the governor the use of the state mansion that had been purchased by Ronald Reagan. He ended up staying in a Best Western hotel for the beginning of his term."[29] As the state struggled with a budget shortfall, Democrats in the senate hoped that by denying Deukmejian access to the governor's mansion (as well as blocking some of his appointments to key executive branch positions), the governor would agree to balance the budget with tax increases instead of deep cuts to education and welfare programs.[30] Through their delaying tactics, the Democrats eventually forced the governor to accept a budget that included a revenue trigger – sales taxes would increase by 1 cent if the state economy did not recover by October 1. Though the trigger was never pulled, the compromise was politically uncomfortable for the governor, and assembly Republicans angrily charged Duekmeijian with caving to Democratic demands. The

---

[28] Interview with Larry Thomas, press secretary and campaign manager to California governor George Deukmejian, conducted by telephone by Thad Kousser and Justin Phillips, June 30, 2009.

[29] Ibid.

[30] Wallace Turner, "Governor's House Is Political Pawn," *New York Times*, May 8, 1983.

ability of the legislature to force "Iron Duke" into a compromise that was inconsistent with his political brand was a clear demonstration of its newfound power in the budgetary arena.

In his third year in office, the governor's State of the State was notable for the brevity of its policy agenda. Deukmejian offered only four policy proposals, but – consistent with our finding that longer agendas lead to a lower rate of success – his close focus paid off. In response to his proposal for new enforcement tools to combat child abuse, legislators sent him a package of bills that allowed child abuse victims to testify outside the courtroom via two-way closed-circuit television, banned probation for those convicted of using obscene materials while committing lewd acts with children, and instituted a five-year sentence enhancement for kidnapping a child under 14.[31] His call for new measures to help women victimized by domestic violence did not appear to lead to any major laws in this area, though without definitive proof of failure, we coded its fate as unknown.[32] Governor Deukmejian's third policy proposal was more incremental than bold, but was successful. He asked for legislation "to encourage innovative methods of meeting local needs such as bond pooling, lease purchase and private construction."[33] His goals were met by bills authoring new revenue bonds to meet San Diego County's future transportation needs[34] and a major deal, brokered with Senator Foran, to give cities and counties $125 million of federal oil revenues for road repair.[35] Finally, the governor failed in his fourth proposal to create the Department of Waste Management to deal with toxics. The plan, the governor's "top priority,"[36] was dealt its final blow late in the session, when "assembly Democrats for the second time that year rejected Gov. George Deukmejian's plan to create a new state agency to control toxic

---

[31] Leo C. Walinsky and Jerry Gilliam, "Sacramento's Year: 40% of Bills Made It into the Lawbooks," *Los Angeles Times*, October 6, 1985, p. A3.

[32] We did not find any clear successes in journalistic searches for bills on this topic, and none were listed in the wrap-up of major crime legislation contained in Leo C. Walinsky and Jerry Gilliam, "Sacramento's Year: 40% of Bills Made It into the Lawbooks," *Los Angeles Times*, October 6, 1985, p. A3.

[33] "Governor's State of the State Address," *Assembly Journal*, January 8, 1985, Sacramento: California State Assembly, p. 106.

[34] Kenneth F. Bunting, "County Marks Wins and Losses at Half Time for Legislature," *Los Angeles Times*, September 23, 1985, p. SD-A1.

[35] Richard C. Paddock, "Flurry of Vetoes Shows Governor's Conservative Bent." Los Angeles Times, October 4, 1985, p. A3.

[36] Carl Ingram and Jerry Gillam, "For Deukmejian, Session Was Like a Rollercoaster," *Los Angeles Times*, September 15, 1985.

waste."[37] Overall, the governor met with two definitive victories and one clear failure on his limited policy agenda.

On the budget, Gov. Deukmejian proposed more and won often, perhaps because of the executive's inherent advantage in budgeting as well as a sharp increase in tax revenues resulting from a now-booming California economy. The governor had also developed a working relationship with Democrats in the legislature. Fred Silva, the senate leader's fiscal advisor, remarked at the time that "after three years, it was clear he [Duekmejian] was a little more willing to talk.... He used to draw this line in the dirt and now the wind has blown it away."[38] In 1985, Deukmejian was able to secure an on-time budget, a feat that had become increasingly rare after 1966. His proposals to spend the state's surplus – including a 10 percent increase in education spending, increases in funding for higher education, raises for law enforcement officers, and an 8 percent increase in safety net benefits – were well received by the Democratically controlled legislature. Indeed, many of these proposals reflected the priorities of Democratic leaders as much as those of the Republican governor. This does not, however, mean that Deukmejian was not forced to compromise. For example, when it came to his proposed raise for law enforcement officers, the legislature forced the governor to agree to raises for all state employees. We were able to track down the final outcome for 9 of the governor's 15 budget proposals. On these, he secured six full passes and three compromises.

8.4.2. *Pete Wilson (1993)*

Governor Pete Wilson, Deukmejian's Republican successor, underwent a similar evolution in his leadership style that often led him to meet his legislative adversaries halfway. After his election in 1990, the former marine, state assemblyman, San Diego mayor, and U.S. senator presented a lengthy set of proposals that would expand the role of government. "If you look at the inaugural address and his first State of the State, you'll see a very ambitious agenda," points out his communications director, Dan Schnur. He'd been getting budget warnings, but the budget bottom fell out in the spring of 1991. Everything that he proposed had to fall

---

[37] Richard C. Paddock and Leo C. Wolinsky, "Workfare Passes; Toxic Plan Loses," *Los Angeles Times*, September 15, 1985, p. A1.

[38] Richard C. Paddock, "Governor Dips into Surplus to Finance Spending Bills," *Los Angeles Times*, October 6, 1985.

by the wayside."[39] The budget became the focus of California politics as the nation went into recession and the Golden State's defense industry collapsed owing to post–Cold War cuts in military spending and base closings. Wilson was forced into bruising fights with the legislature, digging in his heels against taxes in his first year and then striking a deal that contained revenue increases in his second year (a deal that he later regretted). "It was only the third year," Schnur remembers, "that Wilson figured out how not to give away the store or burn the village."

The agenda contained in his 1993 State of the State address fit both Wilson's evolving approach to governing and the state's difficult economic times. "Today I want to speak exclusively of jobs," announced Wilson.[40] Rather than proposing any major programs or initiatives, the governor asked for a mere three policy changes. The first, reflecting his focus on jobs, was a call to restructure the state's competitive technology program so that California would be better positioned to secure federal defense conversion money.[41] The legislature responded with the changes Wilson requested as well as numerous other bills helping defense-related companies convert to other businesses. Echoing a proposal made by past governors, Wilson also called for reforms to the state's worker's compensation program that would both reduce fraud and lower costs for employers. His proposal passed in July, long before the legislative session ended.[42] The governor's third policy item – a growth management plan that would make it easier for builders to obtain permits – did not clear legislative hurdles until the waning days of the session. When it finally passed, it had an unlikely set of sponsors that included a moderate Democrat, an environmentalist, and a pro-business Republican.[43]

According to Gov. Wilson's communications director Kevin Eckery, working with a professional legislature (especially one controlled by the opposition) required constant strategizing and collaboration. The number of agenda items was kept small, and those that made it into the State of

[39] Interview with Dan Schnur, communications director to Gov. Pete Wilson, conducted by telephone by Thad Kousser, July 7, 2009.

[40] "Governor's State of the State Address," *Assembly Journal*, January 6, 1993, Sacramento: California State Assembly, p. 65.

[41] Money from the federal government was made available to states (on a competitive basis) to help industry redirect defense research and development toward commercial markets.

[42] George Skelton, "Last Chance for a Good Impression," *Los Angeles Times*, September 9, 1993, p. 3.

[43] Ibid.

the State address had been carefully developed, often in consultation with lawmakers.[44] Joe Rodota, a Wilson cabinet secretary, told us, "The Wilson administration would get the legislation to the point where people [even Democrats] would want to come carry the bill for the governor." The goal was to create strong bills that were hard even for the Democratic majority to oppose.[45] It is clear, as our model of the policy game suggests, that Wilson was strategic when it came to formulating his agenda, and his strategic behavior paid off with a policy batting average of 100 percent.

Wilson's resolve was also tested every year in budget negotiations, which, during his administration, usually devolved into very lengthy staring matches. The year 1993, however, was the one year during his governorship in which the budget was adopted on time. In his State of the State, Wilson proposed a modest set of seven budgetary items, all of which were tax cuts. Governor Wilson's proposals included a range of targeted tax breaks aimed at boosting small business, increasing research and development, and incentivizing investment in manufacturing equipment. With Democratic speaker Willie Brown often brokering deals with Wilson and business leaders, the budget and tax break bills passed with shockingly strong bipartisan majorities.[46] One summary of the session began, "The California Legislatures 1993 session so exceeded the expectations of those trying to fix the battered economy that it is being described as a watershed in the state's posture toward business."[47] Wilson did not win on every one of his budget proposals. His State of the State urged legislators not to extend a temporary half-cent sales tax increase due to expire on June 30, but Wilson ended up signing a six-month extension and agreeing to a public vote on a permanent increase.[48] This was one of a pair of compromises, and one proposal fell by the wayside, but the governor also won four impressive budget concessions from legislators for a win rate of 85 percent. While Gov. Wilson sported impressive batting averages in negotiations over policy and budgetary items, his overall number of successes was noticeably lower than that of governors who served prior

[44] Interview with Kevin Eckery, communications director to Gov. Pete Wilson, conducted by Thad Kousser in Sacramento, May 5, 2009.
[45] Interview with Joe Rodota, cabinet secretary to Gov. Pete Wilson, conducted by telephone by Thad Kousser, July 16, 2009.
[46] Dan Morain and Daniel M. Weintraub, "State Legislator OK Business Tax Breaks," *Los Angeles Times*, September 12, 1993, p. 1.
[47] Donald Woutat, "State's Help for Business Seen as Watershed Shift," *Los Angeles Times*, September 13, 1993, p. A1.
[48] Daniel M. Weintraub and Eric Bailey, "Wilson, Leaders Seek Statewide Sales Tax Vote," *Los Angeles Times*, June 21, 1993, p. 1.

to legislative professionalization. Wilson did well by setting forth a small agenda and working closely with lawmakers from both parties.

8.4.3. Gray Davis (2001)

Wilson was succeeded by another military and political veteran, Gray Davis, who, after serving in Vietnam, took a tour of duty as Jerry Brown's chief of staff and then climbed the rungs of statewide office into the governorship in 1998. The state's first Democratic chief executive since 1982, Davis faced enormous pressures from liberal lawmakers and interest groups whose bills had been stymied for so long by Deukmejian and Wilson. According to one senator serving at this time, this created a challenge from the beginning. "Gray Davis' tenure gets overshadowed by the recall and the energy debacle," says Pat Johnston, "but he also had to deal with the pent-up demand that came with 16 years of Republican governors."[49]

Early in his administration, Davis was able to hew to the center and pass a number of education reforms, some of which had significant opposition both from fiscal conservatives and from teacher's unions. He did so by taking advantage of his electoral mandate and the strength that comes with any governor's first year in office. Explains his communications director, Phil Trounstine, "Gray had won a very strong election, and polling showed that education was the most important issue for Californians, so he was well-positioned to push it as a central issue. A new governor's strongest moment is in the afterglow of an election."[50] When asked why he succeeded, Davis gave credit to the simple power of a mandate. "I was successful with the legislature in 1999 because I won by 20 percentage points in 1998," stated Davis. "If I'd won by one percent, we couldn't have moved my reform agenda. The momentum of a mandate helps you get things done."[51]

By 2001, however, the momentum of the mandate had ebbed as the Davis administration was swamped by a pair of crises. First, California witnessed an economic downturn that resulted from the collapse of the high-tech sector which had been "the driving force of the state's booming economy" (Block 2006, p. 82). Second, the state experienced

---

[49] Interview with former California state senator Pat Johnson, conducted by Thad Kousser in Sacramento, June 22, 2009.

[50] Interview with Phil Trounstine, communications director to Gov. Pete Wilson, conducted by telephone by Thad Kousser, July 8, 2009.

[51] Interview with Gov. Gray Davis, conducted by Thad Kousser in Los Angeles on May 28, 2010.

the delayed impact of a disastrous electricity deregulation bill that had been passed during the Wilson administration. In 2000, large regions of California experienced power blackouts, and the state was forced to raise the electrical bills of residential customers by 40 percent and commit to expensive long-term electricity contracts with out-of-state utilities (Gerston and Christensen 2004). Davis's public approval ratings plummeted quickly, from 62 percent in January of 2001 to 44 percent in May.[52]

Davis's 2001 State of State was deeply shaped by the electricity crisis, demonstrating how the agendas of governors are often held captive by events beyond their control. Of the 17 policy proposals in his speech, all but two addressed the production, regulation, and conservation of electricity. Despite high public demands for action, the governor saw more policy defeats than victories. Though the legislature heeded his calls to restructure the boards of electricity system operators and for $5 billion in bonds to build additional power-generating facilities, most of his proposals died in committees. Davis met with more success outside of this challenging policy area. His call to send 200,000 teachers to a Professional Development Institute was answered by the passage of AB 466, which sent 176,000 teachers and 22,000 aides to math and reading instructional programs.[53] He also signed into law a modified version of his plan to include 290,000 working parents in the state's Healthy Families health care program. Overall, Davis had a policy win rate of 50 percent, notably lower than that of his predecessors.

On the budget, Davis had more difficulty than Wilson working with legislative leaders to cut deals, even though they were his copartisans. In fact, one of the governor's early fiscal successes came from working across the aisle. "During the budget negotiations one year, a legislator named Jim Cuneen came to me and said that I want to vote for your budget, but I'd really like to see the R&D tax credit rise," remembers Davis, recalling the plot he hatched with Republican Cuneen. "I said I'd love to see it rise, too, but if I propose that, I won't get any credit with the Republican caucus. You have to get your caucus to demand three things in the budget, including this. I'll go to the Democratic caucus, which has members from the Bay Area who would also like to see it go up, and say, look, this is the least offensive thing the Republicans are asking for, let's

[52] Mark DiCamillo and Mervyn Field, "Davis' Standing with Californians Has Plummeted," San Francisco: The Field Poll, May 25, 2001.
[53] Timm Herdt, "New Law Tightens Approach to State's Standard Testing," *Ventura County Star*, October 13, 2001, p. A9.

give it to them. And that's what we did."[54] To move agenda items, Gray Davis, like other modern California governors, was forced to strategize with lawmakers across party lines.

Ultimately, though, even this type of strategizing does not guarantee success. On his 2001 budget items, Davis earned two full passes, two compromises, and two outright defeats. His batting average in the budget game was only 50 percent, the lowest of any of our California governors. Davis defeats came, surprisingly, in education. His proposal to add 1,300 algebra instructors to the state's teaching corps fell victim to declining fiscal revenues. Davis also proposed giving junior high schools $770 per student to increase the length of the school year by 30 days. When state revenues were not as strong as forecasted in January, this idea fell by the wayside. "Because of the tight budget," read one report that was sure to delight students, "Davis agreed to postpone the entire longer-year program."[55]

The next year, the budget only grew worse, and while short-term borrowing by Davis and the legislature avoided a fiscal meltdown and enabled him to win narrow reelection in 2002, the drive to recall him began one week later. Californians began to sign the recall petitions as another budget deficit opened up, Davis approval continued to drop, and, crucially, Republican congressman Darrell Issa contributed $3 million worth of funding for paid signature gatherers (Kousser and Chandler 2008). The recall qualified for the ballot, and with Arnold Schwarzenegger on the ballot to replace him, Davis lost his fight to stay in office by a 55 to 45 percent margin, becoming only the second governor to be recalled in U.S. history.

8.4.4. *Arnold Schwarzenegger (2006)*

Though he had been active in government-sponsored fitness programs and chaired a successful proposition to fund after-school services (2002's Prop. 49), Schwarzenegger was still very much the political outsider when he swept into office in the recall election of October 2003. Schwarzenegger's charisma, larger-than-life persona, and plentiful campaign funds brought him immediate electoral success. He came to office very much the political maverick and was dubbed "The People's Machine" (Mathews 2006). Yet, in his first year in office, "this ultimate outsider pursued

[54] Interview with Gov. Gray Davis, conducted by Thad Kousser in Los Angeles on May 28, 2010.

[55] Jennifer Kerr, "Low-Performing Middle Schools Are Budget Priority," *Ventura County Star*, July 1, 2001, p. A4.

a surprisingly traditional insider strategy" (Chandler and Kousser 2008, p. 220). Like other successful governors, he engaged directly with legislators, alternately charming them in the smoking tent that he erected inside the capitol's courtyard and threatening recalcitrant lawmakers in the run-up to the 2004 legislative contests. He cut deals with powerful interest groups, reaching agreements with the California Teachers Association and the California Correction Peace Officers Association, the twin pillars of Sacramento politics, and then united with the state's Democratic leaders to pass a $15 billion bond to close a budget gap. His first 100 days and the succeeding months led to policy and budget victories, keeping his approval ratings high (Chandler and Kousser 2008).

Emboldened by his success (and perhaps falling victim to the same hubris that has led other popular governors to push too far), Schwarzenegger used his 2005 State of the State address to launch a series of dramatic and very conservative policy initiatives, including cuts across the budget, reform of public employee pensions, merit pay for teachers, and the creation of an independent redistricting commission. He declared war on all of the groups and legislators with which he had made peace the year before. Schwarzenegger was conscious of his decision, predicting that his opponents would "organize huge protests in front of the Capitol" and "call me cruel and heartless."[56] He was right on both accounts but had not calibrated how effective these actions would be. He soon saw how stubborn a professional legislature, backed with allied interest groups, could be. None of the major proposals in his State of the State passed, and when he took them to the ballot in a special election in fall 2005, all failed again. From January through June 2005, his approval ratings fell by 30 points (Chandler and Kousser 2008).

Schwarzenegger reversed course in his 2006 State of the State, announcing his "postpartisan" strategy by unveiling a policy agenda that was populated largely by liberal and moderate proposals. At its core were six items that, when combined, amounted to a $70 billion public works program financed by state-issued bonds. This program was much more expansive even than the one favored by Democrats in the legislature.[57] After the governor gave a speech at that year's Martin Luther King Jr. breakfast in San Francisco, Democratic mayor Gavin Newsom observed, "He's becoming a Democrat again. . . . He gets it, he's learned

---

[56] Carla Marinucci, "Governor's Call to Arms Causing Deep Divisions," *San Francisco Chronicle*, January 9, 2005.

[57] Peter Nicholas, "Gov. Gets Earful from GOP," *Los Angeles Times*, January 12, 2006.

his lesson.... He's running back, not even to the center – I would say center-left."[58]

This new approach paid off in a moderate amount of legislative success. Of the six infrastructure proposals, the legislature passed one in full, gave the governor compromises on three, and killed the remaining two. Ultimately, lawmakers took a more fiscally moderate route than the governor, delivering to Schwarzenegger a public works program that looked more like the package Democrats originally proposed. The legislature also forced Schwarzenegger to compromise on his proposed minimum wage increase (passing a larger increase than the governor wanted) and rejected the governor's most conservative policy proposal – a constitutional debt ceiling. The end result was a policy batting average of 44 percent. While not spectacular, this record represented a substantial improvement over the previous year's debacle. In budgeting, the governor did substantially better, securing a full pass on each of his three proposals. Again, he called for changes to the status quo that were likely to appeal to the Democratically controlled legislature as well as the ideological leanings of the state electorate. These included increased funding for arts, music, and physical education and the cancellation of a scheduled tuition increase at state universities.

8.5. Summarizing Gubernatorial Success Before and After Proposition 1-a

To prevent the richness and detail of these case studies from masking broader trends in gubernatorial success, we summarize the records of governors serving before and after the legislature professionalized. Heeding the lessons of Chapter 6 to look both at success rates and the scale of agendas, we report, for each set of governors, their mean "batting average" along with the mean number of executive proposals passed.[59] These summaries are reported in Table 8.1. In the appendix to this chapter, we provide more detailed information for each governor.

The summary of budget proposals shows just how much Proposition 1-a reduced governors' ability to dictate the details of the state's spending plan. Among governors who served prior to legislative professionalization – Earl Warren, Goodwin Knight, and Pat Brown – the

---

[58] Carla Marinucci, "'New' Schwarzenegger Gets Surprisingly Warm Welcome," *San Francisco Chronicle*, January 17, 2006.

[59] To calculate batting averages and the raw number of successes, we code proposals that ended in a compromise as half of a success.

TABLE 8.1. *Success of California Governors, Before and After Legislative Professionalization*

	Before professionalization	After professionalization
Budget proposals		
Mean batting average	90%	78%
Mean policy successes	14.0	4.1
Policy proposals		
Mean batting average	76%	57%
Mean policy successes	10.5	4.9

mean batting average on budgetary items was a whopping 90 percent. Each moved a substantial number of fiscal proposals, and all enjoyed a high rate of success. After professionalization, however, governors performed less strongly. Among the four modern governors in our sample, the mean batting average fell by 12 points to 78 percent. Even more striking, the average number of budget successes for governors dropped from an impressive 14 per year prior to professionalization to a notably more modest 4.1 afterward.

These declines should come as no surprise. When lawmakers hired large fiscal staffs both in legislative budget committees and in the Legislative Analyst's Office, they gained the ability to conduct an independent analysis of the executive spending plan. Most importantly, with longer sessions stretching well past the budget deadline, legislators gained the patience to hold out, as demonstrated in Figure 8.1. The legislature's new mettle cost modern governors a great deal of the budget writing influence that their predecessors had enjoyed.

Furthermore, Table 8.1 shows that governors (postprofessionalization) also faced a tougher road with their policy agendas. Again, this can be clearly seen in batting averages and in the number of policy victories. The three governors who served before the passage of Proposition 1-a recorded a win rate of 76 percent on the policy items in their State of the State addresses. After professionalization, the batting averages of California chief executives fell to 57 percent. We observe a similar pattern in their average number of policy success, which dropped by more than half, from 10.5 per year to 4.9. This trend is a surprise. Our models of interbranch bargaining did not anticipate that legislative patience would alter gubernatorial success on policy items. This pattern was not present in our cross-sectional analysis of gubernatorial success in 52 State of the State addresses (see Chapter 4).

Of course, it is possible that the patterns of decreased gubernatorial success shown in Table 8.1 can be explained by temporal differences in the types of proposals included in governors' public agendas. It may be that governors, prior to Proposition 1-a, populated their State of the State addresses with smaller, easy-to-pass items, while more recent governors called for bolder change. This would certainly create the appearance that legislative professionalization has eroded the power of California chief executives, when in fact it has had no such effect. To address this possibility, we estimate a regression model of gubernatorial success for the seven California chief executives included in our case study. In this model, the units of analysis are the 144 individual State of the State proposals for which we were able to determine a clear final outcome. The model, like those presented in Chapter 4, controls for the scale of a proposal (ranging from 1 to 5), whether the proposal is a political reform, the total number of proposals included in the governor's agenda, and whether the governor is bargaining with a legislature controlled by the opposition party. Most importantly, we include a dichotomous variable indicating whether the governor served before or after Proposition 1-a.

To save space, we do not report the full results of the model here. However, they very clearly confirm the findings in Table 8.1. Even after controlling for features of individual agenda items, we find that the ability of governors to prevail in interbranch bargaining declined after the passage of Proposition 1-a. This is true in both the policy and budget games. Interestingly, the impact of Proposition 1-a appears greatest when it comes to fiscal matters.[60] The results of our regression model indicate that the probability of successfully securing a full pass on a typical budget proposal fell 43 points after professionalization, while it fell 31 points for a typical policy item. The regression also confirms three of our earlier findings: (1) governors are more likely to succeed on budget as opposed to policy proposals (this is also evident in Table 8.1), (2) proposals that address political reform are very unlikely to be adopted, and (3) proposals that represent a larger change to the status quo are less likely to make it through the legislature than agenda items that are smaller in scale.

While batting averages and the number of executive successes declined after professionalization, so did the size of governors' public agendas. Before Proposition 1-a, the average agenda consisted of 24 policy proposals and nearly 14 budget items. After Proposition 1-a was adopted, the size

---

[60] To test for differing effects, the model includes an interaction between *Budgetary Proposal* and *Professional Legislature*.

of executive agendas fell by over 50 percent, to a mere eight policy proposals and eight budget items. This drop in agenda size further indicates
the waning strength of California governors. In the divide-the-dollar logic
of our budget game, there are only so many cents to go around. As the
legislature becomes more patient, the ability of a governor to extract fiscal
concessions from lawmakers declines. In anticipation of gaining a smaller
share of the figurative dollar, it makes sense for modern Golden State
executives to begin asking for fewer items. Indeed, in our cross-sectional
analysis of 52 State of the State addresses (presented in Chapter 3), we
uncovered a similar correlation – as session length grows, the number of
budgetary items governors propose declines. A similar logic may hold for
the policy game, though we do not develop this in our theoretical model.
As the legislature becomes stronger, governors may need to make larger
side payments to get their desired policies. This could force governors to
ask for fewer agenda items in their State of the State addresses to avoid
spreading their political capital across too many proposals.

Indeed, anecdotal evidence from the preceding case studies appears
to confirm our intuition. Prior to legislative professionalization, California governors crafted large and ambitious agendas. While they lost
on some of their most controversial proposals, such as Gov. Warren's
call for universal health insurance or Gov. Brown's proposal to prohibit
racial discrimination in housing, they managed to accumulate records
of impressive legislative achievement. After 1966, however, a legislature
transformed and strengthened by professionalization drove a harder bargain. The relationships between California chief executives and lawmakers became more contentious as the legislature demanded a greater say in
policy and fiscal matters. The modern governors who managed to secure
a respectable legislative batting average did so by going small – offering
modest agendas that appealed to the ideological preferences of lawmakers. These governors, by necessity, strategized with legislative leaders and
vetted agenda items in ways that would have been unimaginable to their
predecessors.

8.6. Conclusion

Proposition 1-a transformed the California legislature from a citizen
house into a professional body. Its passage set the stage for lawmakers
to dramatically lengthen legislative sessions, pay themselves high salaries,
and hire expert lawyers and policy analysts. The proponents of professionalization argued that it would empower legislators to the detriment

of Golden State governors. Were they correct? If so, was the effect of professionalization most pronounced on budgetary items, as our theoretical models suggest it ought to be?

Our comparison of the outcomes of interbranch negotiations before and after Proposition 1-a indicate that professionalization has indeed strengthened the legislature. Legislators became more patient bargainers in budget negotiations once lawmaking became a full-time, well-paid job. This is evidenced by the striking growth in late budgets that occurred once Proposition 1-a was ratified by voters. After professionalization, governors were also much less successful at moving budget proposals through the legislature. Simply put, patient lawmakers were now willing to challenge the governor on fiscal matters. Somewhat surprisingly, they also dug in their heels on matters of policy. Since the adoption of Proposition 1-a, California governors have averaged fewer policy successes and lower policy batting averages. This particular finding was not anticipated by our theoretical model of policy negotiations, nor is it present in any of our cross-sectional analyses from prior chapters. But at least in California, whether bargaining over budgets or policy, governors have been less successful at moving their agendas through the professionalized legislature than through the citizen body that preceded it.

While the adoption of Proposition 1-a has provided us with a unique opportunity to study the consequences of legislative professionalization, we should take care to once again note the limitations of this analysis. Because much has changed about California and its politics over the past 60 years, the long historical look we undertake here is far from an ideal natural experiment. In particular, skeptical readers are likely to point to the presence of divided government (in the context of increasing partisan polarization) as an alternative cause of declining gubernatorial success. Of the three governors in our sample who served prior to 1966, all bargained with a legislature that was controlled by their copartisans; of the four who served after 1966, only one – Gray Davis – enjoyed similar circumstances.

Though we cannot fully address this concern, we note three mitigating factors. First, in our regression analysis, we still observe an effect of professionalization even after controlling for the increased presence of divided government. Second, unified government is by no means a guarantee of success. During the administration of Gray Davis, Democrats controlled both the legislative and executive branches, but Davis emerged from the 2001 legislative session with the lowest overall batting average of any governor in our sample. His total number of bargaining successes was very similar to that of other postprofessionalization governors, each of whom confronted a hostile legislature controlled by the opposition party. Third, all governors in our sample experienced at least a de facto form of divided government on budget issues. Over the entire course of our study, California's constitution required a two-thirds vote in each chamber to pass a budget (Kousser 2010). None of the governors enjoyed a legislative majority large enough to be able to ignore members of the opposition party on fiscal matters. For these reasons, we do not believe that the increasing prevalence of divided government undermines our findings.

Ultimately, we are confident in concluding that legislative professionalization fundamentally reshapes the balance of power between the executive and legislative branches in state government. Though Chapters 4 and 5 provide strong evidence that professionalization undermines a governor's ability to secure victories in negotiations over budget proposals and the size of government, our analysis of California indicates that the impact of professionalization may extend to the policy game as well. This means that when Gov. Pat Brown signed the ballot measure in favor of Proposition 1-a, he was indeed signing away many of the powers of his office. Nowhere is this more apparent than in the 2011 State of the State address of his son and eventual successor as California governor, Jerry Brown. A half century after his father's address confidently asked lawmakers to pass 58 items, Jerry Brown, facing a transformed legislature and tougher economic times, "unveiled no new policy proposals" and requested just one thing – a statewide vote on a tax increase.[61] Perhaps his speech was an implicit admission that California governors had reached their era of limits.

8.7. Appendix

The first two columns of Table 8.2 show the total number of policy and budgetary proposals made by each California governor included in our case study. In general, the number of total executive proposals declines after the legislature was professionalized. The second and third columns report the number of proposals for which we were able to identify a final outcome. We were more successful at determining these outcomes for recent governors. The likely reason for this increase is that for more recent

---

[61] Evan Halper and Anthony York, "Brown Argues for His Budget Plan in State of the State Address," *Los Angeles Times*, February 1, 2011.

TABLE 8.2. *Agendas and Success of the Governors Used in the California Case Study*

Governor	Policy items	Budget items	Coded outcome policy items	Coded outcome budget items	Policy success	Budget success
Before professionalization						
Earl Warren (R)	27	6	12	5	9 (75%)	5 (100%)
Goodwin Knight (R)	8	15	7	10	5 (71%)	9 (90%)
Pat Brown (D)	38	20	36	20	28 (78%)	17.5 (88%)
After professionalization						
George Deukmejian (R)	4	15	4	9	3 (75%)	7.5 (83%)
Pete Wilson (R)	3	7	3	7	3 (100%)	6 (85%)
Gray Davis (D)	17	6	13	6	6.5 (50%)	3 (50%)
Arnold Schwarzenegger (R)	9	3	9	3	4 (44%)	3 (100%)

governors, we have access to a larger number of journalist sources. To prevent our analysis from being biased against governors who served earlier in the twentieth century, all of our summary statistics of gubernatorial success exclude proposals for which we could not find news coverage. The fifth column reports the total number of policy successes (with a full pass counting as 1 and a compromise counting as 0.5) and, in parentheses, the governor's policy batting average. The sixth column reports the same information, but for budget proposals.

9

Governors and the Comparative Study
of Chief Executives

I have suffered a series of problems with regard to the Administration bills which I have drafted. The problems have arisen, I believe, primarily because the legislators selected to sponsor the bills have not been sufficiently informed about the contents of the bills. For instance, Senator Dunn sponsored and introduced the Urban Aid bill without realizing that Elizabeth was the only city which would not receive an increase. Assemblyman Pellechia sponsored and introduced the Uniform State Building Code without knowing that it would preclude his beloved plumbing code. I think we can do something to prevent the embarrassment and hard feelings which result from such situations.

    – internal memo from Ark Winkler, Assistant counsel to New Jersey governor Brendan Byrne, March 26, 1974

Members of the Legislature have requested that they be forewarned, if possible, of announcement pertaining to major departmental expenditures, new projects, etc . . . that affect their respective districts.

    – Memo from Jeff Ketterson, secretary to the cabinet, administration of Gov. Brendan Byrne, February 1, 1974

Internal memos from the first year of New Jersey governor Brendan T. Byrne's administration show that governors can and do make mistakes, complicating the efforts of observers and scholars to predict executive productivity. The almost comical mistakes noted in the Byrne memos – failing to inform key sponsors of potentially embarrassing details contained in the governor's bills and failing to notify lawmakers prior to major budgetary announcements affecting their districts – reveal a new governor and his administration struggling to master the informal and often perplexing levers of executive power. Sometimes, governors struggle early in their terms, as Byrne did, but eventually study their craft well enough to move major legislative initiatives. After tripping over mundane matters like building codes, Gov. Byrne went on to compile a record of major successes such as the preservation of 20 percent of New Jersey's lands through the Pinelands Protection Act, the expansion of the Meadowlands sports complex, the creation of the New Jersey Transit System, and the passage of an income tax directed toward school funding (see the Byrne Archive; Rosenthal 1990). Other governors move in the opposite direction. California's Gray Davis and Arnold Schwarzengger both met with tremendous success on their initial agendas but later faced frustration as their political capital faded and legislative relations soured. The same hurricane that revitalized Mississippi governor Haley Barbour's political fortunes effectively ended the career of Louisiana's Kathleen Blanco.

No two governors share the same story. As a result, it is tempting to claim that the exercise of executive power is idiosyncratic and that the study of governors should embrace biography and case studies, while resisting systematic quantification and formal models of policy making. Yet, as this book demonstrates, an investigation of dozens of governors across many states can uncover predictable patterns despite the personal quirks and serendipitous arcs of individual chief executives. Each statehouse may seem like its own world, but its inhabitants are not sui generis. Governors all must meet the common challenge of facing nearly unlimited responsibility for governing their states (at least in the eyes of voters), while holding only limited constitutional powers. They also share a toolbox for overcoming their institutional disadvantages. At the beginning of the legislative session, state chief executives have the ability to lay out an agenda for lawmakers, and then, at the end of the session, they can use their veto pen to cast judgement on bills that survive the lawmaking process. In between, governors must rely on a diverse set of tools to cajole, threaten, and sway lawmakers into giving them what they want. In these tools, both constitutional and ephemeral, lie the powers of American governors.

The summary of our empirical results contained in Table 9.1 shows which tools matter, and when. It highlights our key finding – that policy and budget proposals follow distinct logics, dictated by the consequence of bargaining failure. Because states must pass budgets or face political pain and eventual government shutdowns, legislators are forced to come to the bargaining table. Governors are most successful in budget negotiations, performing especially well when they can be more patient because

TABLE 9.1. *Summarizing the Powers of American Governors*

Question	Finding	Type of evidence
Are governors more successful in negotiations over budgetary or policy proposals?	Budgetary proposals	Success on 1,088 State of the State proposals, including 612 policy proposals and 476 budget proposals; 28 states; 2001 and 2006 (Chapter 4) Success on proposals by seven California governors (Chapter 8)
When are governors most likely to prevail in negotiations over policy proposals?	Copartisans hold many legislative seats When the governor: • is popular with state voters • is serving in her first term • is serving in her legacy year • does not have presidential ambitions • proposes a more modest agenda	Success on 612 policy proposals from State of the State addresses; 28 states; 2001 and 2006 (Chapter 4) Natural experiments created by Hurricane Katrina and "coingate" (Chapter 6)
When are governors most likely to prevail in negotiations over budgetary proposals?	When the governor: • is bargaining with a part-time legislature • proposes a more modest agenda	Success on 476 budget proposals from State of the State addresses (Chapter 4) Success of proposals by seven California governors (Chapter 8)
Can governors shape the size of state government?	Yes, especially when negotiating with a part-time legislature	Budget data from 48 states from 1989–2009 (Chapter 5)
Does the item veto allow governors to constrain spending? Does the item veto give governors leverage to move their own agendas?	No clear evidence that the item veto gives governors either negative or positive powers	Budget data from 48 states from 1989–2009 (Chapter 7) Natural experiment created by *Rants v. Vilsack* (Chapter 7)

the legislature only meets part time or, in many cases, when they are serving their last year and looking to sure up their legacy. These findings point to the critical importance of fiscal deadlines – when drastic consequences loom, political combatants can be shifted off of even the most calcified positions. The imperative to avoid a late budget turns appropriations bills into moving vehicles that can carry with them items that might not, under normal circumstances, easily pass. At the federal level, the Fenno rule (Kiewiet and McCubbins 1988) means that Congress and the president do not face the same pressures to agree on a new budget, and thus the president is unlikely to enjoy the same advantages in the fiscal arena as his state-level counterparts.

Negotiation over executive policy proposals is a very different game. Because lawmakers can often live with the status quo policy, they need not even come to the bargaining table. This means that governors often struggle to pass their policy items, particularly if they lack a large number of partisan allies in the legislature. When governors hold the sticks and carrots that influence legislators, such as high approval ratings, the glow that comes in the first term, the steadfastness that arrives in a governor's legacy year, and a credible veto pen, they can more successfully move their policy agendas. When they cannot provide these incentives, they often fail. Some governors embrace the inevitable, calling for ambitious but doomed policy proposals to score points with voters or key backers. Barack Obama's fall 2011 jobs plan, pronounced dead on arrival in Congress but clearly aimed at the 2012 contest, provides a presidential example of this dynamic. In issuing his jobs plan, Obama was merely following the path already taken by one of his rivals when Mitt Romney, as governor of Massachusetts, proposed a plethora of conservative ideas to one of the nation's most liberal legislatures. Neither President Obama nor Gov. Romney met with much success.

Overall, by distinguishing between budget and policy fights in theory and in our empirical models, we show that what governors bargain over often determines both what they get and how they get it. This distinction is revealed in our analysis of 1,088 policy and budget proposals from 52 State of the State addresses. Chapter 3 asks what governors propose in these speeches, while Chapter 4 tracks whether they are successful. Table 9.1 lays out our findings in detail. It lists our main research questions in the first column, our central findings next, and, in the final column, reports the types of evidence that we draw on to reach each finding. Quite often, multiple sources of evidence provide consistent support for a set of findings. Summarizing our results helps us answer a question that scholars and observers have long asked: are there strong governorships, or just strong governors? The primary factors that drive gubernatorial success, whether in the budgetary or the policy sphere, are specific to individual governors and to the times in which they serve. Governors do well early and at the end of their careers, when they are popular, if they keep their agendas brief, and when they have partisan allies in the legislature. None of these has much to do with the formal powers of a governor's office. The one institutional factor that exerts a strong and consistent influence on a governor's lawmaking success is the professionalism of the legislature, not any facet of executive power. Indeed, in our data, there is no link between the most widely used measure of governors' institutional powers – the GIP index created by Thad Beyle – and gubernatorial success. The correlation of his GIP measure with batting average is a statistically insignificant 0.006, and if we include Beyle's index as an explanatory variable in our regression models, it never emerges as a meaningful predictor of outcomes.[1] In any state, a governor who manages her powers and agenda well has the opportunity to enjoy legislative success.

In Chapter 5, we move to a broader sample to generalize our conclusions about budget bargaining. Looking at 48 states from the 1989 fiscal year through 2009, we compare the size of the governor's proposed budget to the size of the enacted budget, drawing on reports compiled by the National Association of State Budget Officers. What we observe when looking across the nation over two decades parallels what we find in our analysis of recent State of the State analysis: governors are strong in the budgeting sphere and especially strong when they negotiate with citizen legislators. When they negotiate with part-time lawmakers holding sessions as short as those in New Hampshire, for every dollar of fiscal change that they propose, governors are able to secure 90 cents. Yet, where legislative sessions are longer, making lawmakers more patient in the budget staring match, chief executives meet with less success. Negotiating with a full-time body meeting as long as California's legislature, every dollar in spending changes proposed by a governor turns into only 60 cents in the final enactment. This reminds us that legislative structure – a factor that is absent from traditional measures of gubernatorial power

[1] We use Beyle's index of institutional powers from 2001 and 2005 to explain batting averages from our 2001 and 2006 State of the State addresses, taking our powers measures from Thad Beyle, "Gubernatorial Power: The Institutional Power Ratings for the 50 Governors of the United States," accessed at http://www.unc.edu/ beyle/gubnewpwr.html in September 2011.

(Schlesinger 1965; Dometrius 1979; Beyle 1983, 2004) – is an important determinant of executive influence.

We move from statistical models to case studies in Chapter 6, using a pair of natural experiments to probe the complex dynamics that connect a governor's approval ratings to her lawmaking performance. Each case poses a puzzle. After Hurricane Katrina, Louisiana governor Kathleen Blanco's popularity plummeted, but her legislative batting average rose. Ohio governor Bob Taft also saw a rise in his batting average after an economic downturn and a damaging political scandal sent his approval ratings toward the lowest levels ever recorded for a governor. How did they survive to govern effectively? By looking deeply into each case, we show that a first glance at overall batting averages can be deceiving. What we find is that both governors succeeded by reducing the ambition of their policy agendas. Governor Blanco retreated to a budget game by shifting the focus of her State of the State address from policy to fiscal issues. The policy proposals that Blanco did offer were smaller in scale and more consistent with the ideological leanings of key lawmakers than were those she made while she was popular. Governor Taft, while not transforming his agenda as radically as Blanco, scaled back by reducing quite dramatically the number of policy proposals in his State of the State. Quantifying these factors into each governor's impact score, we see a predictable pattern. The overall impact of each governor dropped quite notably, along with his or her poll ratings. That being said, both governors still were able to move key policy as well as fiscal items, testimony to the fact that governors are not always captive to their approval ratings.

Chapter 7 combines quantitative analysis with a case study to ask whether the item veto confers a negative or positive power on governors. Are the 44 governors who have the power to delete individual expenditures able to control state spending? The existing literature generally finds no evidence that the item veto leads to spending restraint. Probing stories of the item veto's use and the testimony of those who use it, we argue that it should only trim state expenditures in cases when governors are frugal and when they have enough partisan allies to sustain their item vetoes against a legislative override. Perhaps because these cases are relatively rare, our quantitative analysis yields suggestive results but no definitive statistical evidence that the item veto helps governors cut spending. Neither do we find any clear evidence that governors are able to leverage item veto threats into support for passing their own legislative programs. This is confirmed by a natural experiment that draws on a court decision,

Rants v. Vilsack, that reduced the item veto powers of Iowa governors. We find that the court's decision did not harm the prospects of gubernatorial proposals in the legislature.

Finally, Chapter 8 uses the passage of Proposition 1-a, which radically transformed the California legislature from a citizen house into a professional body, to study the effects of legislative professionalization on gubernatorial success. The results of this case study are consistent with our quantitative models showing that governors face more resistance when they negotiate with professional legislatures. We track the success of State of the State proposals made by seven California governors, beginning with Earl Warren in 1945. The three governors who served when the state still had a citizen legislature consistently succeeded in moving their very ambitious agendas. The four governors who had to negotiate with professional lawmakers faced more difficulties in moving both their policy and budget agendas. Our close look at Golden State governors in both eras confirmed the overall themes of the book: that governors perform better on the budget than in policy battles and that, in either realm, they must use every formal and informal power at their disposal to fashion their ideas into law.

9.1. Toward a Comparative Study of Executives

Gauging the success of governors as we have done here not only enables us to better understand their role in American government but also allows us to situate them among the world's chief executives. The methods that we employ, long applied to presidential studies, are now being used in recent work in the comparative politics literature. "We still know very little about the extent to which chief executives can produce policy changes through acts of government that carry the force of law," writes Saiegh (2010, p. 2). "While the study of presidential legislative success in the United States has a long and fruitful tradition, these analyses seldom provide systematic comparisons with other countries." Saiegh reports "box scores" of chief executives across the globe and urges a comparative, cross-national approach to studying executive power. We agree and also urge that scholars look at the 50 cases of executive power in American statehouses, bringing national, comparative, and state politics into conversation. All fields could benefit. Studies of presidents have developed elegant theories and sophisticated empirical measures that can often be applied and adapted to other chief executives. Comparative scholars will find familiarity in the large number of cases and institutional variation

TABLE 9.2. *Comparing the Success Rates of Chief Executives'*
Legislative Agendas

Type of executive	Success rate
American presidents, Truman through Clinton Average success of presidential proposals Source: Rudalevige (2002)	45.4%
American presidents, Eisenhower through Clinton % of presidential initiatives that became law Source: Edwards and Barrett (2000)	41.2%
American governors, 28 states in 2001 and 2006 Average success rate on all State of the State proposals	52.1%
Latin American presidents, 8 presidential systems Passage rate of executive initiatives in lower house Source: Saiegh (2010)	57.6%
European prime ministers, 9 parliamentary systems Passage rate of executive initiatives in lower house Source: Saiegh (2010)	79.6%
Chief executives in mixed systems, five mixed systems Passage rate of executive initiatives in lower house Source: Saiegh (2010)	76.0%

provided by the American states and comfort in the otherwise similar systems in which governors serve. The presidential literature, often plagued by its small number of cases and looking for ways to evaluate counterfactual scenarios, might look to the states more often.[2]

As a first step toward a comparative study of chief executives, Table 9.2 draws on all three literatures to show the success rates of different leaders in moving their legislative agendas. First, it reports that U.S. presidents, depending on the era and the measure employed, find congressional support for 41 or 45 percent of their proposals. Governors do a bit better, passing on average 52 percent of their combined legislative and budget agendas. Yet, both types of American executives lag behind their counterparts in the rest of the world. Latin American presidents are successful on about 58 percent of their proposals, while the leaders of Europe, mixed and parliamentary, pass 76 percent and 80 percent of their agendas through lower houses.

[2] Few works on the presidency consider governors. For instance, Oxford University Press's 590-page, 16-chapter Institutions of American Democracy volume on *The Executive Branch* (Aberbach and Peterson 2005) could not find room for a single chapter, or even an index entry, on governors.

These patterns remind us that both governors and U.S. presidents are – when it comes to moving their legislative programs – much more like Latin American presidents than European prime ministers. Chief executives in the western hemisphere typically face the same checks and balances of a separated-powers system and cannot rely on the support of a friendly parliament. The differences within our hemisphere are also predictable. Since many Latin American presidents are allowed a more direct role in the lawmaking process than chief executives in the United States (Payne et al. 2002; Aleman and Tsebelis 2005; Saiegh 2011), they are more successful. Do the Latin American presidents with the strongest formal powers do the best? Within the United States, given our finding that legislative professionalism weakens executive power, it should not be surprising that presidents see the lowest passage rates when they negotiate with Congress, one of the most professional legislatures in the world. Is that what accounts for the difference between presidents and governors, or do governors do better because they are often more popular than presidents and hold powers, like the item veto, that presidents lack? Each field of study has clearly yielded important and theoretically relevant findings through its traditional focus: by making comparisons across countries with the same democratic system, from president to president, or from governor to governor. Yet, illuminative patterns and intriguing new questions are revealed when executive performance is viewed through a wider lens.

9.2. Toward a New Agenda in Gubernatorial Research

Recognizing that governors have much in common with other chief executives across the world reminds us that we can use the extraordinary research design provided by the American states to test fundamental questions of political science. These tests, though grounded in the empirics of the states, should be motivated by the same questions that drive scholars of presidential and comparative politics.

The wide variation in governing structures across states opens up opportunities to see how executives function in different types of democratic systems. Do governors play the same role in states that are "hybrid democracies" (Garrett 2005), blending elements of direct and representative democracy, as they do in states that lack the initiative process? At earlier points in American history, states dominated by a single party operated in dramatically different ways from competitive, two-party states (Key 1949). How differently did governors govern in those states, or in nonpartisan and multiparty states? In this book, we find strong evidence that executive power declines as legislative professionalism rises, but the exact nature of this relationship – is it driven by session lengths, by salaries, or by staffing resources? – could be further investigated. Scholars could also test a new finding from the comparative politics literature advanced by Saiegh (2011). He identifies "two major factors that shape [executive] lawmaking: the unpredictability of legislators' voting behavior, and the availability of resources to engage in vote buying" (Saiegh 2011, p. 6). Does unpredictability or, perish the thought, the potential for vote buying predict gubernatorial success rates?

An influential stream of research has shown that state politics provides an especially useful laboratory to test theories of representation. Scholars could use the many measures of citizen ideology to probe the links between executive power and representation (Erikson et al. 1993; Berry et al. 1998; Brace et al. 2002; Lax and Phillips 2009). Where governors are strong, do we see a tighter translation of voter preferences into policy, or are legislatures instead the bodies that most closely mirror the people? Recent works that have put all state legislators on a common ideological scale (Shor et al. 2010; Shor and McCarty 2011) open up many new ways to study the executive branch, since governors who answer the same political attitude surveys as legislators could be placed on this scale. Do governors sit at the center or at the ideological extremes of a state's spectrum? In states with greater partisan polarization, are governors stymied in the legislature or left as the states' only uniting force? How does polarization interact with the other factors that determine executive influence?

The global economic crisis that began in 2008 hit states, with their balanced budget requirements, particularly hard. How they dealt with this fiscal shock can reveal important lessons about which political systems lead to greater policy responsiveness. Did the states that delegate greater powers to their chief executives witness quicker and more decisive reactions to the fiscal crunch? In which type of state did the policy reaction – the mixture of spending cuts versus taxes – most closely resemble public preferences? Does the density of interest group organization (Gray and Lowery 1996) slow or speed the pace of fiscal policy change, and how does it affect the congruence between mass opinion and state policy? Finally, how does electoral feedback work under different regimes of executive power? Did the governors who were most influential over the initial reactions to recession face, as President Obama did, the largest party losses in the 2010 elections?

The motivating question that began this book was fundamentally comparative: can America's chief executives, possessed of fewer formal powers to move an agenda than leaders in most other political systems, effectively govern? We find that a seat in the governor's chair is no guarantee of success. When political dynamics work against a governor, legislators can take advantage of the checks and balances built into America's statehouses to halt executive power at every turn. Some governors fail miserably. Yet others can succeed spectacularly, particularly if they enjoy a great deal of political capital, are bargaining with a citizen legislature, or have many partisan allies in the legislature. Importantly, governors consistently perform better on the budget than in policy negotiations. Overall, governors win on just over half of their proposals, putting them slightly ahead of American presidents but behind Latin America's more powerful presidents and Europe's prime ministers. The American system of checks and balances constrains but does not cripple its chief executives.

References

Aberbach, Joel D., and Mark A. Peterson. 2005. *The Executive Branch*. Oxford: Oxford University Press.

Abney, Glenn, and Thomas P. Lauth. 1985. "The Line-Item Veto in the States: An Instrument for Fiscal Restraint or an Instrument for Partisanship?" *Public Administration Review* 45:372–77.

Abney, Glenn, and Thomas P. Lauth. 1997. "Research Notes: The Item Veto and Fiscal Responsibility." *Journal of Politics* 59(3):882–92.

Abrams, Burton A., and William R. Dougan. 1986. "The Effects of Constitutional Restraints on Governmental Spending." *Public Choice* 49:101–16.

Advisory Commission on Intergovernmental Relations (ACIR). 1987. *Fiscal Discipline in the Federal System: National Reform and the Experience of the States*. Washington, DC: ACIR.

Aldrich, John H., and James S. Coleman Battista. 2002. "Conditional Party Government in the States." *American Journal of Political Science* 46:164–72.

Aleman, Eduardo, and George Tsebelis. 2005. "Presidential Conditional Agenda Setting in Latin America." *World Politics* 57:396–420.

Alt, James E., and Robert C. Lowry. 1994. "Divided Government, Fiscal Institutions, and Budget Deficits: Evidence from the States." *American Political Science Review* 88:811–28.

Alt, James E., and Robert C. Lowry. 2000. "A Dynamic Model of State Budget Outcomes under Divided Partisan Government." *Journal of Politics* 62:1035–70.

American Political Science Association, Committee on American Legislatures. 1954. *American State Legislatures; Report of the Committee on American Legislatures*. Belle Zeller, editor. New York: Crowell.

Banks, Jeffrey S., and John Duggan. 2006. "A General Bargaining Model of Legislative Policy-making." *Quarterly Journal of Political Science* 1(1):49–85.

Bell, Charles G., and Charles M. Price. 1980. *California Government Today: Politics of Reform*. Homewood, IL: Dorsey Press.

Bernick, E. Lee, and Charles W. Wiggins. 1991. "Executive-Legislative Relations: The Governor's Role as Chief Legislator." In Erik B. Herzik and Brent W. Brown, editors, *Gubernatorial Leadership and State Policy*. New York: Greenwood Press.

Berry, William D., Evan J. Ringquist, Richard C. Fording, and Russell L. Hanson. 1998. "Measuring Citizen and Government Ideology in the American States, 1960–93." *American Journal of Political Science*, 42(1):327–48.

Besley, Timothy, and Anne Case. 2003. "Political Institutions and Policy Choices: Evidence from the Unites States." *Journal of Economic Literature* 41:7–73.

Beyle, Thad. 1983. "Governors." In Virginia Gray, Herbert Jacob, and Kennith N. Vines, editors, *Politics in the American States*. Boston: Little, Brown.

Beyle, Thad. 1992. *Governors and Hard Times*. Washington, DC: Congressional Quarterly Press.

Beyle, Thad. 2004a. "Governors: Election, Campaign Cost, Profiles, Forced Exits and Powers." In Keon S. Chi, editor, *The Book of the States*, 2004 ed., vol. 36. Lexington, KY: Council of State Governments.

Beyle, Thad. 2004b. "The Governors." In *Politics in the American States*, Virginia Gray and Russell L. Hanson, editors. Washington, DC: Congressional Quarterly Press.

Beyle, Thad, and Margaret Ferguson. 2008. "The Governors." In *Politics in the American States*, Virginia Gray and Russell L. Hanson, editors. Washington, DC: Congressional Quarterly Press.

Bond, Jon R., and Richard Fleisher. 1990. *The President in the Legislative Arena*. Chicago: University of Chicago Press.

Bowler, Shaun, and Todd Donovan. 2008. "The Initiative Process." In Virginia Gray and Russell L. Hanson, editors, *Politics in the American States: A Comparative Analysis*, 9th ed. Washington, DC: Congressional Quarterly Press.

Bowling, Cynthia J., and Margaret R. Ferguson. 2001. "Divided Government, Interest Representation, and Policy Differences: Competing Explanations of Gridlock in the 50 States." *Journal of Politics* 63(1):182–206.

Boyarsky, Bill. 2008. *Big Daddy: Jesse Unruh and the Art of Power Politics*. Berkeley: University of California Press.

Brace, Paul, and Barbara Hinckley. 1992. *Follow the Leader: Opinion Polls and the Modern Presidents*. New York: Basic Books.

Brace, Paul, Kellie Sims-Butler, Kevin Arceneaux, and Martin Johnson. 2002. "Public Opinion in the American States: New Perspectives Using National Survey Data." *American Journal of Political Science* 46(1):173–89.

Brady, Henry E., and David Collier, editors. 2004. *Rethinking Social Inquiry: Diverse Tools, Shared Standards*. Lanham, MD: Rowman and Littlefield.

Brambor, Thomas, William Roberts Clark, and Matt Golder. 2006. "Understanding Interaction Models: Improving Empirical Analyses." *Political Analysis* 14:63–82.

Brown, Robert, 1995. "Party Cleavages and Welfare Effort in the American States." *American Political Science Review* 89:23–34.

Burns, Nancy, Laura Evans, Gerald Gamm, and Corrine McConnaughy. 2008. "Pockets of Expertise: Institutional Capacity in 20th-Century State Legislatures." *Studies in American Political Development* 22:229–48.

Cain, Bruce E., and Thad Kousser. 2004. *Adapting to Term Limits: Recent Experiences and New Directions*. San Francisco: Public Policy Institute of California.

Cameron, Charles M. 2000. *Veto Bargaining: Presidents and the Politics of Negative Power*. Cambridge: Cambridge University Press.

Canes-Wrone, Brandice. 2001. "The President's Legislative Influence from Public Appeals." *American Journal of Political Science* 45(2):313–29.

Canes-Wrone, Brandice. 2006. *Who Leads Whom? Presidents, Policy, and the Public*. Chicago: University of Chicago Press.

Canes-Wrone, Brandice, and Scott de Marchi. 2002. "Presidential Approval and Legislative Success." *Journal of Politics* 64(May):491–509.

Carey, John M., and Matthew Soberg Shugart. 1998. *Executive Decree Authority*. New York: Cambridge University Press.

Carey, John M., Gary F. Moncrief, Richard G. Niemi, and Lynda W. Powell. 2006. "Term Limits in the State Legislatures: Results from a New Survey of the 50 States." *Legislative Studies Quarterly* 21(1):105–36.

Carter, John R., and David Schap. 1990. "Line-Item Veto: Where Is Thy Sting?" *Journal of Economic Perspectives* 4(2):103–18.

Caruso, Joe. 2004. *Reflections on a Late Budget*. Loudonville, NY: Sienna Research Institute.

Chandler, William, and Thad Kousser. 2008. "Governors, Geography, and Direct Democracy: The Case of Arnold Schwarzenegger." In Frederick Douzet, Thad Kousser, and Ken Miller, editors, *The New Political Geography of California*. Berkeley, CA: Institute of Governmental Studies Press.

Citizens Conference on State Legislatures. 1971. *State Legislatures: An Evaluation of Their Effectiveness*. New York: Praeger.

Clarke, Wes. 1998. "Divided Government and Budget Conflict in the U.S." *Legislative Studies Quarterly* 23(1):5–22.

Clingermayer, James C., and B. Dan Wood. 1995. "Disentangling Patterns of State Debt Financing." *American Political Science Review* 89(1):108–20.

Clucas, Richard A. 2003. "California: The New Amateur Politics." In Rick Farmer, John David Rausch Jr., and John C. Green, editors. *The Test of Time: Coping with Legislative Term Limits*. Lanham, MD: Lexington Books.

Clucas, Richard A. 2007. "Legislative Professionalism and the Power of State House Leaders." *State Politics and Policy Quarterly* 7(1):1–19.

Cohen, Jeffrey E., Jon Bond, Richard Fleisher, and John Hamman. 2000. "State Level Presidential Approval and Senatorial Support." *Legislative Studies Quarterly* 15(4):577–90.

Collier, David, Henry E. Brady, and Jason Seawright. 2010 "Outdated Views of Qualitative Methods: Time to Move On." *Political Analysis* 18(4):506–13.

Collier, Kenneth, and Terry Sullivan. 1995. "New Evidence Undercutting the Linkage of Approval with Presidential Support and Influence." *Journal of Politics* 57(1):197–209.

Council of State Governments. 2005. *The Book of the States*, 2004–2005 ed., vol. 37. Lexington, KY: Council of State Governments.

Council of State Governments. 2010. *The Book of the States*, 2010 ed., vol. 41. Lexington, KY: Council of State Governments.

Council of State Governments, Committee on Legislative Processes and Procedures. 1946. *Our State Legislatures: Report of the Committee on Legislative Processes and Procedures.* Chicago: Council of State Governments.

Covington, Cary R., and Rhonda Kinney. 1999. "Enacting the President's Agenda in the House of Representatives: The Determinants and Impact of Presidential Agenda Setting Success." Presented at the annual meeting of the Midwest Political Science Association, Chicago.

Cox, Gary W., Thad Kousser, and Mathew McCubbins. 2010. "Party Power or Preferences? Quasi-Experimental Evidence from the American States." *Journal of Politics* 72(July):799–811.

Crew, Robert E., Jr. 1992. "Understanding Gubernatorial Behavior: A Framework for Analysis." In *Governors and Hard Times*, Thad Beyle, editor. Washington, DC: Congressional Quarterly Press.

Dallek, Matthew. 2004. *The Right Moment: Ronald Reagan's First Victory and the Decisive Turning Point in American Politics.* Oxford: Oxford University Press.

Dawson, Richard E., and James A. Robinson. 1963. "Interparty Competition, Economic Variables, and Welfare Policies in the American States." *Journal of Politics*, 25:265–89.

de Figueiredo, R. J. P., Jr. 2003. "Budget Institutions and Political Insulation: Why States Adopt the Item Veto." *Journal of Public Economics* 87:2677–701.

Diamond, Jared. 1999. *Guns, Germs and Steel.* New York: W. W. Norton.

Dodd, Lawrence C., and Sean Q. Kelly. 1989. "Legislators' Home Style in Traditional and Modern Systems: The Case of Presentational Style." Presented at the annual meeting of the Midwest Political Science Association, Chicago, IL.

Dometrius, Nelson C. 1979. "Measuring Gubernatorial Power." *Journal of Politics* 41:589–610.

Douzet, Frederick, and Kenneth P. Miller. 2008. "California's East-West Divide." In Frederick Douzet, Thad Kousser, and Ken Miller, editors, *The New Political Geography of California.* Berkeley, CA: Institute of Governmental Studies Press.

Dunning, Thad. 2005. "Improving Causal Inference: Strengths and Limitations of Natural Experiments." Paper presented at the annual meeting of the American Political Science Association, Washington, DC.

Dye, Thomas R. 1984. "Party and Policy in the States." *Journal of Politics* 46:1097–116.

Dye, Thomas R. 1966. *Politics, Economics, and the Public: Political Outcomes in the American States.* Chicago: Rand McNally.

Edwards, George C., III. 1980. *Presidential Influence in Congress.* San Francisco: Freeman.

Edwards, George C., III, and Andrew Barrett. 2000. "Presidential Agenda Setting in Congress." In Jon R. Bond and Richard Fleisher, editors, *Polarized Politics: Congress and the President in a Partisan Era.* Washington, DC: Congressional Quarterly Press.

Erikson, Robert S., Gerald C. Wright, and John P. McIver. 1993. *Statehouse Democracy: Public Opinion and Policy in the American States.* Cambridge: Cambridge University Press.

Erikson, Robert S., Gerald C. Wright, and John P. McIver. 2007. "Measuring the Public's Ideological Preferences in the 50 States: Survey Responses versus Roll Call Data." *State Politics and Policy Quarterly* 7(2):141–51.

Feldman, Daniel L., and Gerald Benjamin. 2010. *Tales from the Sausage Factory: Making Laws in New York State.* Albany: State University of New York Press.

Fenno, Richard F. 1966. *The Power of the Purse: Appropriations Politics in Congress.* Boston: Little, Brown.

Ferguson, Margaret R. 2003. "Chief Executive Success in the Legislative Arena." *State Politics and Policy Quarterly* 3(2):158–82.

Ferguson, Margaret R. 2006. *The Executive Branch of State Government: People, Process, and Politics.* Santa Barbara, CA: ABC CLIO.

Ferguson, Margaret R., and Jay Barth. 2002. "Governors in the Legislative Arena: The Importance of Personality in Shaping Success." *Political Psychology* 23(4):787–808.

Ferguson, Margaret R., and Joseph J. Foy. "Unilateral Power in the Governor's Office: Beyond Executive Orders." Paper presented at the 2009 annual Conference on State Politics and Policy, Chapel Hill, NC.

Field Poll. 2003. Release No. 2081. San Francisco: Field Research Corporation.

Field Poll. 2004. Release No. 2143. San Francisco: Field Research Corporation.

Fiorina, Morris. 1996. *Divided Government.* 2nd ed. Boston: Allyn Bacon.

Fiorina, Morris P., and Samuel J. Abrams. 2008. "Is California Really a Blue State?" In Frederick Douzet, Thad Kousser, and Ken Miller, editors, *The New Political Geography of California.* Berkeley, CA: Institute of Governmental Studies Press.

Fording, Richard C., Neal Woods, and David Prince. 2001 "Explaining Gubernatorial Success in State Legislatures." Presented at the annual meeting of the American Political Science Association, San Francisco.

Forsythe, Dall W. 1997. *Memos to the Governor: An Introduction to State Budgeting.* Washington, DC: Georgetown University Press.

Garand, James C. 1988. "Explaining Government Growth in the United States." *American Political Science Review* 82(3):837–49.

Garand, James C., and Kyle Baudoin. 2004. "Fiscal Policy in the American States." In Virginia Gray and Russell L. Hanson, editors, *Politics in the American States.* Washington, DC: Congressional Quarterly Press.

Garrett, Elizabeth. 2005. "Hybrid Democracy." *George Washington University Law Review* 73:1096–130.

Gelman, Andrew. 2008. "Scaling Regression Inputs by Dividing by Two Standard Deviations." *Statistics in Medicine* 27:2865–73.

Gelman, Andrew, and Jennifer Hill. 2007. *Data Analysis Using Regression and Multilevel-Hierarchical Models.* Cambridge: Cambridge University Press.

Gerston, Larry N., and Terry Christensen. 2004. *Recall! California's Political Earthquake.* New York: M. E. Sharpe.

Gosling, James J. 1986. "Wisconsin Item Veto Lessons." *Public Administration Review* 46:292–300.

Gray, Virginia, and David Lowery. 1996. *The Population Ecology of Interest Representation: Lobbying Communities in the American States*. Ann Arbor: University of Michigan Press.

Gross, Donald A. 1991. "The Policy Role of Governors." In Erik B. Herzik and Brent W. Brown, editors, *Gubernatorial Leadership and State Policy*. New York: Greenwood Press.

Haggard, Stephan, and Mathew D. McCubbins, editors. 2001. *Presidents, Parliaments, and Policy*. Cambridge: Cambridge University Press.

Herzberg, Donald G., and Alan Rosenthal, editors. 1971. *Strengthening the States: Essays on Legislative Reform*. New York: Doubleday.

Herzik, Eric. 1991. "Policy Agendas and Gubernatorial Leadership." In *Gubernatorial Leadership and State Policy*, Eric B. Herzig and Brent W. Brown, editors. New York: Greenwood Press.

Ho, Daniel E., Kosuke Imai, Gary King, and Elizabeth A. Stuart. 2007a. "Matching as Nonparametric Preprocessing for Reducing Model Dependence in Parametric Causal Inference." *Political Analysis* 15:199–236.

Ho, Daniel, Kosuke Imai, Gary King, and Elizabeth Stuart. 2007b. "Matchit: Nonparametric Preprocessing for Parametric Causal Inference." *Journal of Statistical Software*. http://gking.harvard.edu/matchit/.

Hofferbert, Richard I. 1966. "The Relation between Public Policy and Some Structural and Environmental Variables in the United States." *American Political Science Review* 60(1):73–82.

Holtz-Eakin, Douglas. 1988. "The Line Item Veto and Public Sector Budgets." *Journal of Public Economics* 36:269–92.

Iowa General Assembly. 2003. "The Constitutionality of the Governors Item Veto of Provisions of House File 692." Des Moines: Iowa Legislative Services Agency Legal Services Division.

Jacobs, John. 1997. *A Rage for Justice*. Berkeley: University of California Press.

Jacobs, John, and A. G. Block. 2006. "The Governor: Managing a Mega-State." In Gerald C. Lubenow, editor, *Governing California: Politics, Government, and Public Policy in the Golden State*, 2nd ed. Berkeley, CA: Institute of Governmental Studies Press.

Jacobson, Gary C. "The Polls: Polarized Opinion in the States: Partisan Differences in Approval Ratings of Governors, Senators, and George W. Bush." *Presidential Studies Quarterly* 36(4):732–57.

Kennedy, Leo F. 1970. "Legislative Organization and Services." In *The Book of the States, 1970–1971*, vol. 18. Lexington, KY: Council of State Governments.

Kernell, Samuel. 1986. *Going Public: New Strategies of Presdiential Leadership*. Washington, DC: Congressional Quarterly Press.

Kernell, Samuel, and Gary C. Jacobson. 2006. *The Logic of American Politics*, 3rd ed. Washington, DC: Congressional Quarterly Press.

Key, V. O., Jr. 1949. *Southern Politics in State and Nation*. New York: Knopf.

Kiewiet, D. Roderick, and Mathew D. McCubbins. 1988. "Presidential Influence on Congressional Appropriations." *American Journal of Political Science* 32:713–36.

Kim, Henry, and Justin H. Phillips. 2009. "Dividing the Spoils of Power: How Are the Benefits of Majority Party Status Distributed in State Legislatures?" *State Politics and Policy Quarterly* 9(2):125–50.

King, Gary, Robert O. Keohane, and Sidney Verba. 1994. *Designing Social Inquiry: Scientific Inference in Qualitative Research*. Princeton, NJ: Princeton University Press.

King, James D. 2000. "Changes in Professionalism in U.S. State Legislatures." *Legislative Studies Quarterly* 25(2):327–43.

Klarner, Carl E., and Justin H. Phillips. 2010. "Overcoming Fiscal Gridlock: Institutions and Budget Bargaining." Presented at the annual meeting of the Midwest Polical Science Association, Chicago, IL.

Kousser, Thad. 2002. "The Politics of Discretionary Medicaid Spending, 1980–1993." *Journal of Health Politics, Policy, and Law*, 27:639–71.

Kousser, Thad. 2005. *Term Limits and the Dismantling of State Legislative Professionalism*. Cambridge: Cambridge University Press.

Kousser, Thad. 2010. "Does Partisan Polarization Lead to Policy Gridlock in California?" *California Journal of Politics and Policy* 2(2), Article 4.

Kousser, Thad, and Justin Phillips. 2007. "The Roots of Executive Power: Explaining Success and Failure in the Legislative Arena." Presented at the annual meeting of the Midwest Political Science Election, Chicago.

Kousser, Thad, and Justin H. Phillips. 2009. "Who Blinks First? Legislative Patience and Bargaining with Governors." *Legislative Studies Quarterly* 34(2):55–86.

Kousser, Thad, Jeff Lewis, and Seth Masket. 2007. "Ideological Adaptation? The Survival Instinct of Threatened Legislators." *Journal of Politics* 69:828–43.

Krehbiel, Keith. 1991. *Information and Legislative Organization*. Ann Arbor: University of Michigan Press.

Krehbiel, Keith. 1998. *Pivotal Politics*. Chicago: University of Chicago Press.

Lax, Jeffrey, and Justin Phillips. 2009. "How Should We Estimate Public Opinion in the States?" *American Journal of Political Science* 53(1):107–21.

Light, Paul. 1982. *The President's Agenda*. Baltimore: Johns Hopkins University Press.

Lipson, Leslie. 1939. *The American Governor from Figurehead to Leader*. Chicago: University of Chicago Press.

Lowry, Robert C., James E. Alt, and Karen E. Ferree. 1998. "Fiscal Policy Outcomes and Electoral Accountability in the American States." *American Political Science Review* 92:759–74.

Lubenow, Gerald C., editor. 2003. *California Votes*. Berkeley, CA: Berkeley Public Policy Press.

Lupia, Arthur, and Gisela Sin. 2008. "How the Senate and the President Affect the Balance of Power in the House: A Constituitonal Theory of Intra-chamber Bargaining." Manuscript, University of Michigan.

Masket, Seth. 2007. "It Takes an Outsider: Extra-legislative Organization and Partisanship in the California Assembly, 1849–2006." *American Journal of Political Science* 51:482–97.

Mathews, Joe. 2006. *The People's Machine: Arnold Schwarzenegger and the Rise of Blockbuster Democracy*. New York: Public Affairs.

Mayhew, David R. 1974. *Congress: The Electoral Connection*. New Haven, CT: Yale University Press.

Mayhew, David R. 1991. *Divided We Govern*. New Haven, CT: Yale University Press.

McAtee, Andrea, Susan Webb Yackee, and David Lowery. 2003. "Reexamining the Dynamic Model of Divided Partisan Government." *Journal of Politics* 65:477–90.

McCarty, Nolan M., and Keith T. Poole. 1995. "Veto Power and Legislation: An Empirical Analysis of Executive and Legislative Bargaining from 1961 to 1986." *Journal of Law, Economics, and Organization* 11(2):282–311.

McCarty, Nolan, Keith T. Poole, and Howard Rosenthal. 2006. *Polarized America: The Dance or Ideology and Unequal Riches*. Cambridge, MA: MIT Press.

McMahon, E. J. 2005. *Breaking the Budget in New York*. Albany: Empire Center for New York State Policy.

Meyers, Roy T. 1997. "Late Appropriations and Government Shutdowns: Frequency, Causes, Consensus, and Remedies." *Public Budgeting and Finance* 17:25–38.

Morehouse, Sarah McCally. 1998. *The Governor as Party Leader*. Ann Arbor: University of Michigan Press.

Morgenstern, Scott, and Benito Nacif. 2002. *Legislative Politics in Latin America*. Cambridge: Cambridge University Press.

Morrow, James D. 1994. *Game Theory for Political Scientists*. Princeton, NJ: Princeton University Press.

National Association of State Budget Officers. 2002. *Budget Processes in the States*. Washington, DC: NASBO.

National Conference of State Legislatures. 2005. *NCSL Backgrounder: Full-Time and Part-Time Legislatures*. Washington, DC: National Conference of State Legislatures.

National Legislative Conference. 1961. *American State Legislatures in the Mid-Twentieth Century: Final Report of the Committee on Legislative Processes and Procedures of the National Legislative Conference*. Chicago: Council of State Governments.

"Natural Experiments in Political Science." 2009. Special Issue of *Political Analysis* 17(4).

Neustadt, Richard. 1960. *Presidential Power; The Politics of Leadership*. New York: John Wiley & Sons.

Nice, David C. 1988. "The Item Veto and Expenditure Restraint." *Journal of Politics* 50:487–99.

Osborne, Martin J., and Ariel Rubinstein. 1990. *Bargaining and Markets*. San Diego, CA: Academic Press.

Ostrom, Charles W., Jr., and Dennis M. Simon. 1985. "Promise and Performance: A Dynamic Model of Presidential Popularity." *American Political Science Review* 79:334–58.

Overby, L. Marvin, and Thomas A. Kazee. 2000. "Outlying Committees in the Statehouse: An Examination of the Prevalence of Committee Outliers in State Legislatures." *Journal of Politics* 62:701–28.

Overby, L. Marvin, Thomas A. Kazee, and David W. Prince. 2004. "Committee Outliers in State Legislatures." *Legislative Studies Quarterly* 29:81–107.

Patashnik, Eric M. 1999. "Ideas, Inheritance, and the Dynamics of Budgetary Change." *Governance: An International Journal of Policy and Administration* 12:147–74.

Payne, Mark J., Daniel Zovatto, Fernando Carrillo Florez, and Andres Allamand Zavala. 2002. *Democracies in Development: Politics and Reform in Latin America*. Washington, DC: IADB.

Peery, George, and Thomas H. Little. 2003. "Views from the Bridge: Legislative Leaders' Perceptions of Institutional Power in the Stormy Wake of Term Limits." In Rick Farmer, John David Rausch Jr., and John C. Green, editors, *The Test of Time: Coping with Legislative Term Limits*. Lanham, MD: Lexington Books.

Persily, Nathaniel, Thad Kousser, and Pat Egan. 2002. "The Political Impact of One Person, One Vote: Intended Consequences, Perverse Effects, and Unrealistic Expectations." *University of North Carolina Law Review* 80:1291–352.

Phillips, Justin. 2005. *The Political Economy of State Tax Policy: The Effects of Electoral Outcomes, Market Competition, and Political Institutions*. Unpublished dissertation.

Phillips, Justin. 2008. "Does Direct Democracy Weaken Party Government?" *State Politics and Policy Quarterly* 8(2):127–49.

Polsby, Nelson W. 1968. "The Institutionalization of the U.S. House of Representatives." *American Political Science Review* 62(March):144–68.

Posner, Daniel N. 2004. "The Political Salience of Cultural Difference: Why Chewas and Tumbukas Are Allies in Zambia and Adversaries in Malawi." *American Political Science Review* 98(4):529–45.

Powell, Richard J. 2007. "Executive-Legislative Relations." In Karl T. Kurtz, Bruce Cain, and Richard G. Niemi, editors, *Institutional Change in American Politics: The Case of Term Limits*. Ann Arbor: University of Michigan Press. p. 134–47.

Primo, David. 2002. "Rethinking Political Bargaining: Policymaking with a Single Proposer." *Journal of Law, Economics, and Organization* 18:411–27.

Quinnipiac University. 2001. "Senator Clinton's Approval Tops 50% for First Time, Quinnipiac University Poll Finds." Hamden, CT: Quinnipiac University.

Rivers, Douglas, and Nancy L. Rose. 1985. "Passing the President's Program: Public Opinion and Presidential Influence in Congress." *American Journal of Political Science* 29:183–96.

Rogers, Diane Lim, and John H. Rogers. 2000. "Political Competition and State Government: Do Tighter Elections Produce Looser Budgets." *Public Choice* 105:1–21.

Romer, Thomas, and Howard Rosenthal. 1978. "Political Resource Allocation, Controlled Agendas, and the Status Quo." *Public Choice* 33:27–43.

Rosenthal, Alan. 1974. *Legislative Performance in the States: Explorations of Committee Behavior*. New York: Free Press.

Rosenthal, Alan. 1990. *Governors and Legislators: Contending Powers*. Washington, DC: Congressional Quarterly Press.

Rosenthal, Alan. 1998. *The Decline of Representative Democracy: Process, Participation, and Power in State Legislatures*. Washington, DC: Congressional Quarterly Press.

Rosenthal, Alan. 2004. *Heavy Lifting: The Job of the American Legislature*. Washington, DC: Congressional Quarterly Press.

Rosenthal, Alan. 2009. *Engines of Democracy: Politics and Policymaking in State Legislatures*. Washington, DC: Congressional Quarterly Press.

Rubin, Donald B. 1973. "The Use of Matched Sampling and Regression Adjustment to Remove Bias in Observational Studies." *Biometrics* 29:185–203.

Rubin, Donald B. 1979. "Using Multivariate Matched Sampling and Regression Adjustment to Control Bias in Observational Studies." *Journal of the American Statistical Association* 74:318–28.

Rubinstein, Ariel. 1982. "Perfect Equilibrium in a Bargaining Model." *Econometrica* 50:97–109.

Rubinstein, Ariel. 1985. "A Bargaining Model with Incomplete Information about Time Preferences." *Econometrica* 53:1151–72.

Rudalevige, Andrew. 2002. *Managing the President's Program: Presidential Leadership and Legislative Policy Formulation*. Princeton, NJ: Princeton University Press.

Rudalevige, Andrew. 2005. "The Executive Branch and the Legislative Process." In *The Executive Branch*, Joel D. Aberbach and Mark A. Peterson, editors. Oxford: Oxford University Press.

Sabato, Larry J. 1978. *Goodbye to Goodtime Charlie: The American Governorship Transformed, 1950–1975*. Lexington, MA: Lexington Books.

Saiegh, Sebastian. 2010. "Political Prowess or Lady Luck? Evaluating Chief Executives' Statutory Policy Making Abilities." Manuscript, University of California, San Diego.

Saiegh, Sebastian. 2011. *Ruling by Statute: How Uncertainty and Vote Buying Shape Lawmaking*. New York: Cambridge University Press.

Schlesinger, Joseph A. 1965. "The Politics of the Executive." In *Politics in the American States*, 1st ed., Herbert Jacob and Kenneth N. Vines, editors. Boston: Little, Brown.

Scuddler, Jeffrey A. 2005. "After *Rant's v. Vilsak*: An Update on Item-Veto Law in Iowa and Elsewhere." *Iowa Law Review* 91:373–400.

Selten, Reinhart. 1975. "Reexamination of the Perfectness Concept for Equilibrium Points in Extensive Games." *International Journal of Game Theory* 4:25–55.

Shor, Boris, and Nolan McCarty. 2011. "The Ideological Mapping of American Legislatures." *American Political Science Review* 105:530–51.

Shor, Boris, Christopher Berry, and Nolan McCarty. 2010. "A Bridge to Somewhere: Mapping State and Congressional Ideology on a Cross-Institutional Common Space." *Legislative Studies Quarterly* 35:1–32.

Sigelman, Lee, and Nelson C. Dometrius. 1988. "Governors as Chief Administrators: The Linkage between Formal Powers and Informal Influence." *American Politics Quarterly* 16(2):157–70.

Sittig, Robert F. 1977. "A Perspective on State Legislative Reform." In Susan Welch and John G. Peters, editors, *Legislative Reform and Public Policy*. New York: Praeger.

Smith, Mark A. 1997. "The Nature of Party Governance: Connecting Conceptualization and Measurement." *American Journal of Political Science* 41:1042–56.

Squire, Peverill. 1988. "Career Opportunites and Membership Stability in Legislatures." *Legislative Studdies Quarterly* 13:65–82.

Squire, Peverill. 1992. "Legislative Professionalization and Membership Diversity in State Legislatures." *Legislative Studies Quarterly* 17(1):69–79.

Squire, Peverill. 2007. "Measuring State Legislative Professionalism: The Squire Index Revisited." *State Politics and Policy Quarterly* 7(2):211–27.

Squire, Peverill, and Keith E. Hamm. 2005. *101 Chambers: Congress, State Legislatures, and the Future of Legislative Studies*. Columbus: University of Ohio Press.

Thompson, Joel, and Gary Moncrief. 2003. "Lobbying under Limits: Interest Group Perspectives on the Effects of Term Limits in State Legislatures." In Rick Farmer, John David Rausch Jr., and John C. Green, editors, *The Test of Time: Coping with Legislative Term Limits*. Lanham, MD: Lexington Books.

Tsebelis, George and Jeannette Money. 1997. *Bicameralism*. Cambridge: Cambridge University Press.

van Assendelft, Laura A. 1997. *Governors, Agenda Setting, and Divided Government*. New York: University Press of America.

Wahlke, John C. 1966. "Organization and Procedure." In Alexander Heard, editor, *State Legislatures in American Politics*. Englewood Cliffs, NJ: Prentice Hall.

Wildavsky, Aaron, 1966. "The Two Presidencies." *Trans-Action* 4:7–14.

Wilson, E. Dotson, and Brian S. Ebbert. 2006. *California's Legislature*. Sacramento, CA: Office of the Assembly Chief Clerk.

Winters, Richard. 1976. "Party Control and Policy Change." *American Journal of Political Science* 20(4):597–636.

Wright, Deil S., F. Ted Hebert, and Jeffrey L. Brudney. 1983. "Gubernatorial Influence and State Bureaucracy." *American Politics Quarterly* 11(2):243–64.

Wright, Gerald, and Brian Schaffner. 2002. "The Influence of Party: Evidence from the State Legislatures." *American Political Science Review* 96:367–90.

Index

CPSIA information can be obtained
at www.ICGtesting.com
Printed in the USA
LVHW100748260722
724417LV00002B/129